Coast Guard Action in Vietnam:

STORIES OF THOSE WHO SERVED

by

CWO4 Paul C. Scotti, USCG (Retired)

Coast Guard Action in Vietnam
© 2000 Paul C. Scotti
Published by Hellgate Press

All rights reserved. No part of this publication may be reproduced or used in any form or by any means, graphic, electronic or mechanical, including photocopying, recording, taping, or information storage and retrieval systems without written permission of the publishers.

HELLGATE PRESS
a division of PSI Research
P.O. Box 3727
Central Point, Oregon 97502-0032

(541) 245-6502
(541) 245-6505 fax
info@psi-research.com e-mail

Cover design: J. C. Young

Scotti, Paul C.
    Coast guard action in Vietnam : stories of those who served / by Paul C. Scotti.
      p. cm.
    Includes bibliographical references and index.
    ISBN 1-55571-528-1 (paper)
      1. Vietnamese Conflict, 1961-1975—Personal narratives, American. 2. Vietnamese Conflict, 1961-1975—Regimental histories—United States. 3. United States. Coast Guard—History—Vietnamese Conflict, 1961-1975. I. Title.

DS559.5 .S387 2000
959.704'3373—dc21   00-056728

Printed and bound in the United States of America
First Edition 10 9 8 7 6 5 4 3 2 1
Printed on recycled paper when available.

*Dedicated
to*

*all Coast Guard combat veterans
and the families who awaited
their return*

Paul Carl Scotti

Paul Scotti's two destinations in life were to serve his country and to write. Through a remarkably diverse thirty-year military career he reached them.

In 1960, at age 17, after graduating from John Jay High School (formerly Manual Training High School) in Brooklyn, New York, he enlisted in the United States Air Force seeking glory in the air, but instead found bliss on the ground in the medical corps, specifically as an X-ray technician. Four years later he left the service for college. However, school could not satisfy his yearnings for travel and adventure. To fulfill a longing for the sea he joined the United States Coast Guard in 1965.

He requested to be trained as a weapons specialist and volunteered for Vietnam War duty. Both wishes came to pass. Gunner's Mate Second Class Scotti rode the Coast Guard's 82-foot long patrol boats from May 1967 to April 1968, the period of the heaviest American fighting of the war. Along with his shipmates he toughed out monsoon seas and lonely, wearisome patrols looking for North Vietnamese and Viet Cong infiltrators. He dueled a North Vietnamese patrol boat—machine gun to machine gun—and took part in cornering an armed North Vietnamese trawler trying to reach decimated forces in South Vietnam with weapons and medicine shortly after the enemy's failed Tet Offensive in 1968.

In 1971, Scotti made a career course change, switching from pistol to pen, when he became a Coast Guard journalist, an occupation that required an individual not just to write, but also to take photographs and answer questions from news reporters.

Scotti was promoted to chief warrant officer with the designation of public information officer in 1981. Throughout his period in the Public Affairs field, Scotti always seemed to be where big news happened. Wherever he went he earned the trust and respect of reporters. Incidents in which he was spokesperson include the Coast Guard–directed search and recovery operations in the Space Shuttle *Challenger* disaster; the sinking of the Coast Guard buoy tender *Blackthorn* after a collision with a tanker; and the ship collision with the Sunshine Sky Bridge, which sent a thousand-foot span into the water along with the vehicles on it at the time. These latter two incidents took place in Tampa Bay (Florida), both with high loss of life.

His final tour of duty provided an interesting change of pace as one of the Coast Guard's two officers tasked with liaison to the motion picture and television industries. Although based in Los Angeles, California, he regularly found himself somewhere else on filming location as technical advisor and problem solver between his Service and the production company.

He retired from active duty on November 1, 1991 and continues to travel and write. *Coast Guard Action in Vietnam* is his third book. He previously wrote *Seaports: Ships, Piers and People* and *Police Divers.* You are liable to meet him and his wife, Liz, as they crisscross the United States in their motor home visiting their children, grandchildren, and friends.

Foreword

I served as an active duty member of the United States Coast Guard for nearly 22 years, precisely between the beginning of the "Vietnamization" and *Operation Desert Shield* in 1990. My recollections of service in the nation's oldest continuous seagoing armed force do not include combat or combat support in the theater of war. I heard about it, but I was not there.

In *Coast Guard Action in Vietnam,* Paul C. Scotti neatly defines the attitudes, customs, and policies that helped this small operational organization, with so many missions, survive and succeed in the Vietnam War. I was weaned on the dicta: "You have to go out, you don't have to come back"; "If we can't make it we'll find a way to do without it"; and the ever popular, "We who have done so much with so little for so long will soon do everything with nothing forever." This work tells me that the Coast Guard's imagination, creativity, stamina, and dedication to institutional principles were the difference in overcoming logistical, cultural, and philosophical obstacles, as well as an enemy who refused to conduct himself in ways consistent with traditional warfare.

Factual, yet based on the humanitarian emotions that are central to the Coast Guard's purpose, this is the story of a little known—yet absolutely critical—job done to stem the coastwise flow of clandestine personnel, materials, and critical information into South Vietnam. Coast Guard men, ships, aircraft, and technology in Vietnam upheld all but two of the eight basic missions traditionally reserved for those who wear The Shield: icebreaking was never at issue in Vietnam, and it is safe to say that little emphasis was placed on recreational boating safety in those hectic days.

Paul C. Scotti focuses on the other critical missions and the Coast Guard's absolute insistence on excellence in performance of those duties, beginning with military readiness in support of *Market Time* and the myriad other operations in more than eight years of Coast Guard involvement. Merchant marine safety, law enforcement, marine environmental protection, and aids to navigation were afterthoughts in the grand scheme of American involvement in the protection of South Vietnam from Communist influence from the north. Someone had to do them, quickly and effectively. Combat search and rescue was refined to a high art during the Coast Guard's involvement, and Scotti takes you into the minds of the men whose lives go on the line that others may live, braving not only the elements but the enemy as well.

If anyone was ever uniquely suited to tell the story of the Coast Guard in Vietnam, Paul C. Scotti is that person. A career military man with experience in the Air Force medical corps before joining the Coast Guard, Scotti served aboard the 82-foot patrol boats in Vietnam as a gunner's mate, then changed his specialty to journalist in the latter half of his lengthy active duty career. He was there, he was part of the story, and now he has told that story in a way that both Coast Guard veterans and laymen alike can understand and appreciate.

Both a detailed after-action report and maritime war story of high adventure, *Coast Guard Action in Vietnam* is the definitive work on the subject, and one long overdue. Though largely alive with the recollections of those who were there and performed so well yet with so little recognition, the story recounts the courage, despair, bravery, humor, and pathos felt by those whose jobs were—as Captain Francis Van Boskerck characterized in the service's march "Semper Paratus"—the paradoxical "to punish or to save."

The time will come again when the Coast Guard will be called upon to do much with little, to "rig," innovate, stretch, and manufacture its way into the vital support of the Navy and other maritime interests that has been documented in the past. Then, as in Vietnam and conflicts back to the earliest days of the Revenue Cutter Service, the courage, devotion, skill, and character of Coast Guard men and women will be the glue that holds it all together. Paul C. Scotti has written one Coast Guardsman's proud look at his service's vital—though little known—activities in a most difficult struggle, half a world away from home.

Kent E. Fisher
Lieutenant Commander
U.S. Coast Guard (Retired)

Contents

1. Introduction **1**
2. Somebody, Get the Coast Guard! **5**
3. Port Dangers **23**
4. Trawler! **41**
5. Squadron Three **57**
6. The Navigation Masters **79**
7. Attack on *Point Welcome* **101**
8. Mariner Problems Aplenty **113**
9. Combat Search and Rescue **127**
10. Always Ready, Always Humane **145**
11. GQ! **163**
12. Vietnamization—The End of the Line **183**

Epilogue **197**
Glossary **203**
Chronology **205**
Appendix A: Squadron One Cutters **209**
Appendix B: Squadron Three Cutters **213**
Appendix C: Other Cutter Deployments **217**
Appendix D: USCG Patrol Boat: 82-Footer **219**
Appendix E: Statistics **221**
Source Notes **223**
Bibliography **227**
Index **231**

Overview map of Southeast Asia
(Courtesy of U.S. Naval Historical Center)

Coast Guard Action in Vietnam:
stories of those who served

CHAPTER 1

INTRODUCTION

Most military exploits sleep in forgotten files or dwell in the fading memories of living participants, unless a symbol saves a deed from institutional bondage to become timeless legend. For instance, United States Marine Corps files are thick with records of tenacious combat, yet one such fight—no more murderous than many others—lives on in memory across generations. A photograph taken of victorious marines planting the American flag during the capture of Iwo Jima Island from the Japanese in World War II immortalized the fighting image of the Marine Corps, and because of it Iwo Jima will always be remembered.

In the main, though, military people take part in less renowned adventures. As such, individuals who distinguish their outfit through dedicated service and personal sacrifice must find their reward in knowing that they did their job well. But, when up against a general perception that their service did not even take part in an extremely combustible era of American history, such inner solace fails to satisfy.

The Vietnam War, directly or indirectly, touched the lives of most Americans for more than a decade. It dominated all other news in all media every day, with television making the biggest impact by turning its audience into witnesses of war's destruction and death. In spite of this saturated coverage, people are surprised to learn that the United States Coast Guard served in Vietnam. What the Coast Guard did in Vietnam is little known, perhaps because Coast Guardsmen toiled for other military branches. While its performance was privately held in high regard, interservice pride restrained the other services from giving the Coast Guard much public notice. More than that, without an Iwo Jima–like imagery, numbers simply overwhelmed the smallest of the armed forces. Whereas a few thousand Coast Guardsmen served in Southeast Asia, tens of thousands of Army, Air Force, Navy, and Marine Corps members took part. Nonetheless, aroused by their own *esprit de corps,* wherever Coast Guardsmen appeared, mission success improved.

The character of the conflict in Vietnam was not so much survival between two Asian countries as it was a bloody turf fight between Communism and its worldwide nemesis, the United States. Communist-ruled North Vietnam wanted to absorb non-Communist South Vietnam, and the United States was not going to let that happen uncontested. In the beginning, America had expected that advisory and material support alone would suffice for South Vietnam to hold off the North, but the South continually lost territory. South Vietnam's military confidence needed bolstering if the country was to be saved.

The obvious, if less preferred, action to take was to send in more troops—not just to advise, but to fight. As a result, American military strength in South Vietnam increased from 900 in 1960; to 11,300 in 1962; to 16,300 in 1963; to 23,200 in 1964; to 59,900 in 1965; leaping to 385,000 in 1966; and reaching its peak of 543,400 in 1969.[1]

Most of the soldiering by the United States happened inside South Vietnam, with periodic search and destroy assaults and clandestine escapades into bordering countries. Aviators, less restrained by boundaries, attacked North Vietnam, Laos, and Cambodia throughout the war. Thailand avoided fighting on its soil, but, in friendship to the United States, opened the country to American military units. Into this far from finished convoluted Southeast Asian tapestry the Coast Guard returned to combat for the first time since World War II. Unlike during World War II, when the Coast Guard shifted from the Treasury Department into the Navy Department as the government assembled its full military and industrial resources to defeat the enemy, during the Vietnam conflict the Coast Guard stayed put.

This time the government chose to take on the enemy with piecemeal strategy, treating it more like a regional infestation of insect pests by retaliating with selective force to specific threats. As such, the Coast Guard became a "job center," dispatching temporary help and equipment. When the Navy needed vessels, it telephoned the Coast Guard; when the Army needed assistance protecting ports, it telephoned the Coast Guard; and when the Air Force needed helicopter pilots, it telephoned the Coast Guard.

The Coast Guard tackled five important areas in Vietnam: enemy movements over water, port security, aids to navigation, safe and expeditious merchant shipping, and search and rescue. Thus, serving as combatant and consultant—Coast Guardsmen fought and taught!

North Vietnam's surrogate troops in South Vietnam, the Viet Cong, could not win skirmishes without a sure resupply conduit from North Vietnam, and they had one by sea. A trip lasting some 170 days over land took only a few days over water. The easy infiltration of South Vietnam's long stretches of sandy beaches, secluded coves, and networks of rivers and canals allowed steel-hull trawlers to dump tons of munitions directly on land or into junks waiting offshore.

South Vietnam's naval vigilance was as productive as a derelict ship. Night patrols were made with great reluctance, while day patrols were aimless. The Junk Force, responsible for inshore detection, committed merely 40 percent of its craft to patrolling, and most of them just chugged out of sight and then anchored.[2] Naval passivity may be attributed to pique. The Army dominated all military affairs, and showed such low regard toward the cloutless Navy that it shunned the prudent tactic of using naval craft to transport soldiers to battle sites. Understandably, as naval leadership pouted, ennui permeated all commands. It would take a full-time American naval commitment to tighten coastal surveillance. A decision to do so was made shortly after the fumbling about in Vung Ro Bay.

On the morning of 16 February 1965, a U.S. Army helicopter reported a camouflaged vessel along the central coast south of Qui Nhon, in Vung Ro Bay. It took nine days for combined South Vietnamese military forces to get collected to destroy the North Vietnamese supply trawler and capture what offloaded cargo remained. Without the unrelenting goading by infuriated American advisors, the operation would have taken longer, if it would have been accomplished at all.

In March, the U.S. Navy began the task of taking the sea away from the Viet Cong's provisioners by using what aircraft and ships it had handy until the counterinfiltration players of *Operation Market Time* were in place. On 11 May, the operation received significant power when South Vietnam gave the Americans authority to stop, search, and seize any vessel within the three-mile Territorial Zone (TZ), and to search and seize suspicious vessels in the three- to twelve-mile Contiguous Zone (CZ).

For this mission, the primarily deepwater-oriented U.S. Navy had to confront its blind spot and, for inshore patrolling, come up with the shallow-draft vessels that it historically disdained maintaining. The Coast Guard, noted for boat handling in confined waters, responded to a Navy request for boats by sending twenty-six 82-foot patrol boats with crews. Later, when the Navy ran short of oceangoing ships to cover the offshore blockade zone, the Coast Guard again came to the Navy's side with more cutters.

The U.S. Army found itself with the monumental job of overseeing the endless amounts of ammunition and equipment arriving at South Vietnamese ports. Ships and cargo needed protection from sabotage and attack. Safety was also a serious concern. Vietnamese dockworkers did not allow U.S. Army commanders restful sleep when they handled explosives as incautiously as they did bags of rice. Catastrophe could have come anytime. So, unabashed, the Army asked the Coast Guard for dangerous-cargo handlers to supervise unloading and storage, and for port security experts to advise on terrorist countermeasures.

Maritime navigational aids in the United States are taken for granted because they always seem to be there, but South Vietnlam had trouble just keeping its relatively few in order. When new channels and harbors began popping up in South Vietnam like spring flowers, a call went to the Coast Guard to handle this matter. Also, the need for an all-weather, reliable electronic navigation system for aviators to locate their position as well as their target brought Coast Guardsmen in to build and run such a network.

With 98 percent of the military cargo sent to Vietnam arriving in merchant ships, thousands of merchant seamen made long trips to a steamy climate with poor "shore leave" prospects. This and other factors brought out the worst behavior in some crew members, causing shipping delays. It became the Coast Guard's job to resolve misconduct, weed out the incompetent, and keep the ships sailing.

In the fierce air war over Southeast Asia the U.S. Air Force alone lost 2,254 aircraft.[3] The airplanes were replaceable, but lives were not, and extraordinary efforts were made to recover aviators. Confronted with a helicopter pilot shortage for its recovery squadrons, the Air Force borrowed top rescue helicopter fliers from the Coast Guard.

More than 8,000 Coast Guardsmen served in Southeast Asia during the Vietnam War. Here is the story of what they did there.

CHAPTER 2

SOMEBODY, GET THE COAST GUARD!

It was dark and they were watchful. During the day they had heard jets screaming in attack dives and helicopters beating their way from one hot spot to another. Those sounds, along with the muffled thuds of bombs and artillery shells into the green countryside, were the right background acoustics for a war movie. But this was not theater and the Coast Guard cutter slow-running the river was not in the United States on search and rescue patrol.

Seventeen miles south of Saigon, flanked by hostile shores, the USCGC *Point White* (WPB 82308) tiptoed along the Soirap River. On the east bank lay the Rung Sat Special Zone (RSSZ), 400 square miles of dense mangrove swamps and jungle crisscrossed with narrow waterways: a Viet Cong haven where recruits trained, engineers assembled explosives, and medics treated wounded. Cargo ships passing through the RSSZ en route to Saigon sometimes had to run a gauntlet of recoilless rifle and automatic weapons fire. On the west bank lay the flat, broken land of the Mekong Delta region, an area rich in rice cultivation and Viet Cong infestation. Because the RSSZ lacked sufficient food and water sources, the Viet Cong crossed to the Mekong Delta for these needs. As a prelude to a joint American and South Vietnamese plunge into the RSSZ to wrest away the enemy's domination, Coast Guard 82-foot patrol boats were diverted from their usual coastal surveillance to intercept these resupply crossings. Two cutters began cruising the river during daylight hours on 7 March 1966, each accompanied by a pair of Junk Force boats. They returned to base at night and followed the same routine the next day. But, on the third day, the patrols continued around the clock. In an effort to mislead enemy observers into thinking his cutter was leaving again, Lieutenant Eugene J. Hickey Jr. turned the *Point White* for the river entrance in the established routine, but at dark his blacked-out vessel crept back up the river. Except for the occasional distant report of a mortar shell explosion, silence enclosed the cutter. The radar antenna making circular sweeps atop the mast gave the alert but tense crew its night sight. Engineman First Class Joseph E. Moody recalled, "We were definitely expecting trouble. We knew we had VC on both sides of the river."

At 2100 hours they heard rifle shots nearby. Hickey kept his men calm while suppressing an urge to investigate and thereby give away their presence. His restraint paid off an hour and fifteen minutes later when radar showed something behind them moving out of a canal on the east bank. Hickey swung the cutter about, shouted a target bearing to Moody on the bow machine gun, and throttled up to full speed. At less than 200 yards away Moody picked out a bulge on the water. Above him, the siren blared, followed shortly by the South Vietnamese liaison officer shouting halt commands through a loudhailer. Hickey flipped on the powerful searchlight, throwing a harsh glare on a 25-foot motorized junk flush with armed men. The junk began sparkling. Moody's thumbs reacted by crushing the horseshoe-shaped trigger, flashing out responding muzzle blasts. Although the distance between the two craft closed fast, neither side slackened their firing. As one Coast Guardsman arriving at his battle station bent to grab his helmet, a bullet passed over him, penetrating three cardboard-encased white phosphorus mortar rounds in the ammunition locker, sending up sparks and wisps of smoke. When 30 feet away, Hickey spun the helm hard left, skidding his starboard bow into a violent glancing blow against the junk. A surge of water from his wake followed. The one-two punch knocked several Viet Cong overboard. As the vessels separated, the junk came into Gunner's Mate Second Class Lester K. Gates's sights on the starboard aft machine gun. Guided by tracer rounds, his accurate fire began churning the target into a cloud of splinters. A moment later there was an explosion. A body flew into the air and splashed into the water. The shooting ceased. Two men stood in the stern sheets with hands raised.

The two Junk Force boats arrived in time for the mop-up. Coast Guardsmen pulled from the river a survivor burned head to foot, with only his back unscathed. They placed him on deck, making him as comfortable as possible. Hickey edged the cutter alongside with the idea of salvaging the slowly sinking junk, but not all the Viet Cong had given up. One of them, lying wounded on his back, jacked a round into his rifle and fired at Moody, who shot back. Although Moody hit him several times, the guerrilla got off another shot before a Vietnamese sailor leaned over from his junk and finished him off. Efforts to stop the flooding were thwarted again when another Viet Cong began firing from a narrow opening in the forward cockpit. By the time the Coast Guardsmen worked into position for a clear killing shot the junk was awash. It soon sank. Of the 16 Viet Cong, four were taken alive. The man who had been badly burned was the commanding officer of a large training camp and, judging from the size of his armed escort, it appeared that more than an ordinary supply run had been interrupted. Even in war, kindness has influence. The next day ashore, when the *Point White* crewmen saw the burned prisoner again, he told them how much he appreciated their compassion, and that if he lived, Americans would always be his friends.

From 1962 to 1966, Admiral Edwin J. Roland held the post of Coast Guard commandant. Anticipating that eventually his forces would be fighting in Vietnam, he stepped up training in this area to put an edge on their military skills. His good friend, Marine Corps Commandant General Wallace M. Greene, had a painting in his office depicting Marines landing in the swamps of Florida by boat. Greene would point to that artwork and say to Roland, "Here you are. Here's the Coast Guard landing the Marines in the Seminole War." Then they talked of ways of getting the Coast Guard into Vietnam carrying the Marines up the rivers and routing the Communists. However, even before Roland became commandant, the U.S. Navy had sensed that before the muddle in Southeast Asia cleared it would be using its sea service kin. "Somebody, get the Coast Guard!" were likely the words used in November 1961 when a

In the aftermath of a river gunfight between a Viet Cong junk and the *Point White*, the cutter's skipper, Lieutenant Eugene J. Hickey Jr., shows the dents in one of the several 81-mm mortar projectile casings hit by enemy fire. The rifle on the right was taken from the attackers. (Courtesy of U.S. Coast Guard)

Navy-led study group was assembling to leave for Vietnam. The Joint Chiefs of Staff had directed Commander-in-Chief, Pacific (CINCPAC), to look into the South Vietnamese Navy's poor performance against enemy infiltration. Rear Admiral Henry S. Persons, deputy chief of staff for Plans and Logistics, CINCPAC, heading up the review team, wanted a Coast Guard perspective. Commander John B. Speaker Jr., assistant to the Chief of Staff, U.S. Coast Guard Headquarters, Washington, DC, landed in Saigon with the group on 10 November. Speaker likely became the first Coast Guardsman to go to South Vietnam in direct relation to that country's struggle to remain non-communist.

His blunt report to the Commandant portrayed a South Vietnamese Navy devoid of resolve. He found shipboard maintenance extremely poor, the food bad, and shipboard drills and training rarely carried out. At any time half the Sea Force could not sail because of machinery breakdowns. Coordination with the Army was nonexistent. Speaker found the breakdown problem the same in the River Force, which was also below strength and assigned the "poorest of personnel." His only favorable words went to the Junk Force, which showed some success against coastal infiltration. Based upon the group's findings, Persons recommended better personnel training and shipyard maintenance supervision, navy representation on the government's military staff, and stepped-up construction of vessels for the Junk Force. Sound measures without a doubt, but like bones without connecting ligaments, useless until the leaders within the South Vietnamese government ceased their individual power schemes and joined together in unifying their military, industry, and citizenry against a North Vietnamese takeover.

Before Speaker returned to Washington, Persons had him stop in Honolulu to tell CINCPAC what the Coast Guard could do to help. One of Speaker's comments was that if the United States joined the fighting, Coast Guard cutters were available, and were best used in the hands of Coast Guardsmen. In 1965, another Coast Guard officer reaffirmed Speaker's words. Commander James A. Hodgman, a liaison officer on the staff of the Chief of Naval Operations, was queried by that office on what the Coast Guard could contribute to stopping infiltration into South Vietnam. Hodgman answered in his 11 March memorandum, "Coast Guard personnel and ships are ready...to contribute to any effort...in the national interest.... Coast Guard AVPs, PCs and PBs could be dispatched to the South China Sea with a minimum reaction time."

For a long time, the U.S. Army in Vietnam contended that most of the supplies reaching the Viet Cong were coming in by sea. The U.S. Navy disagreed, on the basis of insufficient evidence. That position became moot when a gun-running North Vietnamese trawler was found and destroyed in Vung Ro Bay in February 1965. In the aftermath, General William C. Westmoreland, Commander, U.S. Military Assistance Command, Vietnam (COMUSMACV) called a conference in Saigon on 3 March to devise a joint United States and South Vietnamese naval patrol to counter the problem. Thus was born *Operation Market Time,* in which the Coast Guard would be an important part. The Secretary of the Navy wrote the Secretary of the Treasury on 16 April:

> *The U.S. Navy is confronted with a new and difficult problem.... The Navy must insure that logistic support via sea does not reach the Viet Cong in South Vietnam from North Vietnam, from communist countries, or communist sympathizers.*
>
> *At the present time, Seventh Fleet units are being employed to prevent sea infiltration into South Vietnam. However, we find such ships suffer major disadvantages in conducting patrols against shallow draft junks. We are therefore attempting to locate a source of more suitable patrol craft. Such characteristics as high speed, shallow draft, sea keeping ability, radar, and communication equipment are important characteristics.*
>
> *In investigating possible sources of suitable craft it has occurred to us that the Coast Guard may have some patrol craft available which the Navy Department may be able to use.*

Coast Guard and Navy officials met to discuss the type and number of boats, and how to use them. On 29 April, President Lyndon B. Johnson authorized Coast Guard units to operate with the Navy in Vietnam. That evening the decision was announced to the public. Coast Guardsmen were amazed how fast things moved following the announcement. Within days cutters pulled into shipyards for modification and in three weeks were hoisted aboard freighters for transfer to the Philippines. Crews had orders to report for training in two weeks. These men did not know that when the president signed the memorandum approving the Navy–Coast Guard venture he was not consenting to a notion, but a plan already drawn up and agreed to by all parties that only awaited a presidential okay to enact. Accordingly, when the public learned of the decision, the cutters had already been selected, and matters of administration, logistics, and training worked out.

The Coast Guard patrol force was designated Squadron One. It would have two hundred forty-five men (47 officers, 198 enlisted) and seventeen patrol boats.[1] The cutters chosen had 82-foot, 10-inch steel hulls, twin screws, and two diesel engines propelling at 17 knots. Men with orders for Vietnam processed through the Coast Guard base in Alameda, California, where on 27 May a ceremony formally established the squadron.

Newspaper editorials generally lauded sending over the Coast Guard, expressing little surprise. By comparison, the news jolted some Coast Guardsmen, such as the men on the mess deck of the USCGC *Point Gammon* (WPB 82328) docked in San Francisco Bay, who heard over radio news that *Gammon* was battle-bound. One of them told a *San Francisco Chronicle* reporter, "There were three of us here and we nearly had heart attacks." Another crew member told a *News-Call Bulletin* reporter, "I'm supposed to get married today—wait 'till she hears about this."

The 82-footer, or WPB, carried an eight-man enlisted crew, but for this duty another enlisted man and two officers would be added. With the deployment dates only a short time away, the Coast Guard preferred keeping the experienced stateside crews intact and filling in with volunteers where needed. Few men asked for reassignment; instead, most reacted as those on the USCGC *Point Arden* (WPB 82309), based in Point Pleasant, New Jersey. "Not one of the crew wants off or would change his assignment with any other servicemen," said Chief Boatswain's Mate Donald Edwards. Boatswain's Mate First Class Edward Royer said, "I'll go wherever the boat goes." Seaman Richard Horne, speaking for himself and a shipmate, commented, "We wouldn't change this chance for the world." Thomas Ward, an engineman, said, "This is my work and I'm ready." Chief Engineman Robert Clements, a pragmatist, said, "For me, the assignment is just like any other call, only for longer." He added that the only reaction from his children came from his 12-year-old son, who was afraid that he might leave before he had the television repaired.[2] There was no shortage of volunteers, the enlisted billets went fast, and young eager officers calling Headquarters to sign on were disappointed to hear that orders for commanding and executive officers were all taken, mostly assigned before the word went public. The surplus volunteers would have to wait a year for their turn as replacements.

That the patrol boats were hastened off to shipyards can be attested to by the USCGC *Point Banks* (WPB 82327) crew. Having just pulled into their Woods Hole, Massachusetts, home port after two arduous weeks at sea, which included assisting a

U.S. Navy icebreaker taking on water, the vessel was ordered to a Boston shipyard, giving the crew little chance to comprehend their status and no chance to see their families.

Modifications were made in armament and in making room for the larger crew. The forecastle 20-mm gun mount was replaced with an 81-mm mortar topped with a .50-caliber machine gun. Four .50-caliber machine gun stands were installed aft of the deckhouse—two amidships and two astern. A pair of ready service mortar ammunition boxes found their niche in front of the deckhouse behind the forward mount. On the fantail, a steel frame was welded to the deck to stock five thousand rounds of machine gun ammunition. The accommodations for 10 were expanded to 13, allowing for an 11-man crew, a Vietnamese liaison, and an extra rider. Into a hold went a larger freezer for carrying more food, allowing the vessel to remain at sea longer.

The Navy considered physical and mental conditioning critical for their aviators, boat crews, and advisors. In preparing them for adversity and the possibility of capture, they underwent vigorous training. There were some variations over the years, but in the main, Coast Guardsmen underwent five weeks of preparation. The first week they formed up at the Alameda base for physical checkups, inoculations, and briefings on legal and pay matters such as wills, powers of attorney, tax deductions, and extra allowances. On Treasure Island, a nearby Navy base, they took refresher training to protect themselves against nuclear, biological, and chemical warfare. In a damage control exercise they became sodden trying to stop a ship with simulated battle damage from sinking. Then they shipped out to U.S. Naval Amphibious Base, Coronado, California, near San Diego, joining more than a hundred others for the three-week Counterinsurgency, Survival, Evasion, Resistance to Interrogation, and Escape (COINSERE) Course. Some Coast Guardsmen felt that this was the roughest part of their entire Vietnam experience.

It began easily enough with five days of lectures on Vietnamese culture and Communist aggression. The next week the scene moved to Camp Pendleton Marine Corps Base, where matters became physical, with long hilly hikes and lots of weapons handling. They fired pistols, rifles, shotguns, and machine guns. They took them apart and put them together. For many it was their first experience in throwing a live hand grenade.

Week number four stressed survival, and men lost seven to fifteen pounds confronting privation and abuse. Parachute segments were their sole materials for shelter and bedding. The first day they lived off what they could catch along the seashore. The next morning they were transported to chilly mountain elevations.

In learning to live off the land they sampled the vegetation. Finding most of it unpalatable, they spit it out. Because the wild game knew better than to hang around a locale where so many famished servicemen lurked every week, the instructors released rabbits and pigeons for them to capture, kill, and eat. Nights brought little rest. The camp had to guard against harassing attacks by simulated guerrillas. On the fourth day they were broken up into small groups, given a compass and topographical map, and sent off to reach the next campsite—a trek over wayless terrain that lasted the entire day.

Worn-out and hungry, they were now ripe for capture, where their will to resist interrogation would be tested. The last night was a cold camp, no fires were allowed for warmth, or, in the unlikely event there was anything to eat, for cooking. After the camp broke up the next morning the men gathered along one side of a roughly one-square-mile sector set aside for the evasion phase. Upon signal they had three hours to reach "Freedom Village" on the other end, where their reward would be an hour's rest and fresh fruit. However, to get there they had to avoid enemy impersonators hunting them.

Usually, most were captured, some were still on the loose when time ran out, but few ever reached the village. In at least one exercise two of the three men reaching sanctuary were Coast Guard, and most of the other Coast Guardsmen had avoided capture—an impressive ratio considering there were only fifteen Coast Guardsmen out of more than a hundred participating.

Next came imprisonment. A siren brought in the remaining evaders, who were shoved into trucks and hauled to a squalid prison camp. One Coast Guardsman remembered the camp as a dreary clearing in the woods cordoned off by wood stakes connected with tangles of wire. Guards in ugly brown uniforms adorned with a red star were verbally and physically tormenting those captured earlier. The prisoners knelt on the soggy dirt with their arms outstretched in front of them. They were clad only in undershirt and shorts while guards hosed them with cold water. After being forced to crawl into the enclosure through a barbed wire tunnel, new arrivals added their clothes to the heap of others. As they joined their humiliated shipmates, each repeated over and over in his mind that this is only a drill and will end—eventually.

The degradation went on without letup. Although escape was encouraged, anyone caught attempting it earned greater punishment. Throughout the day individuals were taken from the compound for questioning. Some returned coated in mud, as if they had fallen into a vat of chocolate. When the prisoners showed signs of banding together to bolster morale, the leaders were dragged away and not seen again. The men, having signed statements before the training that they would not retaliate against the "instructors," found it hard not to react against the open-handed blows. At the approach of night they were lined up and hoods were put over their heads. With a hand on the shoulder of the person in front of them they were marched off, each man's mind now like a covered cage filled with birds alarmed by a release of repressed fears and phobias. The journey ended inside a spacious building with a high ceiling, where even the softest speech resounded harshly and loudly. Each prisoner was pushed into a dull black box with three-foot sides poked full of small airholes. Inside, the men removed their hoods, but it gave little relief from the growing heat in the sweatbox. Coming from outside the cramped kennels men heard the pathetic cries of men being beaten and whimpering admissions that the United States carries on chemical warfare. Was this really happening? Was it a put-on? A prisoner could not know.

As a prisoner, when your turn came you were told to restore your hood and taken to another box. This one was only shoulder-wide, and you were placed in it in a forward kneeling position that soon cut circulation off to your feet at the ankles. After what seemed a long interval the box opened and you were pushed into a room not much bigger than a storage closet. The hood was yanked away. But all you saw was harsh bright light.

Behind the glare a nasty voice spit out questions, to which you responded as taught, giving only name, rank, service number, date of birth, and religion. The interrogator holding your military identification card knew all this, but wanted to hear things about you and your job. When you did not cooperate he spewed invectives about anyone or anything believed to be important to you, such as your mother, wife, sister, and service. You replied to other questions as trained. "Sir, my country will not allow me to answer that question." This response would promptly bring the interrogator from behind the light to play handball, using you as the ball. You would bear down and take it. When you refused to break down you were returned to the narrow box until they were ready to question you again. When the lid reopened you girded yourself for the next interrogation go-around, but instead you were taken back to your own kennel. You passed and would remain unbothered. Had you been chatty the torment would have increased until either your resistance stiffened or you broke.

Time passed slowly, and sleep was elusive because of the cramped space and the ceaseless wailing of human suffering. Just when you began to question your sanity and began wondering if this were real after all, the boxes were flung open. The course ended. You and your companions trooped off to a makeshift mess hall to eat oatmeal and an apple, about all your debilitated system could handle. You were glad it was over, but unlike many classes, where students happily mingle with the teachers afterward, you had no desire to do this; these instructors seemed to enjoy their sadistic roles too much.

The final week of preparation was back in Alameda, going over material not yet covered: battle first-aid, radio-telephone communications, Squadron One operations, and 82-footer familiarization. With training over, Coast Guardsmen flew to Saigon, where they were given their assignment. However, with the first group, where the whole squadron was preparing simultaneously, it was different. They were not a small cluster of replacements going into an already established operation. Before moving on to South Vietnam these men assembled at the U.S. Naval Base, Subic Bay, Republic of the Philippines, to join their cutters and shakedown for war.

The Coast Guard needed an exceptional officer to put together its first fighting squadron in twenty years, a squadron from which other service members would derive opinions of the Coast Guard's usefulness. The officer had to have the cardinal virtues of prudence, justice, fortitude, and temperance, spiced with luck. The forty-one-year-old Hodgman, having a strong background for the assignment, was chosen. For the previous three years he had been associated with the Navy—two years on liaison duty and one while attending the U.S. Naval War College, in Newport, Rhode Island. Moreover, he was familiar with the Asiatic side of the world, having served in two cutters, aboard one as executive officer and the other as commanding officer, that roamed the Pacific Ocean. His career began when he graduated from the Coast Guard Academy on 7 June 1944 and was assigned to the Coast Guard–manned destroyer escort USS *Marchant* (DE-249) for European and Asiatic convoy duty. A fellow officer described Hodgman as straightforward in nature. That aptly described his orders, which essentially said "Take these men and seventeen cutters, put together some kind of organization, and do what the Navy wants." Lurking between the lines of military jargon one could also sense the unwritten admonition "and don't embarrass us!"

Coast Guard brass had nothing to worry about. Hodgman's performance only added to the service's reputation for excellence in extraordinary times and earned him the Legion of Merit with Combat "V" device. But that would be in the future. For now,

Coast Guard patrol boats were lashed on the decks of merchant ships and transported from the United States to the Philippines, where their crews further readied them for war before sailing the cutters to South Vietnam. (Courtesy of U.S. Coast Guard)

Hodgman had ninety days to whip together a dog patrol to help a relative keep the foxes out of the henhouse of a friend. Hodgman found himself logging more air miles than an international commercial airline pilot over a similar time span as he hopped from Washington, DC, to California, to Hawaii, to Hong Kong, to Vietnam, and to the Philippines, discussing operations and logistics with various commands in smoothing his squadron's transition into the war.

The penultimate phase of Squadron One's readiness took place in the Philippines when Hodgman arrived on 8 June at the sprawling Subic Bay naval base for a major conference on working out the details of the entire interdiction scheme. Three days later the first party of Coast Guardsmen reported in. The boats, like the men, trickled in throughout the month, with the first two cutters arriving lashed to the main deck of a merchant ship on 17 June, and the last of them coming in on 28 June. Coast Guardsmen found the Philippines period grueling, with no time off and workdays 15 hours long. Each cutter received a thorough inspection for hull and equipment failures. Overall, they were in good shape, but there were problems with those not given the required major engineering overhaul before leaving the United States. This fact was revealed during stress maneuvers, such as high speed runs, where failures occurred. So the sickly cutters were bounced in and out of the shipyard for sundry repairs. During this preparation phase additional communications gear and floodlights—the latter for nighttime boarding—were installed on the boats. June melted into July, but for the Coast Guardsmen time seemed one continuous day, broken only by catnaps. They provisioned the boats. They inventoried, separated, tagged, preserved, and packaged spare parts. They performed gunnery exercises, emergency drills, day and night boarding trials, and tactical maneuvering.

When snags hindered them they approached the matter, first with cordiality. If this failed, other methods did not. When told no vehicles were available for their conveyance needs, Hodgman dispatched Lieutenant Richard Fremont-Smith to the transportation section to shake something loose. After being turned down by underlings, Fremont-Smith took the bold, direct approach of going to the senior naval officer in charge, explaining that the squadron only needed the vehicles for a few weeks.

Impressed with the young officer's approach and the combat mission, the Navy captain gave the Coast Guard sixteen new vehicles recently arrived and not yet in use. Other situations called for a "big stick" approach.

With the allocated training time running down fast, a problem surfaced. The fuel farm would not open early enough for the cutters to top off for a full day of underway exercises. Short on patience by now, the Coast Guardsmen told the man running the place that if it was not open when they came by in the morning they would open it. There were occasions when a rigid bureaucracy cut the supply flow of critical items to a trickle and the straight-laced squadron commander led midnight over-a-fence "requisitions."

With the coastal surveillance plan calling for the Coast Guard to watch the northern and southern ends of South Vietnam, Hodgman divided his squadron into two divisions. He would go to An Thoi, near the Cambodian border, to command Division Eleven and run the squadron from there, while Lieutenant Commander Richard J. Knapp would lead Division Twelve in Danang.

At 1600, on 16 July, eight brilliant-white young hulls paraded out of the harbor and collected around their gray, matronly tank landing ship escort, USS *Snohomish County* (LST-1126). Division Twelve began the lengthy crossing to Vietnam, with Coast Guardsmen feeling the same conflicting emotions of excitement and dread experienced by Christopher Columbus and his fifteenth century crew as they, too, sailed toward the unknown.

Fine weather accompanied the uneventful crossing. Even refueling went smoothly. For this evolution the cutters slipped from their circle formation to line abreast of the escort's port beam at 100-yard intervals. The inboard boat then fell into position on the escort ship's starboard quarter, making fuel hose connection while the next cutter in line took station a short distance astern to recover anyone falling into the sea. The lifeguard craft was next to fuel, with another cutter moving into her vacated station. The process averaged 45 minutes for each boat.

At 0700, on 20 July, just 82 days following the public announcement that the Coast Guard was going to war, the first battle-ready units filed into the South Vietnamese naval base at Danang, greeted by high-ranking American and South Vietnamese naval officers. Eight days later, Division Eleven left Subic Bay, but the trip was not pleasant because the nine cutters and their escort, USS *Floyd County* (LST-762), bucked the Southwest Monsoon. Underway refueling occurred in treacherous 30-knot winds and 15-foot seas, taking eleven exhaustive hours. Credit that there were no injuries, loss of life, or vessel damage must be given to skillful Coast Guard and Navy seamanship. During this passage even mundane acts challenged the men. In the 82-footer, the crew's head is squeezed into the bow. It holds a shower stall slightly broader than the average

The cutter *Point Grace* bounds over the seas as she takes on fuel from the escort ship during Division Eleven's crossing from Subic Bay in the Philippines to An Thoi in South Vietnam. (Courtesy of ET2 Gordon Angermeier, USCG)

person. Gunner's Mate First Class Martin J. Kelleher, a burly man of 215 pounds, gave this account of trying to take a shower. "We had a hell of a trip over. We really beat ourselves up. After about three days I couldn't stand myself any longer, so I went to take a shower. The head was up forward. I demolished the shower. I mean the boat is just a-pitching and a-flopping and a-snapping. I mean snap rolls. They had a grab rail and a soap dish in the shower. I'm soaping up—the old sea shower routine—and we took a violent roll and I grabbed that rail and it came off in my hand and I fell backwards and hit that soap dish and it came unglued and gouged my back. So, finally I wound up sitting down. There was no way you could stand up in that thing. That was the only shower I took en route. I tell you it was mean. It was mean."

After five punishing days at sea the convoy rested for 24 hours at the South Vietnamese base on Con Son Island. With less than 250 miles to go they resumed passage on the evening of 30 July. The next day, upon entering the Gulf of Thailand, the *Operation Market Time* task force commander ordered three of the cutters out on patrol and the rest proceeded into An Thoi.

Division Eleven was an isolated operation. After crossing the Gulf, the escort ship dropped her anchor off the point of ice cream cone–shaped Phu Quoc Island. As the cutters nestled up to the ship the men looked at the empty surroundings, gradually coming to the realization that this was it! Home? Thus far all they had seen were rocky islands, sand, and jungle, causing some to wonder about the big rush to get here. The *Floyd County* would serve as support vessel and house the repair force and spare crewmen until the USS *Krishna* (ARL-38) was customized for the task.

On the beach sat the small fishing village of An Thoi and a South Vietnamese Navy base with U.S. Navy advisors. Most of the island rested above South Vietnam's mainland boundary with Cambodia, and both countries claimed rightful ownership of it. Sightseeing on the 25-mile-long island was not recommended. Only three villages were in government control; the Viet Cong dominated everywhere else. Additionally, little of the Gulf's mainland rested in government possession and the multitude of canal outlets along the coastline gave infiltrators the advantage. Though it was far from ideal, this site was the best available in the Gulf for reasons of a deepwater anchorage, a lee from monsoon winds, and proximity to Coastal Surveillance Center, An Thoi. Yes, the Coast Guardsmen were here, and they were not among friends.

Up north, Division Twelve settled into a more populated and hospitable home. Upon arriving in Danang the *Snohomish County* snuggled up against a vacant cement pier at the Vietnamese naval base below Monkey Mountain, with her bevy of cutters nestled alongside. The original plan called for anchoring the division in the harbor once two support barges being outfitted in Subic Bay arrived. Knapp preferred staying shoreside to avoid the inherent logistics headaches that came with separation. When a mutual respect turned into a friendship between Knapp and the Vietnamese base commander, Knapp gained local approval to keep the division where it was. His superiors, given time to observe that the arrangement worked well, did not push him into the stream after all. The division stayed there for more than two and a half years, until the U.S. Navy consolidated its *Market Time* forces further into the harbor.

The extent of enemy seaborne resupply remained uncertain, but at MACV, the premise remained that it was formidable. Estimated figures of how many tons of supplies needed to enter the country daily to keep the Viet Cong effective were being compared with the probability of how much was getting past the current *Market Time* force levels. Although the detection of infiltrators at the ends of South Vietnam seemed strong, the center of the country was vulnerable.

Accordingly, COMUSMACV wanted more forces. At the direction of CINCPAC a study group met in Saigon in September to consider this. Among other recommendations, it called for nine more Coast Guard cutters and an increase in the number of PCFs (patrol craft, fast) ordered into the country to be raised from 54 to 84.

When the U.S. Navy found it needed an inshore patrol boat it went shopping and bought a 50-foot commercial aluminum craft, stuck guns in it, slapped on gray paint, and gave it the nickname "Swift" for its more than 25-knot capability. The Swift boats began arriving in country in October. The study also created Task Force 116, or *Operation Game Warden,* a river patrol force to interdict the enemy in the waterways of the Mekong Delta and RSSZ.

Lieutenant Commander William E. Lehr Jr. was a busy man in Squadron One, with chief of staff, engineering officer, and supply officer duties. In December, he became even busier when Hodgman ordered him back to Subic Bay to shape the men and WPBs arriving there into Division Thirteen. For Lehr the chore was like having to endure the same unpleasant dream again. It was made somewhat less exacting, in that, as the new men became sufficiently trained, some were sent to Divisions Eleven or Twelve and replaced with men from those units, in order to spread experience among the new unit. While the division took form, so too did its operating base at Cat Lo. On a narrow strip of land, with the main road between Vung Tau and Saigon on one side and the river on the other, the base was constructed. From here the cutters would disperse on patrol northeast and southwest of the river mouth leading to Saigon. At 1600 on 19 February 1966, Division Thirteen cutters moved out of Subic Bay escorted by the USS *Forster* (DER-334) toward their place in Coast Guard history. The formation had *Forster* in the center of a circle, with the cutters stationed at a 1,000-yard radius. As did Division Twelve, Thirteen transited under fine weather, but toward the end it had some excitement, which Lehr noted in his division diary entry for Tuesday, 22 February 1966:

At 0130 the formation commenced emergency maneuvers to avoid two Chinese Nationalist steel hull fishing trawlers. The trawlers [were] detected at some distance ahead, but their course was extremely erratic. Initially the formation tried to clear by passing north of the trawlers but they altered course to steer directly into our path. Next the formation turned south so as to pass astern of the fishermen. Again they changed course and headed directly for us. By this time the situation was critical so the CO of Forster *ordered all units to break formation and maneuver independently. There were several hair-raising occurrences when the trawlers passed through the leading semi-circle of the formation. At one point both the* Forster *and* Point League *had to back down to avoid each other as well as the trawlers. Fortunately, there were no accidents.*

By about 0300 all of the scattered units were in formation again. The division was formed in column at that time to make the final 20 mile passage.

That same day the WPBs, on a strong flood tide, entered the river in a column, peeled off at the Cat Lo base, made an impressive 180-degree turn for the assembled audience and moored in three nests of three boats. The welcoming committee included the local mayor, the Vietnamese Third Coastal Zone commander, an honor guard, a police band, and schoolchildren waving American flags. When finished, the new base would be a comfortable setup. For now, it lacked water and fuel sources, sending cutters begging to the many large ships anchored in Vung Tau. In return for fillups the cutters delivered mail for the ships. With thirty percent of the buildings completed, the shore party had sleeping quarters, but meals were a hassle. Until the galley went up the men had to be trucked into Vung Tau to eat. Two days later Lehr turned his temporary command of Division Thirteen over to another officer and returned to his Squadron One troubleshooting chores.

Before the arrival of the Coast Guard cutters, *Operation Market Time* worked as well as torn fishing net. Most of the enemy ships, especially the smaller ones, could easily elude capture because Seventh Fleet ships were restrained by their draft from reaching suspects near the coast. Ten days after Division Twelve reached Vietnam, operational control of *Market Time* was turned over to the U.S. Navy forces in South Vietnam, becoming Task Force 115, a coastal surveillance command composed of sea, air, and shore-based units.

Market Time sectioned the water off South Vietnam into nine patrol areas numbered in order from north to south. They measured 80 to 120 miles long and ran 30 to 40 miles out to sea. Each was further subdivided, with roughly two-thirds of the offshore area as one, and the inshore third diced into sections. For example, in Area Three off the central coast, the large outer zone was 3B, and the inner one was partitioned into 3C, 3D, 3E, 3F, 3G, 3H, and 3I. Three barriers were thrown up to defeat infiltration. The air barrier took the form of naval aircraft flying various tracks reporting and photographing suspects. Destroyer escorts and minesweepers roamed the outer barrier, generally stalking 10 to 15 miles offshore. The inner barrier belonged to the WPBs, joined later by the PCFs. At first, the cutters were strung out in a line along the Demilitarized Zone (DMZ) and the Cambodian border, but as the task force learned more about enemy movements they were assigned random cruising in the inner patrol areas throughout the country. Patrol vessels kept in contact with one of five Coastal Surveillance Centers (CSC): Danang, Qui Nhon, Nha Trang, Vung Tau, and An Thoi. Jointly manned by U.S. Navy and South Vietnamese Navy watchstanders, they passed information and operational orders. The main effort to find the enemy came by visit and search. Every patrol day crews put in hours poking through junks, making it the most dominant part of the daily routine.

The Coast Guard's first enemy kills came on 19 September 1965. Not long after midnight the USCGC *Point Glover* (WPB 82307) ordered a 24-foot motorized junk to stop. It reacted with a foolish attempt to ram the cutter. Upon dodging this tactic the Coast Guardsmen fired into the engine. When the vessel went dead in the water, the five Viet Cong jumped overboard. One was fished from the water by another cutter and taken prisoner, and the others either escaped or drowned. At 2230, near the Cambodian border, when the USCGC *Point Marone* (WPB 82321) closed on a 35-foot junk for boarding, the occupants responded with small arms fire and the fight was on. When the encounter was over, nine Viet Cong were dead, and one critically wounded.

In those engagements the cutters had white hulls, but that was about to change, with an order from *Market Time* headquarters to repaint the WPBs gray. The basis was that gray is less distinguishable, an arguable point depending upon the situation. Naturally, Coast Guardsmen resented the order. They took great pride in their white ves-

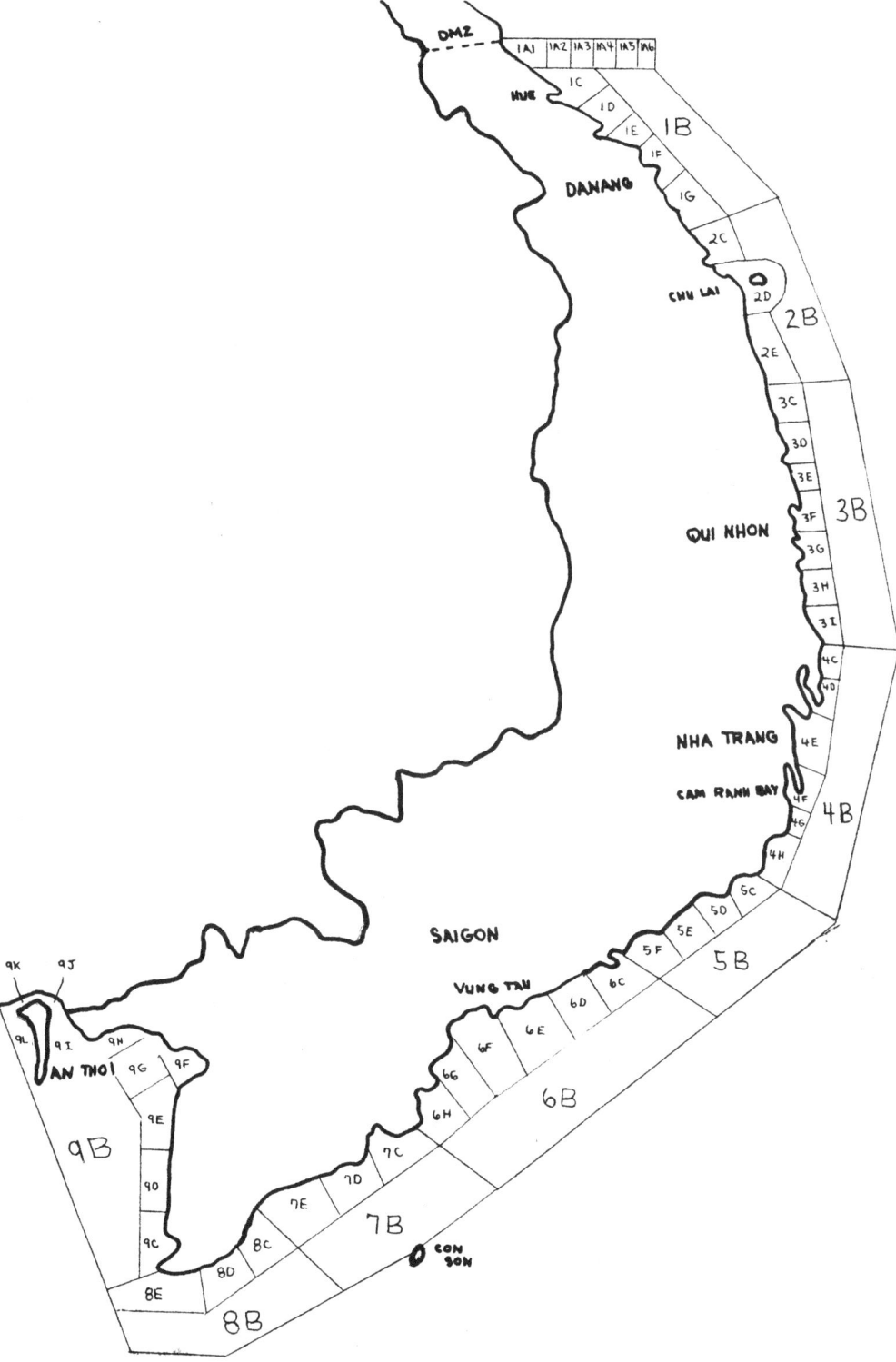

The surface patrol areas of *Operation Market Time* were divided into larger offshore sectors for the ships and smaller inshore sections for the patrol boats.

sels, some reasoning, of course, that if they wanted to be like the Navy, they would have joined the Navy. To retain distinction between the services, Coast Guardsmen experimented with colors and settled upon a vibrant, black-gray shade, giving the cutters a menacing presence. This quieted the grumbling.

At the south end of the country Hodgman was working five jobs. Besides commanding Squadron One and Division Eleven, the Navy put him in charge of directing *Market Time* operations in Areas Eight and Nine and maintaining the supporting units, and named him Fourth Coastal Zone Advisor. South Vietnam was sectioned into four military regions known as Corps. The corresponding Vietnamese naval area in each Corps was called a coastal zone, or district.

The Coastal Zone Advisor's main job of getting two cultures to function in harmony was complicated by weaknesses in leadership and discipline in the South Vietnamese Navy, which often exasperated Hodgman and his successors. A sample of what the advisor was up against comes from this squadron diary entry of 15 December 1965 by Hodgman:

> *Several hours a day are spent in detail on US-VNN coordination and advisory activities. This is quite a business. They pay very little attention to orders from their superiors and if the CO is away everything stops. Right now one of my problems is that one of my advisors knocked loudly on the door of a VNN officer during his siesta and startled him. The VNN officer formally complained to me and is sulking. He has been giving briefings in English but now has decided his English is not good enough and has declined to do so in the future. I have handled the situation without creating a big internal flap but I wasted over two hours before it was settled and he is still unhappy.*

Hodgman's successor wrote that getting Vietnamese Navy officers to communicate with each other is a big problem and getting their naval units to coordinate among themselves is extremely difficult.

Burdened with many command "hats" and with the addition of Division Thirteen, Hodgman felt it impractical for him to continue as squadron commander. He therefore recommended to Coast Guard Headquarters that this post be administered from Saigon, where the U.S. Navy had its headquarters, and that a senior officer be given the assignment. The Navy had no objection to the reorganization. On 31 January 1966, 44-year-old Captain Robert J. Loforte relieved Hodgman as Commander, Coast Guard Squadron One (COMCOGARDRON ONE). Thereupon, when word spread that a Coast Guard officer was in Saigon, a wide variety of people began dropping into the office, with little advance notice. They expounded on problems and demanded to know why the

Coast Guard was doing nothing about them, completely disregarding that this was foreign soil and not the United States. Lean and energetic, with diplomatic sensitivities, Loforte was the right man for the year ahead, when the Coast Guard role in Vietnam would expand into many roles.

CHAPTER 3

PORT DANGERS

THE U.S. NAVY WAS NOT ALONE IN SEEKING OUT THE COAST GUARD. The U.S. Army, with logistical responsibility throughout most of South Vietnam, too, found need for their military kinsmen.

Since fighting troops require an uninterrupted feeding of materials to nourish their mission, proven supply methods sent ships, plump with cargo, across the ocean with conveyor belt regularity. But this orderliness crumbled into disarray at South Vietnam, where the few seaports and shipping facilities were better suited for an early 1900s coastal trade. Saigon, the most commercially developed deepwater port, became the foremost dropoff point. The military buildup moved faster than spring floods, inundating Saigon before measures could be taken to contain and channel the overflow to new ports. Merchant ships floated at anchor for weeks before they were called to offload. Then, when their turn came, their masters watched in dismay as inexperienced, locally hired stevedores gave bombs the same rough handling as dry goods.

Warehouses, few in number, quickly filled to capacity. Crates piled up everywhere, sprawling beyond the wharves and warehouse aprons into the narrow streets, where they hindered trucks trying to squeeze the supplies out of the city. The U.S. Army, in April 1965, activated the 1st Logistical Command for the unwieldy task of absorbing and disbursing the massive supply influx into II, III, and IV Corps.

No waterborne logistics setup succeeds without righteous attention to security and safety. Knowing these areas are the everyday affair of the Coast Guard in safeguarding American harbors, COMUSMACV asked for an evaluation of the Saigon port. Commander Risto A. Mattila of the Ports and Waterways Division left his desk at Coast Guard Headquarters to spend five months appraising the situation. His subsequent report gave as much comfort as reading about the recovery chances of a friend with numerous terminal illnesses. He found a port operation without form.

If the Viet Cong had had any decent organization at the time they could have destroyed crucial materials with the merest of personnel casualties. So many South Vietnamese government agencies were enmeshed in administering the port that any harmony for streamlining seemed unlikely. Every day thousands of people entered and left the port area—a third of them with no legitimate business there. Without a clearance and identification program only happenstance distinguished the friendly from the hostile. The harbor, with its sinuous approaches, could easily have been attacked by light weapons, while the ships made indolent targets for floating mines or swimmers packing demolitions.

Just as bothersome was unsafe ammunition handling. Mattila watched a Vietnamese man expeditiously unload his truck of explosive projectiles by speeding up in reverse, then hitting the brakes to send the heavy shells tumbling to the ground. When questioned about his technique the man remarked that it would be much easier if he had a dump truck. If such carelessness continued, eventually Saigon's port would blow itself up without any enemy effort. Because the U.S. Army had few on active duty with port operations knowledge, soldiers were having to learn while doing, which could turn deadly.

Accordingly, Mattila recommended that the Army accept Coast Guardsmen to supervise ammunition handling and to give port security guidance. A part of this occurred in February 1966, when COMUSMACV asked for Coast Guard Explosive Loading Detachments (ELDs). Port Security, on the other hand, was a contested issue, as neither the Army nor the Navy wanted any part of it.

The 1st Logistical Command, already feeling overburdened, contended that waterside protection belonged on the Navy's duty list. The Navy demurred, arguing that they were there for harbor defense, not policing. Interservice squabbling went unresolved until a mine disabled one freighter and mines were found attached to anchor chains of others at Nha Be. The occurrence drove COMUSMACV to rule that 1st Logistical Command would take charge of all aspects of port security in their Corps areas. Not long after this decision, the commanding general of 1st Logistical Command, Major General Charles W. Eifler, met with Loforte, expressing his concern that his people knew little about protecting a waterfront complex and wanted the Coast Guard's help.[1]

Loforte explained that his service could furnish advisors but the actual security would have to be done by the Army. This satisfied the general, and in July 1966 COMUSMACV sent a message that "an urgent requirement exists for Coast Guard personnel trained in port security." The ELDs arrived first, when 16 eager men stepped off an airplane in Saigon, on 4 June 1966. Their zeal to get going had to simmer a week or so until they became acquainted with people and surroundings. Loforte personally took charge of making the introductions to ensure that everyone understood the purpose of these teams, not only because it fell within his capacity as the senior Coast Guard officer in Vietnam with administrative control over the ELDs, but out of an irrepressible service pride that jumped at the opportunity to peacock. Loforte was like a proud father introducing his sons to a new employer. He knew that "his boys" would bring praise from the Army and heightened respect for the Coast Guard.

The Coast Guardsmen were divided into two teams of one officer and seven enlisted men each. Explosives Loading Detachment #1 went to Nha Be on the river several miles below Saigon, while ELD #2 moved into Cam Ranh Bay. Although they primarily worked at these major ammunition processing sites, the men were also dispatched to obscure out-ports, river ramps, and midstream anchorages. The 1st Logistical Command welcomed them unconditionally, but in the beginning the field commands

Coast Guard Petty Officer Dominic Emelio (right) of Explosive Loading Detachment #2 and his U.S. Army counterpart supervise the safe unloading of ammunition from a ship in Cam Ranh Bay. (Courtesy of U.S. Coast Guard)

did not. Soldiers working the docks grumbled that the Coast Guard was butting into their business and that stateside rules would slow down offloading. Hence, the ELDs not only had to learn the Army mindset and organization, but they also had to overcome the natural resentment toward outsiders. This bias, however, vanished early, aided by common military roots and those inspiring traits that bring on respect: competence, perseverance, and humility.

Their job was hampered mostly by the problems noted by Mattila. Lieutenant (j.g.) Edward G. O'Keefe, officer-in-charge, ELD #1, found security inexcusably lax. He caught South Vietnamese sentries sleeping and watched South Vietnamese lighters draw alongside ammunition ships unsearched. He found South Vietnamese Navy harbor patrols passive and predictable and observed scant supervision of U.S. Army MP (military police) guards on ships. His reports to 1st Logistical Command detailed his findings, but little would change until the arrival of the port security detail.

The ELDs found solutions to some of their stumbling blocks within the Coast Guard family. At Nha Be, where ELD #1 lacked water transportation for getting around to ships, Division Thirteen loaned them a 14-foot boat until the Army came through with one.

The prattle that Coast Guard intervention would retard unloading time was repeatedly proven otherwise. Sharp-eyed Coast Guardsmen spotted equipment weaknesses, fixing them before they could fail at a critical moment. They picked through Saigon port buildings searching for better gear and found wire cargo slings to replace manila ones. They found drop-forged safety hooks to replace cracked or bent handforged ones.

O'Keefe had made a written recommendation that electric forklifts be used between decks on ammunition ships to speed up cargo transfer and improve safety. But, rather than waiting for someone to eventually get around to acting on his suggestion, he went looking on his own. He discovered, shunted out of the way in a somnolent warehouse—their presence and purpose forgotten—44 crated electric forklifts and a hundred batteries to power them. O'Keefe then suggested outfitting a barge to maintain the forklifts and ferry them from one ship to another.

When an ammunition ship arrived for offloading, the usual procedure was for someone from the ELD to meet her officers to explain the ground rules. Because of port layout and enemy presence, these varied from place to place. Items covered included placement of fire hoses, water surveillance lighting, state of readiness for getting under way in an emergency, and smoking regulations. This was followed by an inspection of the cargo handling equipment.

Coast Guardsmen worked alone, or in teams, in 12-hour shifts. Unlike in the United States, where the Coast Guard held federal authority to stop unloading because of safety violations, here the Army was in charge, and an Army counterpart held this capacity. As soldiers learned to respect the Coast Guardsmens' knowledge they usually heeded their recommendations. Later, it became practice for local Army port commanders to delegate to the Coast Guard the authority to stop operations when a serious unsafe practice was witnessed.

The ELDs worked around the clock and every day of the week. A Coast Guardsman might go a month before seeing a day off. Even then, the chance was good that he would end up spending it at some distant place like Pleiku in the central highlands inspecting retrograde cargo—the ammunition returning to the United States. When a Coast Guardsman came aboard ship the hard-edged, uneasy creases on the master's face usually dissolved into soft, assured lifelines. These veteran mariners, familiar with Coast Guard professionalism, felt secure under its direction. When a novice Army cargo supervisor came aboard, a master might pray that his ship got unloaded without blowing up. Captain N.T. Aubert of the USNS *Greenville Victory* was so impressed with the scrupulousness of Boatswain's Mate First Class Albert F. Earle of ELD #1 that he wrote Earle's Coast Guard superiors recommending him for special commendation.

Per routine, the first thing Earle did on boarding the *Greenville Victory* was explain the setup. Aubert, who had been hauling ammunition into Vietnam for five years, wrote that Earle gave one of the finest briefings on the local conditions, dangers, and requirements that he had ever received in any port in Vietnam or elsewhere. At the time, ELD #1 was short-handed, leaving Earle working the ship alone and without relief. Day and night Aubert witnessed the lone Coast Guardsman climbing in and out of holds, peering over the side, and studying the cargo handling, intent on detecting anything that might bring disaster.

The master kept urging Earle to get some sleep, reminding him that he had two officers and a full watch on duty patrolling the decks all the time. If a problem came up he would be called immediately. But Earle continued on, catching a random catnap. Then, shortly before 0400, while he was wresting away heavy shoring blocking access to pallets, a wood beam fell, knocking him out. He was pulled from the hatch and laid on deck, where Aubert applied a cold compress to a bloody head gash. When Earle regained consciousness he refused the aid of a stretcher. With assistance that he grudgingly accepted, he wobbled down the accommodation ladder into a boat taking him for medical treatment.

In one way Aubert felt relief—at least now the man would get his overdue sleep. One can imagine Aubert's surprise later that morning upon seeing Earle back at work on the ship. A whack on the head and 23 stitches were not enough to keep away a Coast Guardsman with a dogged sense of duty.

The ELDs submitted weekly reports to their respective Army commands. For the local commanders these digests were like windows through which they could view the state of port operations without leaving their offices. These synopses itemized what Coast Guardsmen came up against on the job.

There was inattentiveness. A stevedore was injured when a pallet fell on his feet because he was not watching what he was doing. There was belligerence. A Coast Guard officer had confined and placed under guard a nasty merchant seaman for intoxication, smoking, and failure to cooperate. There was negligence. A Coast Guardsman, finding one U.S. Army MP asleep on the fantail during his guard duty, and a second missing from his post, scooped up their weapons for safekeeping and advised the MP desk. Above all else, their knowledge of dangerous cargo made Coast Guardsmen most valuable. They treated explosives as an animal trainer treats a tiger—with wariness. To less informed stevedores—American or foreign—the projectiles tight inside sturdy boxes or the drab green bombs strapped in tiers on pallets had the appearance of withstanding a fair amount of banging about. They felt no menace in the word "explosive" stenciled on them.

Consequently, to some the Coast Guard's strictness in enforcing safety rules seemed extreme. Coast Guardsmen knew, for example, that napalm, a frequent traveler in ships and a fearsome weapon well-reputed for rapidly transforming a target into ashes, is a blend of gasoline and benzene thickened into a glue-like mass with the addition of polystyrene, and housed in a thin-walled casing. While fuzes were not installed until just prior to use in the combat area, they also knew that rough handling easily punctured the metal skin. Once freed, the viscous pale orange liquid presented a serious fire danger because napalm ignites through a broad range of temperatures. If its flammable vapors accumulate in a confined area, an ignition source as small as a lighted cigarette can bring on an explosion. Combustible vapors are the biggest reason for "no smoking" rules.

Coast Guardsmen responded fast to a napalm hazard. When a napalm bomb toppled and split open on the deck on 15 August 1967 they stopped the unloading immediately, resuming only after the syrupy discharge was removed.

In comparison to running down infiltrators in a patrol boat, unloading ships sounds dreary. Yet these dangerous-cargo men were not deprived of excitement. Late one afternoon at the Nha Be anchorage a sling-load of 20-mm high-explosive incendiary ammunition slapped against the hull of the SS *Carroll Victory,* causing the 100-round ammunition cans to plummet into the hold of the barge below. As smoke rose from the damaged containers the Coast Guardsman on the ship grabbed a fire hose, slammed open the nozzle, and rained water into the barge. At the same time, two soldiers on the barge hurried into the hold, snatched up the smokiest can, and ran back on deck and threw it into the river, where it hit the water and exploded.

Gunner's Mate First Class Joseph R. Glenn, after finishing his 12-hour shift one night, was riding to shore in a Korean tugboat with his thoughts mainly on reaching his quarters for sleep. But, when the tugboat passed a docked ship, Glenn was alert enough to spot a sampan and five Vietnamese tucked under her bow. Two of the men were climbing the anchor chain. He drew his .45-caliber sidearm and fired shots to get their attention. The men on the chain dropped into the harbor and the sampan fled. Glenn commandeered the tugboat, chased down the sampan, and then recovered the swimmers. Three of his captives carried no identification. He turned them in and went on his way.

Three Coast Guardsmen showed their mettle on 18 June 1968, when the Viet Cong launched a furious nighttime mortar and small arms strike on the Cat Lai Army Terminal facilities. A cluster of ammunition barges anchored in the Dong Nai River took the initial fusillade, setting a landing craft near the barge afire. Lieutenant (j.g.) William S. Cotter and petty officers Albert F. Earle and Oliver W. Creacy Jr. grabbed helmets and flak jackets and ran from their quarters to their small boat. En route, Cotter signaled a tug coming from the scene to stop. They scrambled aboard to hear that the tug had to desert the fire after her firefighting pump quit. Before long, however, the engineers had the pump working again and the tug headed back, with everyone aware that the landing craft held 55 pallets of dynamite.

Their biggest concern was that if the barge blew it might take nearby ammunition barges with it. Creacy scampered to the top of the pilothouse to man the monitor. Cotter and Earle picked up the hose stretched out on the bow. After knocking out most of the flames, Cotter and Earle jumped into the landing craft, dragging the heavy, water-rigid hose with them to soak down areas they could not reach from the tug. From the tug, Creacy drenched them with water to protect them from the heat and flareups. Once the flames were out Cotter and Earle began tossing the baking cargo overboard. Through it all the Viet Cong had been sniping at the firefighters. But when the attack ended all that the enemy had to celebrate were neck and wrist burns to two Coast Guardsmen. Eifler, well pleased with his ELDs' "highly commendable performance," made his feelings a matter of record in a letter to the Coast Guard praising their tireless efforts in contrary situations. Of their uncommon temperament he wrote, "Their courteous and cooperative attitude has won for them the respect and admiration of all in my command with whom they have come in contact."[2]

Notwithstanding the ELDs' fine work, protests of abusive cargo handling continued to come in. The master of the SS *Queen's Victory* had strong criticism of a U.S. Army longshoreman at the Tuy Hoa sub-port, where he watched bombs dropped and bounced, forklifts jammed into cargo, and widespread smoking in the hatches. He reported continual horseplaying on the job, "such as soldiers throwing empty pop cans at one another, dropping cluster lights on each other, and boxing with every G.I. they pass."

In truth, the territory was too vast for only two ELDs to cover. Eifler wanted at least one more and he wanted it for Qui Nhon. Located between Danang and Cam Ranh Bay, the fourth major deepwater port in South Vietnam had become first in flagrant cargo mishandling reports. One instance involved the SS *Gamon* which, after partially offloading at Qui Nhon, went to Nha Be. There ELD #1 found ammunition scattered all over the holds, evidence of carelessness in securing the reduced load for sea travel.

Eifler personally asked Admiral Willard J. Smith for another ELD when the latter visited South Vietnam. Smith, who had succeeded Roland as Coast Guard commandant, readily offered another team, but that did not mean that it would happen soon, because standard procedures had to be followed. First, manpower ceilings required the Army to find eight soldier positions to drop to replace with Coast Guardsmen. Next, the request had to join the paperwork horde crawling through the layers of chain of command from one side of the world to the other. Still, aware that the petition was being made, the Coast Guard saved some time by going ahead with personnel selection and training. The sloppy cargo processing continued in Qui Nhon, and when Coast Guard ELD #3 arrived in March 1968, a year later, they were too late to prevent one calamity. A few months earlier, alongside the SS *Berea Victory,* a landing craft with its motor idling indulgently awaited its fill of ordnance. Its crew was unaware that it was about to experience ruin through the deadly combination of a lack of know-how and faulty offloading methods. Two 750-pound bombs swaying above the craft slipped from their sling. Upon hitting the boat a low-order explosion flung two soldiers overboard. Two others fled the ensuing fire by scurrying up the Jacob's ladder to the ship.

When the Army coxswain fell dead across the controls his weight engaged the engine and the craft moved slowly away from the ship. Midway between the *Berea Victory* and another anchored vessel a second minor explosion took place, quickly followed by a massive blast that shredded the landing craft. One of the two soldiers earlier thrown into the water died. Only an act of providence prevented the destruction of the ships, with an even greater loss of life.

In I Corps, where the U.S. Navy was in charge, safety standards were no better. In June 1966, when Loforte and Lieutenant Commander Howard H. Istock, commander of Division Twelve, were dinner guests of the admiral running the Danang naval support activity, the admiral related his safety and security problems in anticipation that the Coast Guard might help. The fallout of the evening was that Istock, trained in these areas, would evaluate the port and make corrective suggestions. Furthermore, Division Twelve would send men with explosives handling expertise to help with offloadings when it did not interfere with the division's mission.

This part-time assistance did little to alleviate matters. Ship captains told of persistent negligence with frightened indignation. The master of SS *Longview Victory* repeatedly told Korean civilian stevedores unloading his vessel not to overload slings by placing two pallets of 500-pound bombs in a load. When they ignored him he stopped the unloading. After the work resumed the Koreans retaliated by finding imaginary things wrong with the cargo gear and refused to continue until the equipment was "fixed." Apparently, the doubling up of loads was driven by their being paid for how much tonnage they moved. Another master was emphatic when he wrote in his trip report, "...in Danang every known rule of safety was violated in the discharge of ammunition."[3] Finally, the Navy followed the Army's wisdom in formally asking for Coast Guard assistance, and on 9 June 1968, ELD #4, Danang, was established. Later, there were references to a fifth team, ELD #5, Vung Tau, but that was merely a title for conversational clarity. When ammunition shipments increased in the 1970s ELD members from the other teams took turns working in Vung Tau on temporary duty.

The ELD Coast Guardsman did not fit in any clique; he was an outsider, always "an X among Os." On the waterfront he engaged merchant mariner belligerence, within the Army he dealt with soldier coolness, among the foreign populace he coped with enemy violence, and surrounded by explosives he lived within a spark of annihilation. Engineman First Class Robert J. Yered's experiences sketch this environment. A New Englander, Yered possessed the stalwart regional traits that ideally suited him to dangerous cargo duty. His ability to get along with diverse personalities, his sound judgment, and his fearlessness served him well during his 1967–1968 tour with ELD #1. In July 1967, Yered ordered three intoxicated merchant seamen to stop smoking cigarettes over an open hatch where ammunition was being unloaded. They responded by attacking him, dislocating his shoulder before help arrived. The Coast Guard investigated and pressed charges against the main attacker for assaulting a federal officer. Two months later Yered was in Seattle, Washington, for the preliminary hearing. To the Coast Guard's dismay, the incident was dismissed because the U.S. Attorney's office neglected to have present the Army stevedore who witnessed it. When it became a matter of Yered's word against the mariner's the government had no case. Yered returned to Vietnam disappointed but not deterred.

Some weeks later, an hour past midnight, a South Vietnamese Navy patrol boat thumped against the ammunition ship he was working on. From it came a staggering group of Vietnamese sailors, American soldiers, and merchant seamen carrying and drinking beer. Yered promptly asked that the MP call for assistance to remove the drunken men. Unsure of his responsibility, the MP did nothing. Yered identified himself to two mariners, asking them for their names. In reply one of them tried to hit him but was stopped by a mariner, and the master, who had come on deck. Although the situation dissolved without further violence, Yered had to endure salvos of verbal insults and physical threats from the surly merchant marines until they weaved off to their quarters.

Yered would not forget February 1968. A few minutes after midnight, on the 14th, the Viet Cong sent the Americans St. Valentine's Day greetings that came from the heart, but with a sentiment that was anything but love. Vietnamese stevedores were winching ammunition from the SS *U.S. Tourist,* anchored at Cat Lai, onto barges when recoilless rifle and small arms fire banged into the ship. The clamor sent the stevedores running for refuge, where they huddled in terror of the unwanted company. The two Coast Guardsmen on board immediately had all lights turned off. From the shore, Yered and the ELD #1 officer-in-charge saw the attack and hurried out to the vessel. The four Coast Guardsmen and an Army sergeant put below the two loads of 105-mm artillery shells left on deck. They then coaxed the Vietnamese from hiding long enough to close the hatches in a fire preventive measure and flooded the deck with water. Twenty minutes after the attack began the ship was able to get under way if needed, but the attack ended as it had started—without fanfare. Four nights later, off Cat Lai and under a bright moon, three ammunition ships loafed at anchor on the quiet river while their cargo was transferred into barges. Along the weedy river's edge 300 yards away the Viet Cong slipped into position. As they planted their mortars, lifted recoilless rifles on their shoulder, and pressed their eyes against rifle sights, they did not know that collectively the bellies of the ships held in excess of 30 million pounds of explosives. They just knew that with good fortune they could cause a big boom. The port side of the SS *Neva West* and the ammunition barges next to her faced the enemy. It was 0100, and the Vietnamese stevedores and Army checkers were enjoying a meal-break. Yered was in his cabin cleaning up when explosions erupted around the ship. He ran on deck, making a rapid search for damage. The vessel seemed all right until he looked over the port rail and saw the aft end of a 130-foot barge, which was three-quarters full of 81-mm mortar rounds, on fire.

Through the smoke he could see flashes of small explosions caused by heat. Using a hose laid out by number three hatch, he gushed water onto the blaze, oblivious of the incoming shooting—unlike the stevedores and crew, who stayed in hiding. In the wheelhouse, an Army sergeant kept the base informed by radio and reported enemy positions.

For 15 minutes Yered soaked the barge, then, to get at the flickering beneath the wooden pallets, he made the vertical climb down to the barge, dragging the hose along. Finding that he still could not reach the obscured flames with the hose, Yered shouted to the sergeant that he wanted a bucket. He then stepped among ruptured mortar shells, picking up burning fragments and 60-pound cases and throwing them overboard.

The sergeant came down from the bridge, retrieved Yered's hose, and continued dousing the barge. After a while someone dropped Yered a bucket. He began hurried trips from the side of the ship, where he filled the pail with water draining from the main engine cooling discharge. He carried the water back to the burning cargo.

He did not know how many buckets of water it took to drown the fire, but an hour had passed since the enemy opened up. The attack ceased after MPs, transported by landing craft, chased the Viet Cong from the riverbank. With the fire out and the enemy gone, Yered had a chance to take in the ship's appearance and saw her blackened and holed from wheelhouse to waterline.

Later, he withdrew to the fantail and smoked a cigarette to calm his lingering excitement. Yered reflected briefly on how close a call this had been, then turned his thoughts to his wife and two children back in Massachusetts. The U.S Army had their thoughts, too—of Yered's valor—and awarded him a Silver Star.

The ELDs assuaged one part of the 1st Logistical Command's problem—getting dangerous cargo safely moved off ships. The other part—protecting it—was up to the Coast Guard Port Security and Waterways Detail (PSWD). Following the arrival of the detail's men in Saigon on 15 October 1966, Loforte, in jest, wrote in the unit diary, "...after they had their first look at the port they were ready to ship out—not over. Well, as I told them, there's no other way to go but up on that job."

Three savvy Coast Guard veterans composed the first PSWD. Heading the group was Commander Raymond C. Hertica, a 44-year-old officer who survived the World War II torpedo sinking of his cutter by a German submarine. He was a good choice, a no-nonsense guy who found his relaxation in smoking fine cigars. His thorough port security knowledge, backstopped with a sturdy build and a hardset countenance, conveyed the impression that if his advice was heeded, a great deal of calamity could be averted.

His assistant, brawny Lieutenant Donald G. Kneip, 37, whose promotion to lieutenant commander came through a month later, like Hertica treated port security as earnest business. But in contrast to Hertica he had a spontaneous sense of humor. Kneip usually found something to chuckle about even in seemingly unfunny circumstances, and individuals in his presence would often be seen laughing. Chief Boatswain's

Mate Charles D. Wise rounded out the team. His main job was ensuring that cargo was properly stowed.

At their initial meeting with Eifler, the general told them that they were to improve security at all coastal and river ports, barge sites, and anyplace else where munitions were put ashore in the 1st Logistical Command's jurisdiction. They were amazed at the general's confidence in them, because that meant they had responsibility for 70 percent of South Vietnam.

In reality, it became the entire country when the Navy learned of their usefulness. To begin, however, their first priority was the port of Saigon, which at the time inhaled most of the cargo coming into the nation. They were given open-ended travel orders and status as direct representatives of the general. If local port commanders, or others, tended to shrug them off because they were not U.S. Army, they carried a personal letter from Eifler that left no doubt that any suggestions offered by these Coast Guardsmen were to be accepted as coming from him.

To better understand how to secure Saigon Port they commenced a rigorous scrutiny by foot, jeep, boat, and helicopter. The chaos dismayed them. Clusters of junks and sampans hugged docked ships. Storage facilities were dilapidated and wharves rundown, while mixed cargos made little mountains along the waterfront without regard for their harmony.

The 1st Logistical Command, having had the unfamiliar port security job only four months, had instituted roving patrols ashore and afloat, but from the Coast Guardsmen's perspective they were not precluding anything. Furthermore, no fencing existed between the port and the city, allowing anyone to meander about unchallenged.

Studying the layout as if they were saboteurs, the Coast Guardsmen unanimously agreed that the entire installation could be destroyed simply by starting a fire in the dry season. Moreover, rather than the enemy causing a conflagration, they feared that with so much disregard of safety measures, the odds were greater that one would start accidentally. Without pause, flames would consume the haphazard array of combustibles because of a feeble firefighting defense.

Docks lacked handy firefighting equipment and the port had one fire truck, a pumper with a 400-gallon water supply crewed by Vietnamese and an American advisor. The few tugs available for fighting a fire had only single monitors of limited use. As a consequence, Hertica told the Maritime Administration (MARAD) and Military Sealift Transportation Service (MSTS) Advisory Board to pass the word to all ship captains to have their vessel's firefighting equipment in a "go" state, as they will get little, if any, shoreside assistance in event of a fire onboard.

Hertica had no use for some of South Vietnam's protective forces. He was particularly disgusted with a colonel who claimed responsibility for the harbor's security, other than those portions under U.S. Army control. Hertica noted in his log that the officer's operation consisted of several companies of South Vietnamese Army MPs who spent most of their time eating and gambling. Apparently, the country's premier, Nguyen Cao Ky, held the same opinion, because he fired the colonel on the spot during a port inspection.

There were those trying to do the job right, such as the Vietnamese commissioner, who as Chief of the Harbor Police ran a competent program of land and water patrols though beset by a severe lack of people and equipment. The entire matter was complicated by overlapping jurisdictions of various Vietnamese and American police and military components.

The way it looked to the PSWD, the Army seemed more concerned with pilferage than with infiltration or attack, and with a satisfactory reason. Based upon the estimates given to the PSWD, 5 to 10 percent of United States military cargo and 20 to 50 percent of all United States Agency for International Development (USAID) commodity import cargos were being stolen. While theft itself did not concern the PSWD mission, when port security against infiltration tightened thievery would decline.

Their critical survey of the port took weeks of exhaustive study and legwork. They examined waterfront blueprints and traced the city's storm drain network, from which Saigon expelled its slime into the harbor out of three-foot-wide openings. Concerned that someone would crawl into these befouled passages with demolitions, the PSWD inspected each one to see that they were barred.

This chore had its peril. Below these openings decades of sewage had turned the river bottom into a blue-gray muck, a soggy marinade of countless noisome ingredients that emitted a gagging odor. At low tide, when the river shrank back to uncover her moist belly, the Coast Guardsmen went to work. While squishing his way between the green slime-coated pilings under one pier, Kneip was sucked up to his hips in the thick goo, leaving him helpless. Hearing his call for help, Wise jumped from the pier onto some solid footing, and tossed Kneip a line and dragged him free. No one approached the smelly officer until after he had been sluiced with a fire hose.

They found all the openings barred with iron grills, and from then on the Army checked them regularly for tampering.

Seven and a half weeks after arriving, Hertica turned in his written report for securing the port. He detailed where fences, guard towers, lights, and guards should be placed. He called for a clear zone between An Khanh and the mooring buoys because anyone could walk from shore to the ships over the sampans, junks, and lighters crammed together in that interval.

As for combating fire, if firefighting tugboats could not be procured, landing craft would be decked over and mounted with five 500-gallon-per-minute water pumps matched with a multiple monitor tower. It should be stocked with hoses, nozzles, foam cans, and the like, so that it had the capability to fight any type of ship or dock blaze. Eifler was pleased with the document's comprehensiveness and ordered the recommendations carried out.

While the ELDs worked for the Army command in their location, 1st Logistical Command also had them placed under the authority of the PSWD. A commercial contractor asked for Army approval to backload dynamite from a barge onto a ship to carry it out to sea for dumping. The matter so concerned O'Keefe, of ELD #1, that he sent the PSWD a copy of the letter he had forwarded to the Army that reported he had found deterioration so grave that movement risked detonation. If the transfer was approved it meant that 165 long tons of nervous dynamite would pass through heavily populated areas and past other hazardous cargo-laden ships.

Hertica recommended to 1st Logistical Command that they hold off on an answer until he looked for himself. He was told that the command would support his decision.

Thirty seconds after descending into the hold, a grinding, knee-dropping nitroglycerin headache overwhelmed Kneip. As O'Keefe reported, clear liquid was seeping through the cases. Crystallization would follow, making the dynamite extremely sensitive to movement.

After Kneip came on deck for fresh air, Hertica went down for a look. He recognized a bad situation: a single rifle bullet would obliterate that cargo.

Back on deck the two smiling contractor representatives suggested lunch before the Coast Guardsmen made up their minds. Lunch, of course, would be on the company. That sounded good to Hertica, so they dined at a prominent French restaurant in downtown Saigon, in a cordial atmosphere.

Over a glass of wine and lit cigars following an expensive meal, one of the contractors took a confident puff on his cigar and said to Hertica, "Well Skipper, what do you think about taking that dynamite downriver and out to sea?" Hertica did not answer right away. He took a couple of leisurely puffs on his own cigar, glanced over to Kneip, who sensed what was coming, and looked back at the contented civilians. Then, in his own wry way, he replied, "No fuckin' way!"[4]

The representatives accepted the decision without surprise. Kneip believed that they had thought the Army might let them move the dynamite, before the Coast Guard became involved. Yet, it was worth a try. They were told instead to take the dynamite out to a field and burn it, which they did.

South of Saigon, along the river at Nha Be, only a mile separated the huge petroleum-oil-lubricant (POL) tank farm that supplied virtually all of III and IV Corps from the ammunition ship offload anchorage. Troubled that an exploding ammunition carrier would start a chain reaction that would destroy the tank farm, Mattila, in his survey, proposed shifting the anchorage up to Cat Lai.

When Hertica realized that nothing was being done he pushed hard for the relocation. Despite Hertica's professional judgment, some agencies involved disagreed, believing Cat Lai less secure. Eifler agreed with Hertica and threw his support behind the change. The move eventually took place, although what switched the minds of the reluctant was not the general's desire, but discovery of aiming stakes lining up the ammunition anchorage for Viet Cong mortarmen.

In April 1967, ammunition operations moved up to Cat Lai, and none too soon. Not long afterward two intense attacks on the tank farm in the span of three days caused severe damage. Many believed that had the ammunition ships still been there, the entire POL terminal would have been leveled.

At the same time that the PSWD was trying to make Saigon Port secure, a new multimillion-dollar cargo facility was under development upriver. When finished, it would handle most of the military cargo clogging up Saigon's docks. Commonly referred to as the new port, this title stuck and became its name.

Persistent inspections enabled the PSWD to get many security and safety measures built into Newport. Eifler had complete trust in "his Coast Guard" and he left no doubt among his engineers that they would promptly attend to PSWD projects. As a result, Newport grew into a well-protected installation. This was proven during the failed Tet Offensive of 1968, about which Kneip boasted that at Newport the machine gun emplacements "rolled them [the enemy] up ten deep."

The men of the PSWD applied themselves in places other than Saigon. Security breaches elsewhere wailed for correction, such as at Cam Ranh Bay, where a Vietnamese boy had slipped aboard the SS *Old Westbury* and was caught trying to set fire to a

Commander Raymond C. Hertica (center), Coast Guard Port Security/Waterways Detail, with Lieutenant Commander Walter H. Riddle, USCG, in attendance (right), briefs Colonel Vern E. Johnson, USA (left), 1st Logistical Command Provost Marshal, on the waterfront security situation in Saigon. (Courtesy of U.S. Coast Guard)

napalm bomb. Barge sites were especially vulnerable. These were usually small wharfs where a barge could lay to be offloaded by mobile crane. At the Coast Guard's urging the Army supplied these isolated dropoff points with 500-gallon-per-minute, trailer-mounted firefighting pumps. They visited sub-ports like Phan Rang and Nha Trang, where cargo was plunked down onshore and then shuttled across open beach, without protective cover, to a temporary storage encampment beyond the tree line. When the Army entered the Mekong Delta to attack the Viet Cong, PSWD personnel went along to ensure that logistical security was not neglected.

Port protection is a marriage between security and safety. Shielding against subversion is futile if the destructive end is accomplished through accident or negligence. This is why 80 percent of Wise's job was proper cargo storage, which he taught to soldiers running the warehouses and docks. Although largely a matter of good common sense in segregation and placement, before the PSWD came along little consideration of this logic was employed.

Of course, the necessity to empty the ships backed up in the harbor as fast as possible contributed to turning every clear spot into a cargo heap. It was as if moving trucks had pulled up to a new house and the movers, after stacking furniture and cartons to the ceiling, left everything else cluttered in the yard. In Saigon, Wise saw corrosive liquid–filled drums stacked atop flammable liquid–filled drums pressed against a lumber pile. Had the corrosive fluid leaked into contact with the flammable liquid the result would have been explosive and fiery.

The Coast Guard's presence vastly lessened threats of accidental fire. Hazardous cargo became separated by combustion/flammability, which was made easy by standard color labels. Maximum distance was put between dangerous materials, which included compressed gases, acids, and flammables. Steps were taken to retard a fire from spreading. On wharves and in warehouses, cargos were positioned to allow lanes for firefighters and their equipment. Painted yellow lines marked locations where cargo was prohibited. A limit was placed on the height to which cargo was stacked indoors, to allow overhead water sprinklers to do their job.

One of Wise's successors, Master Chief Boatswain's Mate Ralph H. Carr, picked up the title "fire marshal" when sergeants began asking him to inspect their offices and gathering places such as snack bars for fire hazards.

The Viet Cong did not have to assemble much force to upset the supply flow. Ships presented big, slow targets for a few individuals wedged among the thick riverbank foliage with rocket launchers, happily waiting for one to come poking out from around a bend. This happened below Nha Be, when a vessel with a Japanese crew took five rocket hits in an ambush that killed one crewman and wounded several more. To deter such attacks the PSWD urged helicopter gunship escorts through favorable ambush sites. Once in port, ships had to guard against another menace—the North Vietnamese swimmer commando. This predator's objective was to place explosives on a target and withdraw. Executing this mission demanded endurance, a characteristic shown by a swimmer captured in Cam Ranh Bay, who had been in the water for six hours. Such toughness, combined with patience and a suicidal devotion to duty, made these individuals extraordinary weapons.

A rundown on this stealthy foe reads like a screenwriter's description of a supervillian: "Training of a swimmer-sapper is known to extend upwards to two years. Training includes: swimming, hand-to-hand combat, demolition techniques, sabotage, assassination, kidnapping, reconnaissance, individual weapons, infiltration and exfiltration techniques, political indoctrination.... Scaling a wall or penetrating a wire perimeter with wire entanglements is no real problem to the sapper. He is a master at reconnaissance and at silent approach. Swimming distances of 600 meters underwater or 50 kilometers on the surface is included in his training." This is how the 1st Logistical Command's regulation 190-36, "Security Against Underwater Swimmer Attack," a document prepared by the PSWD, described this formidable antagonist.

The sapper, respected by peers and treated, in general, by the North Vietnamese public with adulation, was well-motivated. With morale higher than most in the North Vietnamese military, his gladsome state of mind soared with successes such as slipping by security at the Binh Trieu ammunition barge site and blowing up one barge, badly damaging another craft, and sending four American soldiers and one South Vietnamese soldier to join their departed ancestors.

The commando did not just splash around looking for a juicy target, plant his charges, and breast stroke to shore to watch the fireworks. His hallmark was great patience. From ten days to a month or more he gave the objective personal scrutiny. A North Vietnamese underwater demolition company consisted of fifty men divided into a headquarters section and three demolition sections. The company, or solely a demolition section, would move into a region, familiarizing themselves with the primary targets. Any assistance needed came from local sources. Through this lengthy

Merchant ships supplying the American forces regularly came under Viet Cong rocket attack in rivers and harbors. (Courtesy of U.S. Coast Guard)

and tedious reconnaissance they learned about locations, patterns, and guard routines. Boat patrols were studied for repetitive tendencies and often the saboteur would boldly swim through the target sector assessing tidal conditions, resting points, and escape routes.

Local confederates sometimes left explosives at a predetermined spot. Dropping them next to a buoy was popular. Another arrangement was to deliver them in small quantities for later assembly and then dangle them off a pier or vessel. But, rather than leave anything to chance, the swimmer preferred towing his demolitions using neutral buoyancy devices so the package floated just beneath the surface. The commando teams set up their hideouts well away from the port to elude detection. Another captured swimmer admitted walking eight hours to reach the point where he entered the water.

The protracted scouting finally ends. It is time for the attack. Monotony transforms into high tension for the sinewy Asiatic leaving shore on a moonless night to become engulfed by the black water. He is attired in swimming shorts, with a sheath knife and two grenades slung around the waist; his only swimming accessory is a clear plastic snorkel tube. He propels himself just below the surface, raising his head only high enough for the eyes to clear for a quick orientation peek. A tethered bag of explosives trails him.

By clinging to the shadows in the lighted harbor he reaches the port quarter of his target, a British tanker. His elation is accompanied by contempt for a stupid enemy who makes this so easy. After placing his charges, he withdraws from Nha Trang harbor. When confident that he is beyond observation, he swims relaxed on the surface. The explosion in the distance brings on a smile; he feels fulfilled. However, this time the allies are fortunate because the explosives were placed next to the engine room, and, although the tanker is disabled, no one is hurt and her volatile cargo of aviation fuel stays intact.

To defend against these attacks the PSWD considered the swimmer's strengths and weaknesses. In his favor the swimmer was hard to detect, submerged quickly, dived deep, could hold a stationary position, and changed directions fast. To the American's advantage the swimmer had to surface to confirm his direction, and though he could hear approaching boats he could not tell from which direction they were coming. He tired faster in colder water, and, being human, feared grenades.

Based upon these observations and experience, the Coast Guard recommended getting as much illumination on the water as possible, and positioning guards in darkness where they could see without being seen. Instructions were issued to shoot into debris that could conceal a swimmer or mines.

The Coast Guard believed scare charges were the best deterrent; that is, dropping concussion grenades into the water at irregular intervals. The most common grenade used against swimmers was the M3A2. With its equivalent of a half pound of TNT it was useful within 71 feet of a swimmer. At 5 feet the blast was lethal; out to 30 or more feet a swimmer was stunned. Beyond 51 feet there was no physical harm, but the loudness of the explosion frightened the swimmer, unaware if he was spotted or not. Sentinels were also told to be on their highest alert for swimmers during slack water or during reduced visibility, periods that favored the enemy.

Each side had their successes and failures. These encounters were, at best, a stand-off until the 1970s, when the Americans turned port security over to the South Vietnamese. Then, swimmer sorties increased, and so did their success rate.

Hertica believed that to prevail against the swimmer, vigilant water patrols were a must. Yet the Army had few craft and most were slow and cumbersome to maneuver. For this reason Hertica advised Eifler to procure 39 PBRs (patrol boat, river). These quick, compact, well-armed shallow water boats had already proved useful in *Operation Game Warden,* the U.S. Navy's warfare against the Viet Cong in tortuous rivers and canals. He also recommended that, while awaiting the PBRs' construction, off-the-shelf Boston Whalers be bought. Eifler concurred and the requisition went out in November, 1966.

Still, what was considered urgent in Vietnam was not always greeted with the same importance in the United States. Late in January, the Department of the Army replied that the Boston Whalers would be ordered, but asked that the number of PBRs be reduced. The $85,000 cost for each boat spawned the reconsideration.

Eifler's staff begrudgingly revised the order to a minimum number of 27. The general, however, knew that fewer boats would impair coverage and that his staff was simply obliging higher authority. He knew that the perceived savings of using fewer boats was specious, because in the long term the government would expend more money replacing materials destroyed by undetected swimmers. Worst of all, there would be needless dying. His reply to the Department therefore was adamant: 39 PBRs—no less.

Under political pressure to keep war expenditures down, the Department needed convincing and asked for a consultation. In March 1966, a Coast Guardsman, Hertica, was sent to Washington in behalf of the 1st Logistical Command, the U.S. Army in Vietnam, and the U.S. Army in the Pacific, to address the landlubbers.

Hertica's approach was direct. He went right to the point: To ward off breaches in port security a boat that could detect, intercept, escort, and fight was paramount. The 31-foot, 21-knot PBR was that component. It could squirm into shallow shoreline recesses where swimmers hide because its waterjet propulsion, unhindered by propellers, struts, and rudders, keep it from snagging on underwater obstacles. With twin .50-caliber machine guns forward and a single .50-caliber machine gun aft, its four-man crew could rip up junks and covering shelter.

Hertica told his audience that just recently, a large dredge had been sunk at My Tho. Two Navy minesweepers had been destroyed and two others heavily damaged in the main channel to Saigon. Swimmers attempted penetration of the Newport installation with 100 kilograms of explosives. Then he drove home his argument, saying that North Vietnam, heartened by these triumphs, had ordered more saboteur squads into South Vietnam.

The Department, convinced that frugality on this matter would backfire, approved the full request. Still, it would be July before the Boston Whalers arrived and not until January 1968 for the PBRs. Ironically, Boston Whalers were plentiful in South Vietnam. In April, the PSWD discovered 26 in a warehouse, but they were purchased with non-appropriated funds for recreational use, causing an exasperated Hertica to write in his log, "We haven't as yet got port security patrol boats, but now we can go water skiing."

The blunt-bowed, homely Boston Whaler was laughed at for its bathtub appearance. Yet critics were impressed with the capability of its foam-filled fiberglass hull to remain afloat even after being carved in two. The 16-foot 7-inch-long boats came only in one color—cream. Thus, the first modification made by PSWD was to paint them a dull black. A pedestal was installed on the bow for mounting an M60 machine gun and a 9.5-horsepower auxiliary motor added to back up the primary 80-horsepower engine.

With the delivery of the boats the PSWD found they had a new job—teaching soldiers to be sailors. They taught engine maintenance and explained what to do if the motor stopped, which happened frequently in the beginning, until it was discovered that detergent oil instead of non-detergent oil was being used. The former fouled the spark plugs.

The training ran its course despite being hampered by missing engine control linkage, incorrect parts assembly by Army maintenance personnel, torrential rains, high winds, and occasional sniper fire. A qualified coxswain could maneuver in strong current and dock without poking holes in the hull. The Army crews became smart about patrolling without establishing a pattern for the enemy to recognize. Despite the Coast Guardsmen's insistence that crewmen wear life jackets, the inevitable tragedy occurred when a Boston Whaler broached in heavy water, throwing its crew overboard. The three men who made it safely to shore wore life jackets; the only soldier without a life jacket, the coxswain, drowned.

The PSWD and ELDs achieved their purpose of giving the Army the knowledge needed to function in an unfamiliar area. The tireless efforts of the Coast Guardsmen seemed too often thwarted by human nature. An example was when Hertica observed a soldier guarding a south perimeter fence by sitting on a woodpile with his back to it. On the previous evening, along the west perimeter, the bottom strand of concertina wire had been cut and yanked aside, leaving an opening to the road beyond it. This discovery was not made until daylight, even though a guard supposedly passed that spot every fifteen minutes or so. But, notwithstanding these incidents, each man who served in these Coast Guard units knew his presence saved life and property.

CHAPTER 4

Trawler!

Elation filled the men, but so did trepidation. It was like knowing that you had won a grand prize but to claim it you had to thrust your hand into a fire to pull it out.

During the night, along the east shore of the Ca Mau Peninsula, a comma-shaped land mass punctuating the nominal separation of the Gulf of Thailand and the South China Sea, the USCGC *Point Grey* (WPB 82324) detected a North Vietnamese trawler trying to reach the Viet Cong on shore with her killing cargo: tons of weapons and ammunition. Hastened by the cutter's discovery, the vessel had missed the inlet she sought and grounded. This was 10 May 1966, still young in America's overt combat participation in the war and its first cornering of a North Vietnamese gunrunner. The cutter's first daylight attempt to reach the stranded trawler was foiled by heavy fire from the infuriated Viet Cong. That sent the meddler dancing clear. Now, hours later, as the cutter approached again, a surreal silence enveloped the trawler's white superstructure and soft blue-gray hull, which melded into a colorless glare under the strong afternoon sun.

She typified her 110-foot class, with elevated forecastle and poop decks bracketing a sunken main deck. Her bow was shaped like a blunt stone arrowhead and her stern like a horseshoe. Instead of a deckhouse shoved to the stern, as on most trawlers, this vessel had it located nearly amidship. A four-man boarding team crouched along the cutter's starboard bow just aft of the mortar–machine gun mount. A U.S. Army major, who was catching a ride back to An Thoi after inspecting defenses at a Junk Force site, swayed the machine gun barrel in a slow sweep of the coastline, where the indiscernible enemy lurked among the mangroves clotting the water's edge. The soldier was filling in for Gunner's Mate First Class Martin J. Kelleher, who hunkered in the boarding party with an open box of grenades resting at his feet. The big, 15-year Coast Guard veteran, who thoroughly enjoyed his profession, played over and over in his mind how he was going to toss the grenades "to clear the deck" of anyone lying in wait. Although the Americans could have readily destroyed the trawler with aerial and naval ordnance, a scarcity of coastal infiltration intelligence made capturing her intact, or at least seizing her documents, a priority. Under this calculated risk, which largely imperiled only the *Point Grey,* the skipper coaxed his cutter through the shallows. She lurched, and after stopping a moment as if to take a deep breath, skidded over a band of mud. Shoved by tide and wind to within shouting distance of land, the trawler, looking as innocuous as any deserted cargo vessel, drew them on...and on...

This chance encounter had begun more than 16 hours earlier at 2200, when the bridge watch spotted two bonfires near the entrance of the Rach Gia River, a mile beyond the *Point Grey*'s upper patrol boundary. Despite intermittent rain squalls the night's warmth made the size of these blazes appear out of place. Suspecting they might be a signal or guidance beacon for small junks running the coastline, the cutter stayed nearby.

What began as a four-day patrol had stretched into six when late word came that their relief would not be arriving the next morning either. As it was, this side of the peninsula was unpopular with Division Eleven boat crews. A cutter had to leave port late at night to effect relief early in the morning, and then, after eight hours of running full speed, reached the sailor's patrol purgatory, a dreary, empty, uncomfortable sea where there was nothing to board, or see, except an occasional cargo junk passing through. It did not matter which monsoon season was in progress. Winds were always roughing up the water, as on this night, where completing a track against the seas took hours and with the seas less than half that time.

For Lieutenant (j.g.) Charles B. Mosher, the commanding officer, this was his first cruise east of the Ca Mau Peninsula. What he knew of the locale came from intelligence reports and his crew. The sum of this was that the sea bottom was an alluvial plain, meaning the depths were shallow and ever changing. As a consequence a craft of their size could not get near the coast, much less into the inlets. But Mosher wanted to know things firsthand, so early in the patrol he tried entering the Bo De River. The nervous fathometer flashed rapid depth changes, showing 20 feet of water under them in one moment, then an instant later only 10. The bottom came up fast, causing the screws to churn silt. But at the river's entrance, when they pushed over a hump, the bottom fell away. The fathometer sighed and blinked 50...60...70 feet. Satisfied that a vessel could penetrate this isolated coast, Mosher took his cutter back to sea.

A little over two hours after sighting the fires they were no longer alone; six miles to seaward, radar showed a steel-hulled vessel clipping along at 10 knots on a southerly heading. Mosher ordered an intercept course. At 0120 *Point Grey* sought her identification through flashing light but received no reply. When they were 400 yards away the cutter's searchlight came on, revealing a fishing trawler with no hull designation or flag.

Some vague markings on the stack gave Mosher the impression that she was Nationalist Chinese and he reported that to the surveillance center. Maybe, he thought, this was merely a case of a non-hostile vessel on her way to fishing grounds that in oriental perverseness was ignoring a busybody occidental. There had been no precedents as to how a gunrunning trawler would react when encountered. The assumption was that upon discovery an infiltrator would either turn for international waters or start shooting and run for the beach. This vessel confounded that reasoning by doing neither. Ironically, in the cutter's mail bin at An Thoi sat an intelligence book with a photograph of a North Vietnamese trawler just like this one. The cutter secured her lights and fell deeper into the blackness to watch the stranger on radar. Displaying no urgency, the trawler ceased moving southward to wander in aimless directions before casually turning for shore. Half an hour later the trawler hove to a couple miles off land from where the bonfires had been seen. The Coast Guardsmen watched to see if someone was coming out to meet her.

Nothing happened until 0315 when the trawler fired up her engines and dashed for the inlet. The cutter pursued, firing mortar illumination rounds to keep the trawler in sight. The trawler's master, showing skilled seamanship, maneuvered into the wind so that the flares blew back over the *Point Grey*.

Mosher, quick to adapt, ordered shorter fuze settings, causing the flares to blossom at lower altitudes and hit the water before his cutter reached them. Hounded by the *Point Grey* and weighed down by a full cargo in unpredictable waters, the trawler's captain was overmatched. Twenty minutes later the vessel apparently grounded. Mosher had hoped that the trawler would fire on him and thus settle outright the question of friend or foe, but her crew remained passive. From 50 feet away the cutter's searchlight probed the longer and higher craft. Although no one was visible on the trawler, Coast Guardsmen glimpsed figures in the shadows of topside gear and piled fishing nets. The South Vietnamese liaison petty officer raised a loudhailer to his lips and called for someone to come out. Finally, a man wearing a dark rain slicker stepped into the clear gesturing that he did not understand.

The swells rocking both vessels made a night boarding dangerous even under agreeable circumstances. Mosher, knowing he was at a tactical disadvantage this close to the larger vessel in the dark, decided the prudent thing to do was move away and wait for daylight before attempting a boarding. He had not reckoned, however, on a rising tide and onshore wind.

By 0500 the invader had been pushed to within 1,000 yards of shore—well into restricted waters. Once again Mosher challenged the vessel with flashing light, reasoning that if she was friendly she would certainly welcome assistance. Ignored, he radioed in that his initial identification was wrong—this vessel claimed no nationality. At daylight the trawler lay 400 yards from shore like an abandoned shoe. Lines dangled down her sides and doors flapped open and closed with the slow motion of the sea. When the *Point Grey* moved in at 0700, the trawler sat perpendicular to shore and gave Mosher the idea that he could use her for a shield on one side or the other from the shore fire he expected. To provide cover for his boarders he had armed men sprawled atop the pilothouse.

But before the cutter could get near, the jungle sparkled as if it had been invaded by hordes of fireflies. Miniature water fountains spurted about the cutter. Bullets hammered the hull before the crew heard what sounded like the crackling of hundreds of firecrackers. Mosher backed out of range to spend the rest of the morning periodically lobbing in mortar shells and making machine gun firing passes on the entrenched Viet Cong. It had become a stalemate, with neither side having enough force to possess the trawler. Evidence of their remoteness was the fact that reinforcements did not arrive until the minesweeper USS *Vireo* (MSC-205) appeared at 1120 and the USS *Brister* (DER-327) showed up at 1145. Their presence, though, provided only moral support, as their deeper drafts kept them well away from the action. Early in the afternoon a succession of air strikes pummeled the Viet Cong until it was believed safe for the cutter to put a towline on the trawler and pull her out, or, in any event, gather up what documents could be found...

On and on drew the cutter. At nearly 1400 Mosher pressed his eyes against the binoculars, trying to stare through the jungle. He saw evidence of the air strikes—bomb fragments and charred foliage—but no Viet Cong, dead or alive. His gaze switched to the trawler, now less than 100 yards from shore. He felt certain that his boat lacked the horsepower to drag out the mired gunrunner; his more immediate challenge was finding enough water to get over the unpredictable alluvial bottom.

Mosher knew, too, that if they were attacked they could not expect suppression fire from *Brister* because they were in her line of fire. A whaleboat from *Brister* accompanied them with the intent to try to reach the trawler should the shoals keep *Point Grey* from doing so. But, judging from the overly cautious distance that *Brister* lagged behind, just as in the morning, *Point Grey* was on her own. The cutter lurched again. Her stern swung to port as the bow momentarily caught on the silt. She sideslipped several yards, snapping Kelleher out of his reverie to glance up at his reassuring Thompson submachine gun slung on one of the mortar ammunition locker dogs. He might need it, before the grenades. The forbidding coast with its dense tangle of trees grew larger as the land came nearer. So did the foreboding among the crew. All tried to suppress the danger alarms going off in their minds, except for the major, who called up to Mosher for permission to reconnoiter by fire. With permission granted he triggered machine gun bursts into the jungle.

Instantly the water about the cutter began splashing. Again, the Viet Cong, unable to maintain restraint any longer, opened fire a trifle too soon. When the major suffered a leg wound, Kelleher jumped up and took over the machine gun. The rest of the boarding party scattered for their action stations. Mosher yanked the throttles full astern, pouring more fuel into the engines than they could burn. Thick smoke gushed out of the aft exhausts, enveloping them in a black cloud and leading those aboard *Brister* to conclude that the cutter had been destroyed. Still in action, but in serious trouble, the *Point Grey,* her propellers finding only mud to thrash, began sliding across the bottom, unable to keep a heading. Incoming fire ripped up the bow and punctured the bridge. The radar screen in front of Mosher went blank when the receiver absorbed the shot that otherwise would have killed him.

Up forward, Kelleher's machine gun became silent when it ran out of ammunition. The Vietnamese liaison petty officer, hustling ammunition, dropped the cans on deck and with his back to shore bent over to yank off the lids. His visage turned from concentration to disbelief, then became a blood mask. A bullet had hit him under the shoulder and drove through his face. He was pulled below for first aid by another crewman bringing up ammunition.

Kelleher looked for his loader, Commissaryman Second Class William N. Kepler, a New Englander like him, and his good friend. He found Kepler on the deck between the mortar lockers, clutching his bleeding left thigh. Kepler had just had the misfortune of being the first Coast Guardsmen wounded in the war. Kelleher pulled him up and yelled at him to get off the bow. In shock and disoriented, Kepler started down the starboard side—the one facing the enemy. As he crawled he heard the frightful sounds of bullets thunking into the boat around him.

Alone now, Kelleher had to be gunner and loader. Knowing he presented a sizable bullseye for the enemy, he rushed through the reloading. In his haste, the ammunition belt twisted, which resulted in the gun jamming when he tried to fire it. Taking a safer course of action, he dropped to his belly, continuing the fight using his submachine gun.

Mosher glanced around to see what had become of the whaleboat and caught sight of its retreating wake. He could barely hear the gun clatter above the screaming engines dragging the squirming hull over the muck. *Point Grey* backed in this excruciatingly slow manner for 200 yards before popping free from the bottom. Grateful for the deep water, Mosher cut the helm for a hard starboard turn, bringing his port machine guns into action. On the bow, with the aid of a shipmate, Kelleher had the machine gun firing once more. The cutter cleared out without further harm and made for *Brister* for a talk to reconsider their approach in the stalemate.

Point Grey resembled a tin can used for target practice. Dozens of holes riddled her bow and deckhouse. Most were small arms size, but the size of some punctures told that they had been up against at least one heavy weapon. Along the bow and below the gunwale, large tears into the paint storage compartment properly impressed a seaman checking for damage. After seeing sunshine streaming through the jagged holes illuminating the paint-splattered mess he reported to his skipper that they would not need lights in the paint locker anymore. The mortar boxes had taken a peppering. Almost a dozen nicked or holed high explosive and flare containers were dumped overboard. Considering the ferocity of the fight, the close range, and the cutter's inability to maneuver, the *Point Grey* was fortunate to escape without a death or major damage. The wounded would heal and return to duty. For the major this was his second Purple Heart Medal. His first came while catching an airplane ride with the Air Force. After this shootout, he vowed to do his future traveling only in Army tanks.

The Viet Cong had wanted the trawler's cargo, while the Americans wanted the cargo and the trawler. By now it had become obvious that neither side would have their way. At 1700 the trawler lay within 50 yards of shore; by dark, she would be shoved up against the trees where the enemy could raid her holds, so orders came from *Market Time* headquarters to destroy her. Around 1800, *Brister, Vireo, Point Grey,* and the newly arrived USCGC *Point Cypress* (WPB 82326) opened up the barrage. From 2,000 yards the cutters pumped out 25 rounds of 81-mm mortar, while *Brister,* 7,200 yards away, fired 37 rounds of 3"/50, and *Vireo* contributed with her 20-mm guns. An air strike followed. The trawler burned and shuddered from secondary explosions until 2030 when a hull-quivering blast tore her in half.

For the men on the *Point Grey,* destruction instead of capture did not diminish the exhilaration of their accomplishment. They had brought down *Operation Market Time*'s first North Vietnamese arms trawler, earned glory for the Coast Guard, and had something to brag about.

For Mosher the honor was somewhat ironic. He had been certain that neither the Coast Guard nor he would get into the Vietnam War. At his previous duty station he was asked by a neighbor when the Coast Guard was going to Vietnam, and Mosher emphatically responded, "It will be a cold day in hell!" The next day came the announcement that his service would be patrolling off South Vietnam. Of course, Mosher wasted no time in volunteering.

This North Vietnamese trawler cornered by the cutter *Point Grey* along the
Ca Mau Peninsula lies in fragments after being destroyed by
naval gunfire. (Courtesy of U.S. Navy)

While the *Point Grey* crew took an overdue respite, *Point Cypress* moved in to discourage the Viet Cong from picking through the debris. Throughout the night she kept the wreckage illuminated with mortar flares and five South Vietnamese Navy junks and a landing ship joined her in using automatic weapons to harass any lingering forces. In the morning *Point Grey* returned to An Thoi for repairs, leaving American and Vietnamese salvage teams combing the crumpled bow and broken stern, which lay in lapping water 60 feet apart. Slowed by bothersome sniping fire and rising tides, it took the salvors three days to complete the job. The middle section, where the bridge had been located, had been destroyed, foiling recovery of logs, charts, and other records holding clues to the trawler's wanderings.

Nonetheless, 74 tons of materials were hauled away, including 15 tons of ammunition. Among the retrievals were: 57-mm recoilless rifles, 12.7-mm antiaircraft machine guns, 7.62-mm machine guns, 60-mm to 120-mm size mortar projectiles, blocks of TNT explosives, and paraphernalia to spread propaganda (projectors, amplifiers, speakers, movies, and pamphlets). The cargo mostly bore Communist Chinese markings, and the late vintage (1965) ammunition led American intelligence analysts to conclude that troops in the Ca Mau region were low on ammunition.

Since 1959, the character of the war had been slowly evolving from hit-and-hide tactics by unorganized guerrillas to one of a North Vietnam–directed takeover. If the Viet Cong were to go up against larger forces and win bigger battles they would need standardized weapons and a steady source of war materials.

The North Vietnamese Army, having entered South Vietnam, also needed resupply. Thus North Vietnam organized to furnish these needs by sea and land. Cramming the fish holds of armed trawlers with munitions and running them clandestinely into South Vietnam complemented the slower land infiltration routes. Smugglers were able to slip in and out of South Vietnam with ease until the Americans showed up.

The loss of the trawler to the *Point Grey* was the first in a number of interceptions that forced North Vietnam to abandon this mode, except in desperation, as was the case following its disastrous losses in the 1968 Tet Offensive. In late February of that year five trawlers left North Vietnam to run the *Market Time* blockade, but as the offensive failed so did this venture. None of them made it through.

Before the chance discovery of a North Vietnamese trawler unloading at Vung Ro Bay in February 1965, no one could prove conclusively that the sea was a major supply route. However, in June 1966, a North Vietnamese political officer attached to a Viet Cong unit in the Ca Mau Peninsula that regularly met the trawlers defected, and confirmed what had long been suspected. He revealed that between 1963 and 1965 42 trawlers reached An Xuyen Province (accomplished by seven or eight different vessels): 20 in 1963, 15 in 1964, and 7 in 1965. The falloff in 1965 was a result of the American naval buildup along South Vietnam.[1]

The trawlers arrived twice a month, but allowing for poor weather and delays in skirting detection, arrival dates were not fixed in advance. However, a pattern of middle and end of the month appearances emerged. Upon receiving a day or two notice of a shipment, Viet Cong security and unloading forces spread out at the meeting place. Lookouts settled into tall trees, scanning for enemy patrols as well as their own vessels.

A gunrunner might approach the coast after 2300, when higher tides enabled her to get over the shoals. A simple flashing light recognition system was employed. Using the designated light color, the number of flashes between vessel and shore had to total the recognition number. If the number was six and the challenge light blinked twice, the proper response was four. A junk then came out and led the trawler to the landing site, where she was camouflaged with foliage. Unloading took place at night, under the glow of acetylene lamps, by the manual exertion of Viet Cong soldiers carrying their burdens across makeshift wood plank gangways. Once emptied, the trawler immediately sailed for North Vietnam and the contraband left behind was moved to nearby caches, where units reported to draw equipment.

The defecting political officer reported that while only 15 or so bunks were in the trawlers, the crew consisted of a skipper, his assistant, a political officer, and 17 to 22 men, with a primary armament of stand-mounted 12.7-mm DShK (Degtyarova Sphagina Krupnokaliberyni) Soviet heavy machine guns, the equivalent to the American .50-caliber machine guns on the inshore *Market Time* patrol craft. Trawlers ran from 88 to 150 feet in length, and each one carried enough munitions to keep several Viet Cong battalions in action for months.

This risky infiltration endeavor fell to North Vietnam's 125th Naval Transportation Group, operating out of Haiphong in secrecy under the guise of a meteorological

A North Vietnamese trawler that had attempted to reach Viet Cong forces with weapons and ammunition floats in captivity in Danang. The rare intact capture on 15 July 1967 was made possible by highly accurate mortar fire from the cutter *Point Orient,* which killed key enemy crew members before they could set off the self-destruct explosives arrangement. (Photograph by author)

outfit. It had been in the smuggling business since at least 1962. The concept of using steel-hulled trawlers—a small, common, inoffensive craft with large carrying capacity and a shallow draft—to penetrate the South Vietnamese coastline was effective until the U.S. Coast Guard and the U.S. Navy raised the risk factor from hazardous to suicidal. "Suicidal" aptly described the 125th's mental outlook. Each trawler was rigged for self-destruction, with explosives placed in at least five locations. These could be detonated from the chain locker, engine room, or after store room. In the trawler that the USCGC *Point Orient* (WPB 82319) played a major role in capturing on 15 July 1967, a ton of TNT was found wired to destroy the vessel. As member of an elite operation, these proud Communist sailors snubbed their naval brethren and proved their fanaticism by blowing up their vessels, and, if necessary, themselves, if capture looked imminent.

After their many successes, the trawler loss on 10 May 1966 was probably looked upon as a fluke by the 125th. Then, 41 days later, the Coast Guard rattled their arrogance again.

Lieutenant (j.g.) Stephen T. Ulmer's year in Vietnam was up. He had served with Division Twelve as operations officer and as executive officer on the *Point Gammon,* but had not reached his goal to command a patrol boat in the war. Like Mosher, he was single, slender, energetic, and adventurous. So while his year group returned home, Ulmer, who had extended his tour of duty to fulfill a longing, went south to Division Thirteen to command the USCGC *Point League* (WPB 82304).

Cargo holds empty, machine guns at rest, a captured North Vietnamese arms trawler sits in Danang as a tourist display. (Photograph by author)

On 18 June 1966, ten days after reporting to the division, Ulmer eased the cutter from her moorings and began his first full war patrol in command. He was going to a stretch of the Ca Mau Peninsula off Vinh Binh Province, more than 100 miles north of where *Point Grey* had her day of glory. Ulmer spent the early part of the patrol scouting close inshore, getting familiar with the area.

But he had another reason for risking grounding or ambush. He needed to get his men some action. He had inherited a boat that been tagged the "Point Loser" simply because she was the only one in Division Thirteen not to have any real combat since arriving in Vietnam four months previously. The label, of course, was unfair: her crew was as professional and as courageous as any cutter's, but often reputations are falsely founded on the basis of uncontrollable circumstances.

Therefore, before morale dipped any lower, before performance became affected, and before the cutter began deserving the nickname, Ulmer needed to find a fight. He was in a good spot for it, too, because the cutter that he relieved had intercepted three Viet Cong junks moving toward the Co Chien River the night before. In the ensuing firefight one junk was blown into splinters, two fled with damage, three Viet Cong were confirmed dead, and two others were likely killed. On the first evening Ulmer probed the Co Chien River, observing traffic and plotting waterway obstacles. Watchful for anything suspicious, they popped a mortar flare over a small island. Nothing happened. The next morning Ulmer followed a Coastal Force junk in to the beach, hoping to entice the enemy to fire on them. Nothing happened. At 2300 that night the cutter crept through the shallows toward the river, only to run aground.

A small portion of the cargo taken from the North Vietnamese trawler captured on 15 July 1967. Among the supplies found aboard were 1,556 weapons and six million rounds of ammunition. (Photograph by author)

During these anxious moments they were like a large lollipop sticking up out of the sand—an easy target. Alert Viet Cong gunners could have reduced the cutter to a smoldering hulk. But again, nothing happened. After working loose Ulmer gave the order to cruise offshore. They had had enough tension for one night. The crew was getting mad. Had somebody clued the Viet Cong in on their reputation? It was as if the foe considered shooting at them a waste of time. Some might have thought Ulmer's dangerous actions put his men in unnecessary jeopardy, but to have any impact on disrupting intracoastal smuggling, an inshore craft needed to work close-in. His tactics were common practice. When Ulmer disappeared into his cabin to grab some sleep he had no hint that *Point League* was about to lose her timid reputation in a big way. During the afternoon, a *Market Time* aircraft had reported an unidentified trawler 80 miles east of Con Son Island, alerting vessels along the Ca Mau Peninsula for an infiltration possibility. At 0245, on 20 June 1966, Engineman Second Class Daniel R. Vaughn's heart beat a little faster when he saw the rectangular pip on the radar screen moving up the coast less than eight miles away. He knew they had hit the jackpot. Ulmer ran up to the bridge and sent the helmsman, Gunner's Mate Second Class Albert J. Wright Jr., to the bow machine gun, then cut the helm for an intercept heading. Four miles away he gave the flashing light challenge. The night visitor responded by turning for shore. Two miles from land she stopped alongside a junk, probably on station to pilot her into the river. But, now only 600 yards away, the *Point League* flicked on her searchlight and broke up the meeting.

Automatic weapons off the captured North Vietnamese trawler. The vessel is visible in the background. (Photograph by author)

The trawler abandoned all navigational caution and fled for the river entrance. Ulmer radioed CSC, Vung Tau, that he was in hot pursuit. By skill or luck the trawler had slipped between a narrow gap in the radar coverage of two outer barrier ships, leaving only the luckless *Point League* in the way of a major arms shipment from reaching the Viet Cong. The 24-year-old, redheaded skipper punched the General Quarters alarm while up forward Wright fired the perfunctory warning shots. The siren's painful wail left no doubt among the trawler crew that somebody was coming for their blood.

On the bridge a radio crackled with an agitated voice from the surveillance center demanding information. Ulmer shouted to the liaison officer, a young South Vietnamese ensign, to tell the voice on the radio that he could not talk right now. The liaison officer, unfamiliar with radio procedure, grabbed up the hand mike, and in his excitement answered, "Sorry, we are very busy. Call back later." In his rush to find a place for the mike he shoved it upside down into an empty coffee cup, jamming the transmitting key open, treating the surveillance center and other units to a firsthand account of the battle.

Shunning any pretext of innocence, the trawler's gunners opened up on the *Point League,* sending an incendiary round smashing inside the bridge, knocking down the executive officer with a shrapnel wound and momentarily stealing Ulmer's night vision. Another bullet plowed a furrow across Wright's ankle. In the short, furious fight Coast Guardsmen turned their gun barrels white hot, aroused by their eager captain shouting, "Shoot!...Get 'em!...Shoot!" A few thousand yards south of the Co Chien

River the trawler's flight ended. Her luck ran out when she ran out of water. They had her now! The jubilant Coast Guardsmen vented months of disappointment with a steady murderous fire into the trawler until her guns fell silent. Nothing more could be done until daylight.

The USCGC *Point Slocum* (WPB 82313) arrived in the area at 0520 and, after a brief conversation with *Point League,* inspected the half-dozen nearby junks on the slim chance of finding the one that had met the trawler. The cutter found only seemingly innocent fishing boats. At 0600, with helicopter gunships overhead, the *Point League* moved in for a closer look at her prize. Although the North Vietnamese had abandoned the trawler, the Viet Cong ashore had not. The cutter and gunships returned the fire coming from the ridges of the sand dunes, their machine guns and rockets whipping the beach into a lethal sandstorm. Moments later, U.S. Air Force F-100s bombed the positions. When an explosion rocked the trawler it was uncertain whether it happened as a result of a preset self-destruct mechanism or some errant ordnance from the aircraft. After the air attack broke off, *Point League* left to replenish her ammunition from USCGC *Point Hudson* (WPB 82322), now on scene, and *Point Slocum* moved onto the firing line. With only two feet of water under the keel, she closed within 800 yards of the trawler before the redoubtable Viet Cong turned guns on her.

A short while later the helicopter gunships returned, inviting Lieutenant B. Foster Thomson III, the *Point Slocum*'s captain, to make another approach to draw fire so they could locate targets. The cutter returned for more sea-to-shore dueling, and in her last firing pass left the spot of heaviest Viet Cong concentration smoking with white phosphorus. At the mortar, Chief Boatswain's Mate Bruce D. Davis suffered burns and shrapnel wounds when small arms fire struck two mortar shells, igniting their increment powder bags. When the *Point Slocum* left to get Davis medical attention, *Point League* and *Point Hudson* moved into place and delivered 52 mortar shells and 6,000 .50-caliber rounds into the beach. It was no contest. This was one arms shipment the enemy would not get, nor deny its capture. Under the relentless air and naval firepower, the Viet Cong faded from the beach, leaving their foes to deal with the burning trawler stranded 50 yards from shore. They probably thought that it was only a matter of time before the flames capturing the stern pilothouse reached into the explosives-filled holds. When she blew, salvage crews would be fortunate to find a firing pin intact. The heat was already playing a ragged melody of small explosions as ammunition cooked off. This was a time for volunteers, a time for bravery against a different kind of enemy, and there was no lack of them. Coast Guardsmen from the three cutters, led by a commander from the USS *Haverfield* (DER-393), now directing on-scene activity, loaded portable firefighting equipment aboard two South Vietnamese Coastal Force junks and moved in on the trawler, hurling water from fire hoses into the choking black smoke and defiant orange flames. At the same time, the cutters spread themselves 500 yards apart with all weapons trained on the beach to suppress any further Viet Cong resistance. When the blaze came under control, *Point League* and *Point Slocum* moved alongside and sprayed water over the cargo holds to keep them cooled down while the firefighters finished putting out the fire. From then on, matters became chaotic as a multitude of American and South Vietnamese naval units joined the cast. The former aided in salvage and intelligence gathering and the latter sought part of the credit and souvenirs.

In one instance, when *Point League* prepared to move away from the trawler in an attempt to tow the vessel, a South Vietnamese landing ship ignored the cutter's warning to stay away and abruptly stopped alongside. Happy sailors scampered across the cutter's deck—behaving like kids released from school for an unexpected holiday—and began grabbing up anything movable on the trawler. The landing ship eventually backed off, but only a few hundred yards, where she still hampered the tow effort. The crewmen that she had left behind were jumping overboard to swim to their ship. Before *Point League* could do anything else she had to fish out some of them to save them from drowning. All the same, the trawler was not budging until lightened by dewatering. It was noon the next day when salvors freed her and she was taken to Saigon to serve the government as a bragging coup, touting that in six weeks nearly 200 tons of munitions had been denied the enemy.

The trawler was sound despite being measled with countless bullet holes and eight mortar-size rents. The charred pilothouse showed signs of a hurried attempt to destroy intelligence: the wheel, compass, engine order telegraph, and sundry navigation gear were missing. By contrast, the clean and recently painted forecastle had been untouched by fire. The engine room showed conscientious upkeep and had ample spare parts on hand. Her main engine was a four-cycle, solid injection, air-started, 225-horsepower, 375-rpm diesel, made in 1963 in Magdeburg, East Germany.

From information found in the navigator's notebook and the engineering log, the voyage started in North Vietnam with a stop in China to take on cargo. The doomed journey to South Vietnam commenced on 14 June. There were 14 bunks in the 99-foot-long vessel. Photographs taken by the aircraft that first detected her showed 11 men visible on deck. In the aftermath, one crewman was found dead in the engine room and South Vietnamese soldiers found the bodies of five others behind the beach. They captured two wounded sailors, but one of them died without regaining consciousness and the questioning of the other brought forth no new information. More than 1,100 pistols, rifles, machine guns, recoilless rifles, and rocket launchers were captured, along with more than 350,000 rounds of ammunition. Most of the weapons were made in Communist China, with a sprinkling of Soviet Union and North Korean models among the lot.

The Coast Guard's interception of two trawlers, compared to none for the Navy, caused one Navy officer to lament, "The Coasties get all the action."[2] Other Navy officers reasoned that the Coast Guard's experience in long, wearisome rescue searches gave them an advantage in maintaining alertness during patrol monotony. The Coast Guard did put together a distinguished record against trawler infiltration. From July 1965 to December 1971, when the cutters patrolled the South China Sea, ten North Vietnamese trawlers were destroyed or captured. Coast Guardsmen engaged the enemy in nine of those ten and in each played a major role in the outcome. Coast Guard vigilance also caused an unknown number to turn back. The success or failure of these arms carriers depended on the level of surveillance and degree of watchfulness along the South Vietnamese coast. As such, appraisal of this aspect of the war is broken down into five periods of activity: (1) Pre–*Market Time* Infiltration (1962–1965); (2) First Trawler Infiltration Era (February 1965–March 1968); (3) Pause in Trawler Infiltration Attempts (March 1968–August 1969); (4) Second Trawler Infiltration Era (August 1969–April 1972); and (5) Final Stage (April 1972–January 1973, cease-fire).[3]

In the Pre–*Market Time* stage, trawler infiltration ran unchecked, with the bulk of the supplies feeding into the Mekong Delta. This period concluded with the discovery of the Vung Ro Bay trawler. From 1965 to 1968, the First Trawler Infiltration Era, all pretext of a local guerrilla struggle dissolved as warfare burst open with a ferocity that spared neither Vietnam, nor Laos and Cambodia.

In this bloodiest period of the conflict, the combatants, in a show of wills, unhesitatingly committed men and equipment to the war, resolving little. During this time, the vitally important trawlers came poking holes in the naval screen, only to fail. Of the twelve detected six were destroyed, two were captured, and four chased off. The desperation for supplies was evidenced by one captain's own desperation. After being spotted, he shunned the prudence of clearing out and tried running for the beach.

In 1965, COMUSMACV estimated that the enemy received 70 percent of its supplies by waterborne infiltration, mostly from trawlers. Three years later COMUSMACV believed that no significant infiltration of troops and supplies was occurring moving in by sea. The pause in trawler infiltration took place from the spring of 1968 to late summer of 1969, when North Vietnam curtailed the attempts and concentrated on the safer alternative of moving supplies through Cambodia. Communist Chinese ships dropped cargoes in Sihanoukville, from where they moved unimpeded into South Vietnam through inland waterways or overland by an expanded Ho Chi Minh Trail through Laos. The Second Trawler Infiltration Era picked up in 1969, after Cambodia's Prince Norodom Sihanouk halted the arms shipments through his country. The first intruder was detected 24 August and was run back into Chinese waters. But North Vietnamese strategists, encouraged by the fact that the United States had begun disentangling itself from the war and gradually turning its *Market Time* vessels over to the South Vietnamese Navy, increased trawler infiltration attempts. Tactics changed, in that, once detected, the trawler would abort the mission to return another time, rather than take a suicidal chance to get through. Thirty-eight infiltration attempts were detected during this era. Thirty-three trawlers aborted, three were destroyed, and two made it through the naval screen.

On 28 August 1970, two weeks after Coast Guard Squadron One ceased to exist, the first trawler since the Coast Guard joined the counterinfiltration effort was believed to have reached her destination. Another success was discovered in March 1971, when an abandoned trawler was found in An Xuyen Province. This vessel was last known to be in Haiphong on 18 December 1970. But Coast Guard Squadron Three was still in business, and sank two of the three trawlers, with the third sunk by the South Vietnamese Navy on 24 April 1972, in international waters.

At this late stage, South Vietnam dropped its policy of waiting until trawlers were within 12 miles of their coast to attack, and now fired on them wherever found. For two reasons no trawlers were detected in the Final Stage: the high seas were no longer a sanctuary and North Vietnamese ports were mined in May 1972, which may have trapped trawlers in these harbors. From American and South Vietnamese accounts it appears that their joint efforts ran the trawler gunrunning program onto the rocks. The assessment is not total without hearing from North Vietnam. In December 1973, an officer who served with Group 125 said that his outfit made 62 successful trips between 1963 and 1973. This would add 20 to the 42 making it to the Ca Mau Peninsula reported by the political officer defector. How many of those 20 took place before

Market Time is unknown, but even if averaged out to two a year for those ten years, the gunrunners' success ratio remains poor.

Market Time lasted from March 1965 to December 1972, with a scorecard of 50 trawler detections—37 aborted, 9 destroyed, 2 captured, and 2 making it through the naval screen. Strangely, *Market Time*'s primary opposite, Group 125, went out of existence a few months earlier, replaced by Group 950, a new infiltration unit that used smaller fishing vessels bought in South Vietnam and carrying documents to operate in South Vietnamese territorial waters. The impact of Group 950 is unclear.

The U.S. Navy put together a sound plan, using a diversity of vessels and aircraft tied to an effective command and control network that choked down major seaborne infiltration. Without question, the Coast Guard made a huge contribution to its success. This is exceptionally notable, considering that, when called upon, Coast Guardsmen, in a sense, grabbed their guns, picked up their boats and plopped them down in the South China Sea. They went to work as if war were an everyday occurrence.

Operation Market Time fared as most Navy–Coast Guard joint operations have for more than two centuries because of one constant: an unconditional devotion to duty by the sailors and Coast Guardsmen on the seas.

North Vietnam's Arms-Carrying Trawlers

Type	Length	Beam	Draft	Speed	Cargo (Tons)	Crew	Armament
SL-2	125'	19'	11'3"	17–20 knots	Unknown	10–13	14.5-mm (3) or 14.5-mm (1) and 12.7-mm (2) and possibly 33-mm (3)
SL-3	88'	18'	8'	12 knots	100	10–15	12.7-mm (3)
SL-4	99'	19'	8'	14 knots (est.)	95 (est.)	10–16	12.7-mm (4)
SL-5	110'	22'	9'	12 knots	100–110	10–15	12.7-mm (?)
SL-6	96'	18'	8'	15 knots	100	10–15	12.7-mm (2) and one probable 14.5-mm
SL-8	150'	27'	12'8"	Unknown	400 (est.)	Unknown	12.7-mm and possibly 23-mm or 37-mm

Source: Erdheim, Judith C., *Market Time*
Center for Naval Analyses, September 1975

CHAPTER 5

SQUADRON THREE

THE NUMBER OF COAST GUARDSMEN ASSIGNED TO VIETNAM service was about to more than double. Two years after acquiring inshore craft for *Operation Market Time* from the Coast Guard, the Navy went back asking for offshore help.

Although there were sufficient barrier ships prowling the deep coastal waters, an urgency to employ seven destroyers—with their longer-range guns for bombarding North Vietnam and for assault operations in the south—kicked over the tidy schedule board. To accomplish this, the Navy figured it would yank seven radar-picket destroyer escorts (DERs) out of *Market Time* to relieve destroyers on duty elsewhere in the world, and use Coast Guard ships and the Navy's new 165-foot-class motor gunboats as DER replacements. An alternative would have been activating DERs from the mothballed fleet, but that would have been time-consuming and expensive. The cutters provided a frugal expediency. In a 10 March 1967 memorandum, the Secretary of the Navy formally asked the Secretary of the Treasury for five cutters for Vietnam duty. Four days later a return memorandum approved the request, but this paperwork exchange merely fulfilled the required administrative process. The Navy and Coast Guard, knowing it would happen, had had their planning staffs working on the deployment particulars for weeks. In fact, on the day of SECNAV's request, Coast Guard Headquarters sent a message out to the field naming the cutters chosen—and their arrival date off the Vietnam coast. These ships would comprise U.S. Coast Guard Squadron Three and stage out of Subic Bay in the Philippines. Thirty different cutters would rotate through the squadron in its nearly five years of existence.

By Coast Guard definition a cutter is any of its vessels 65 feet and longer. They are named as well as numbered. Those under that length are only numbered and called small craft, or boats. "Cutter" comes from the service's original ten vessels, the single-masted, fore and aft rigged sailing cutters of the eighteenth century. A vessel's length is elemental in Coast Guard conversation, replacing its class as an identifier. The remark "I have orders to a two-fifty-five" means that the person is going to a 255-foot-long cutter. When the call came to enter the 1960s battle arena, the Coast Guard's warship fleet was an aged group equipped with much obsolete gear. Had this collection of 327s, 311s, and 255s been human beings, they would have long ago retired from their labors. They were a scramble of pre–World War II and World War II gunboats and seaplane tenders. They were kept in better running order than anyone should have expected by men propelled with a concrete pride that they could do more with less than any other armed service or federal government agency. This belief seemed borne out by the U.S. Congress's propensity to pile upon the nation's smallest military service many diverse missions without any meaningful increase in funding for new equipment and more people.

Even though the wakes of these cutters had migrated across generations, they still carried enthusiastic crews. It was, after all, their ship, and if she performed well and if in the view of outsiders looked sharp, their esteem swelled. The appeal of aged things is that they have existed in a time not experienced, and known only through historiography.

Observably, Coast Guard members tend to be optimists. Maybe it is the search and rescue mission that attracts this personality, but nevertheless, optimists find inspiration in the past and some of these old vessels live in Coast Guard lore.

Foremost among them were the 327s. Named after former Secretaries of Treasury, they personified the mental image of the word "cutter" with their rakish bow and slender beam. In 1936 and 1937, seven of these 2,700-ton ships were built for the Coast Guard. Crews found them a good ride, even in rough seas.

During World War II convoy duty across the Atlantic Ocean, German submariners found them a deadly nuisance. On 22 February 1943, the USCGC *Campbell* (WPG-32), cognizant of 15 to 25 German submarines stalking her convoy, depth charged five of them and rammed a sixth during 12 tense hours. Another 327, the USCGC *Spencer* (WPG-36), sank two German submarines and probably put a third on the bottom before moving to the Pacific Ocean, where she served as flagship in numerous amphibious landings. More than 20 years later these remarkable vessels, still running at a frisky 20.5 knots, were going back into war.

The 311s, not as jaunty in looks with their boxy superstructure, were seaplane tenders constructed for the Navy in World War II. After the war a number of them were transferred to the Coast Guard. They, too, had a notable combat record. The USS *Half Moon* (AVP-26) shot down at least six Japanese aircraft, and in a 33-day period, the airplanes she tendered sank 43 Japanese supply vessels.

Then there were the forlorn 255s. The Coast Guard had prepared a design for a 316-foot cutter that was essentially a "no-frills" 327. But what Congress authorized for construction in the spring of 1941 was shy by 61 feet. Supposedly, Congress held that they were replacements for the 250-foot-long ships given to Great Britain under the lend-lease program and the new vessels had to have similar characteristics. Another theory for why they were shortened is that it was so they could fit through the locks to reach the Great Lakes, thereby giving shipyards of that region an opportunity to bid on the contract. Regardless, they were built in California and Maryland, and under such low preference that the first one went into commission 11 days after Germany surrendered. The 255, snubbed for combat at birth, was getting a chance for a war record near the end of her active duty. Seven modern ships did serve in Squadron Three, but at the time of the Navy's request one had just entered service and the others were still

The first five high-endurance cutters assigned to Squadron Three nest alongside USS *Jason* (AR-8) upon arriving at Subic Bay in the Philippines. The cutters, from left to right, are *Half Moon, Yakutat, Gresham, Barataria,* and *Bering Strait.* (Courtesy of U.S. Coast Guard)

under construction. These sleek, fast, 378-foot cutters, the first new large vessels built for the Coast Guard in 20 years, began going to Vietnam in late 1969.

Squadron Three was officially established on 24 April 1967 in ceremonies at the Navy's Pearl Harbor base in Hawaii. Two days later—their white hulls further purified by the tropical morning sunshine—an impressive formation of five 311s, each carrying more than 160 crewmen, headed out to sea. Old ships, yes, but with contemporary crews and rejuvenated by the trust given them to carry men through war again. They were rejuvenated with the new and uplifting title of High Endurance Cutter (HEC).

Gone were the musty designations of seaplane tenders and gunboats. The Coast Guard had recently standardized its cutter groupings, giving these large cruising cutters a term referring to their greater capacity to remain under way before needing replenishment. The ships of the squadron's first quintet were: USCGC *Barataria* (WHEC-381), Portland, Maine; USCGC *Bering Strait* (WHEC-382), Honolulu, Hawaii; USCGC *Gresham* (WHEC-387), Alameda, California; USCGC *Half Moon* (WHEC-378), New York, New York; and USCGC *Yakutat* (WHEC-380), New Bedford, Massachusetts.

Captain John E. Day, the squadron's commander—whose serious nature was complemented by a granite square jaw—made certain this was no idyllic cruise by holding daily drills. Besides the standard man overboard, abandon ship, fire and collision evolutions, he stressed battle stations and gunnery, and put special emphasis on the joint ship exercises of tactical maneuvering, communications, and underway replenishment.

Day learned the importance of intership coordination for combat potency as a young officer on World War II convoy duty. Since the war, however, cutters worked alone, and now, as part of the U.S. Navy's Seventh Fleet, interaction with other ships would be frequent. Day also had Coast Guard pride in mind and wanted to leave a good impression on the Navy. In this regard he need not have worried.

On 10 May 1967, the squadron sailed into Subic Bay, situated on the west side of Luzon, northwest of Manila. It was the closest major American naval facility to the Vietnamese mainland, some 640 nautical miles away on a straight line, and, therefore, the primary service center for military ships going to and coming from the war. A couple of days later, after Day and his small staff set up headquarters ashore, *Barataria, Bering Strait,* and *Gresham* departed in calm seas for a 15 May rendezvous to relieve patrolling DERs.

Doing anything for the first time fills many with a natural apprehension that is a combination of dread of the unknown and the anxiety over bungling the job. Military training tries to circumvent these stresses through repetition and mental discipline. Still, unfamiliar surroundings tend to spook one's confidence. Only weeks ago the men had been in their own country, where they had family, spoke the language, knew the culture, and knew how to get around. Here, none of that applied. The cure of such foreboding calls for a dose of the familiar and a swallow of action.

It did not take *Barataria*'s crew long to overcome their remoteness jitters. She had just emerged from a vagrant tropical downpour nearing her relief coordinates when from a bridge radio speaker a voice said, "Welcome to the South China Sea." The call had come from *Point Cypress,* operating nearby. The friendly greeting was a timely reminder to the crew that they were not among strangers after all—nearly 500 Coast Guardsmen were already here. The familiarity continued for *Barataria*'s skipper. For Commander Richard M. Morse, going aboard *Forster* to obtain station relief information was like returning to a house he had once lived in. His thoughts spiraled back to the Korean War, when he was part of a group assigned to bring 18 destroyer escorts out of mothballs to be manned by the Coast Guard. *Forster* was the first of them. After a couple of days getting acquainted with the local waters and the details of *Market Time* watchstanding, *Barataria* sailed into An Thoi for a briefing with the task group commander, which turned into something of a family reunion since the task group commander was a Coast Guard officer and Division Eleven was based there. With his crew now more comfortable 12,000 miles from home, Morse wanted action as soon as possible to scrub the remaining uneasiness from their psyche.

When he learned en route to patrol from An Thoi of a report that a U.S. Army Special Forces camp near a river mouth was going to be assaulted overnight, Morse asked for, and received, permission from his superior to stand by the outpost, ready with gunfire support. By 2130 the cutter was in position. The bridge watch spoke in hushed voices so they could immediately hear any radio call for help. Under the forecastle, men in the upper handling room waited for the word to pass projectiles and powder cases to the gun crew above them. Inside the 5"/38 gun mount—virtually a metal shed with a barrel poking out of one side—nine men waited in cramped confinement breathing humid air reeking of machinery grease and shipmates' sweat. Nothing happened. Did the enemy know they were waiting to shred their attack? Was the intelligence wrong? Were there other circumstances forcing the assault's cancellation?

To extend their time on patrol, the U.S. Navy's inshore craft, nicknamed "Swift" boats, would take on fuel, water, food, and a fresh crew from a Squadron Three cutter at sea. (Photograph by author)

Whatever may have been the reason, *Barataria* resumed course at 0300 with a weary and disappointed crew. During the week that followed the men lapsed into the timeless shipboard routine of upkeep to which all seafarers are in bondage anywhere, anytime. Then, on the afternoon of 22 May, the wait to participate in the war ended off An Xuyen Province, where a U.S. Air Force light observation airplane found targets for them.

Barataria's gun cheerfully hurled 45 rounds on Viet Cong emplacements. Far to the north, along the DMZ, the bridge watch on the USCGC *Point Dume* (WPB 82325), tuned to the same radio frequency, cheered when they heard the spotter tell *Barataria* that all shots were on target.

The *Market Time* operation constantly sought ways to tighten its naval cordon with the resources given it. Its leaders recognized that coverage weakness existed from An Thoi to Cat Lo, a 300-nautical-mile spread where these were the only *Market Time* support bases. In between lay an uninviting geography of delta marshlands and tree-entangled shoreline in a thinly inhabited region under Viet Cong dominance.

Early in 1966, the problem was addressed by using the outer barrier ships as mobile bases for the short-range PCFs. As a result, Squadron Three Coast Guardsmen found that, along with everything else, they were storekeepers and innkeepers. Usually two PCFs came under their charge. After 24 hours on patrol the Swift boats met the ship to take on water, fuel, food, and a fresh crew.

One headache in this operation was finding places for the replacement crews of two officers, eight enlisted men, and two Vietnamese liaison petty officers to sleep.

The ships had already used the available space for the additional men assigned them to reach wartime sailing complement. One cutter had the foresight to equip her forward recreation deck with ten extra bunks and housed the PCF crews there, but most sprinkled the extra men in officers', petty officers', and seamen's quarters. The practice of "hot racking"—catching sleep in any bunk not in use, usually a watchstander's—was often the only solution. As for the PCF sailor, it mattered little to him where he slept; just having access to hot food and a hot shower in a space more restful than a small boat in open seas was a welcome respite. The Coast Guard WPBs did not need relief crews, but came alongside for water and fuel if they were going to be out for an extended period.

Ship and boat worked together, sharing their advantages. The ship, with her greater height and combat information center, could observe farther. Still, detection was only Part A; Part B was overtaking suspects, and here the boat, with quickness and a shallow draft, excelled. It made excellent bait, too. The USCGC *Winona* (WHEC-65), a 255, sent two PCFs into a river to attack a heavily fortified position to draw fire. As soon as the enemy opened up on these agile lures *Winona* pounded them with her deck gun. When one PCF took a recoilless rifle hit just above the waterline, the cutter, without a pause in her barrage, sent a small boat over with a repair party, which slapped a patch into place to hold out the water until the PCF made it home.

Just as each cutter adjusted at sea, the squadron staff did so ashore. At the outset, the seven DERs still attached to *Market Time* and the five cutters were separate entities performing the same function under Commander, Cruiser-Destroyer Group 70.8. Two seven-ship DER squadrons out of Hawaii alternated six-month deployments to Southeast Asia as Task Unit 70.8.5. The Coast Guard ships on ten-month home port to home port deployments composed Task Unit 70.8.6.

It soon became evident that two squadrons' staffs in the same office, doing the same thing, was trouble. Not only did it duplicate the work, but it fostered nonproductive competition. It was like two brothers running hardware stores side-by-side, where the stores are owned by their father and all profits go into a family bank account. The inevitable reorganization became official on 1 October when the units merged into CTU 70.8.5, a Coast Guard–Navy unified command. The top post went to the squadron commander having the highest-ranking billet, in this instance the Coast Guard. The DER commander served next in line as chief staff officer. Each leader, however, was still responsible for keeping his ships in a high state of readiness.

Reorganizations are defended by their promoters with bowed heads and soft, assured voices promising better service as the outcome. What really happens—regardless of whether staff is reduced, stays the same, or is increased—is that the pledged efficiency drowns in increased workload. It was no different this time. On top of running the task unit, Captain Day was also designated Commander, Cruiser-Destroyer Group Seventh Fleet Representative, Subic, which meant parenting the average 65 ships in the group when any of them were in the area, which was often. So for the 8 officers and 13 enlisted men on the Coast Guard–Navy staff, the only difference they likely noticed under the new arrangement was less opportunity to go to the head during office hours.

Squadron Three cutters had a different regimen than those of former Squadron One. Their underway percentage was alike, but whereas the WPBs lived in Vietnam, the HECs only visited. When not patrolling in Vietnamese waters, the HEC moored in some other country for duty, maintenance, or rest. If a Coast Guardsman aboard ship calculated how his time in Squadron Three was allocated, he would have found it to be: 70 percent at sea; 20–25 percent moored for upkeep; and 5–10 percent on port call liberty. These figures stayed constant even after the Navy withdrew all DERs from *Market Time* two years later and decommissioned them in an economy move. The task unit was committed to fill five *Market Time* stations, two Taiwan Patrol stations, and Hong Kong Station Ship. *Market Time* patrols varied from 21 to 30 days. The Taiwan stint—pulled solely by the DERs because the HECs lacked electronic countermeasure devices—lasted 28 days, and Hong Kong Station Ship 21 days. This last assignment was something new for the cutters. Including them into this rotation was part of the reorganization, and in December *Bering Strait* became the first HEC to pull this duty. She was the only one of the original five to do so, as the others had completed their tours before their turn came.

Hong Kong, then a British Crown Colony, was composed of an island, a peninsula, and some leased territories along the China coast. Visitors came away from Hong Kong with modern images of thickets of grand hotels, splendid office buildings, concrete apartment complexes, and expensive homes. They recall too, contrasting images of fragile, scrap wood, tin, and tar paper shack dwellings clutching rocky hillsides, and shabby sampan homes clustered by the thousands in corners of the harbor sheltered from typhoons. These sights made it hard to believe that in 1841, when the Union Jack went up claiming the island for Queen Victoria, it was barren, mountainous rock without geographic identity and with few inhabitants. Back then, the British had been prowling for a location to set up a trade center free of China's control, yet close to the mainland and the city of Canton. So when a dispute between English and Chinese merchants could not be amicably resolved, a short, lopsided war resulted in which Great Britain wrested the island from the Chinese emperor and named it Hong Kong, for "fragrant harbor." In the following decades the colony expanded across the strait to the Kowloon Peninsula and absorbed the surrounding small islands to become a dominant world commerce center. Modern China, no longer the military pushover of the 1800s, but a powerful industrialized nation under Communist rule and unbending foe of the Western free world, found it irksome having this capitalistic wart on its elephantine hip. Still, China found advantages in having the English colony next door. She supplied it with food and critically needed water—at a large profit. As a backer of North Vietnam she used Hong Kong to spread anti-American sentiment. An American sailor wandering into the Chinese Trade Fair and Exposition found, along with cultural displays, graphic Vietnam War photographs with enraged captions in English and Chinese deploring the actions of the United States and urging people to confront the tyrant.

Hong Kong also proved a fertile source in securing U.S. dollars and currency easily converted to dollars, which enabled the financing of costly revolutions and terrorism. The United States attempted to keep money out of China's war chest by prohibiting its citizens from buying Communist Chinese goods and services. To this end Chinese goods purchased in Hong Kong had to be accompanied with a Comprehensive Certificate of Origin issued by the British government, guaranteeing that the items were made in the colony or in a non-Communist country.

But none of these wearisome international politics mattered to the tourists. Hong Kong enticed them with exotic sights, good food, shopper's bargains, and the hint of a promising sensual nightlife. To the sailors of the U.S. Navy's Seventh Fleet, Hong Kong was all these, and a chance for some plain old skylarking. Acting as the Navy's agent to help the men enjoy a safe liberty was the Hong Kong Station Ship, or officially, Senior Officer Present Afloat (Administrative), Hong Kong.

Entering Hong Kong by sea for the first time leaves an unforgettable imprint. The harbor is a pause in a long roomy strait with narrow inlets on the east and west. It is bracketed by the mountainous rocks that are Hong Kong Island to the south and Kowloon Peak to the north, making those aboard ship feel like goldfish swimming past whales. The watery expanse that yokes the city halves boils with craft wedged along shore and disarranged across the harbor. Little pierage exists because the angry typhoons that rage through the strait would just tear ships from the docks. Therefore, in crowded anchorages ride freighters, old and rusty, new and sleek. There are warships, gray, white, pale green, short, long, narrow, and wide, all swinging on buoys. To and from the anchorages scurry lighters, launches, vending junks, and walla wallas, the sampan water taxis. From side to side, more than 2,000 times a day, dash big black and white car ferries and smaller green and white people ferries. Passing, simultaneously, through this frantic cross traffic are countless fishing boats, tugs, barges, and coastal freighters headed for other destinations. Amid all this movement rise the sounds of bells, whistles, horns, and the sharp cries of sea birds mixed up with smells of diesel fumes, decaying fish, pungent spices, saltwater, and refuse. Into this melange to pull Hong Kong Station, her hull blissfully white, a Squadron Three HEC treads her way to nestle alongside the somber gray-hulled DER that she is relieving. First priority is linking communications systems with shore and ships in the harbor. Over the weeks ahead radiomen will handle thousands of classified and "plain language" messages to pass on to visiting ships. Some messages include arranging for tug, pilot, and berthing services through the British Port Services Officer.

Next, a status board is set up for keeping track of military vessels. While this is taking place, overzealous tradesfolk are bouncing over the decks offering laundry and other domestic services. One enterprising woman meets each ship to haggle with the executive officer over the quantity of scrap brass she will accept for removing the garbage and painting the hull. At the same time her female workers peddle soft drinks on the fantail and her business partner is inducing patronage at their bar by announcing free drinks for all hands the first night. Handpicked Coast Guardsmen hustle down the gangway with night sticks, white webbed belts, and black armbands marked with the bright gold letters "SP." This is the shore patrol party heading for instructions at the Royal Navy's provost marshal's office, where they will be shown persuasive ways to deal with the unruly. The British preferred that the U.S. Navy take care of their own, and, in keeping with this approach, promoted close liaison with civilian authorities to work out special problems. Generally the station ship detailed an officer and ten enlisted men, who stayed ashore the entire time, lodging in a hotel. Divided into port and starboard duty sections, they worked from 0730 until 0130, after liberty had expired. Visiting ships fleshed out this small permanent force by daily assigning men to walk the beat. The policy toward sailors on liberty weighed in their favor. They were to be treated as fighting men on a well-earned holiday and assisted as much as possible. Most sailors were appreciative and constrained their misbehavior. A 255, the USCGC *Androscoggin* (WHEC-68), was station ship when 3,500 sailors were loose ashore. That night only seven formal misconduct reports were logged.

After all the briefings are done, all the protocol visits completed, and all the necessary files and equipment transferred, the DER slips away, leaving the cutter to settle into the life of a bobbing administrative office. With the arrival of each military ship, the cutter sends over a launch with a welcoming team to greet the newcomer, passing along the rules of conduct, points of interest, and purpose of the station ship. In spite of this being a hectic assignment, Coast Guardsmen still found opportunity to ride a water taxi to Kowloon, or Victoria, on Hong Kong Island, to get in on those shopping bargains they had heard about. They also spread goodwill by bringing aboard Chinese orphans to watch cartoon movies and stuff their tummies with ice cream. Hong Kong was also a pleasant spell for the deck force because someone else got to paint the ship. They watched with amazement the Asians applying paint with wrapped bundles of frayed silk. It was messy, and even though it did the job, the deck force pledged to stick with their brush and roller technique.

On Hong Kong Station Coast Guardsmen filled roles as radio broadcaster, postmaster, doctor, policeman, supply clerk, public relations director, and nursemaid, but found it a welcome diversion from laborious *Market Time* patrols and the confinement of ship life. In some ways, shipboard environment is like monastery life. Both members live in a community residence that is also their workplace, each abiding by stringent rules of conduct, and following a prepared daily schedule. Although a sailor's seclusion is not as absolute as a monk's, because his time away from people comes in chunks, he looks forward to the solitude on the empty sea, where duty may be demanding but is largely free of surprises. In brief, it is an escape from the complexities of shore living.

A monastery emphasizes individual contemplation. By comparison, a crew is based on teamwork, and goaded by such announcements over the loudspeaker as "The speed which General Quarters was set was good, all stations were manned and ready in three and one half minutes—except for gunnery." This, of course, prompts the embarrassed gun gang to catch up with the rest of the team next time. In essence, the Squadron Three cuttermen were, for ten months, cloistered in a steel enclave. A ship is expected to go where needed, do what is ordered, and get the job done. The men inside function like cells inside a human body, keeping it alert, healthy, and purified. Hence, shipboard life consists of repetitive cycles of watchstanding, maintenance, and cleaning. Each morning and afternoon, the crew musters by divisions on the fantail. Each person is accounted for and information is passed down the chain of command. Then it is on to work. Periodic personnel inspections are held to check for compliance with grooming and uniform standards, and regular material inspections of the ship are made by the commanding officer. Cleaning is an endless, inglorious task, necessitated in part to prevent disease transmission in the close quarters and to eliminate fire hazards. But sometimes the crew will feel that the tidy work is being carried beyond reason and lets it be known in tacit ways. The crew may have been sending such a message the time one HEC mentioned in the Plan of the Day that, in one week, 24 swabs had been misplaced or lost, leaving only 10 remaining on board.

Seafarers, traditionally men, have been tagged throughout the ages with a nefarious reputation in the lusty regard for women. While the twentieth century sailor may be sedate compared to tenth century Vikings or eighteenth century Caribbean pirates, it does not mean he is indifferent to women. Having to live apart from women naturally makes the longing for them greater than in circumstances where feminine companionship is available. Aboard ship women are a constant topic of discussion, and the inside of many lockers are brightened with female pinups taken from sexy magazines. It can be anticipated that, after extended periods away from females, sailors will at times neglect the usual propriety shown in public toward them. The skipper of one cutter stopping in Hawaii en route to Southeast Asia, knowing that among the welcomers on the pier would be ladies in grass skirts and halter tops, traditional Polynesian attire, wisely warded off any ill will by admonishing his men to be in full uniform of the day and not to make salty comments toward the women—who were the wives of Coast Guardsmen stationed there.

Patrolling in the South China Sea confronted Coast Guardsmen with other adversaries besides the Viet Cong. Bright sun and debilitating tropical heat were two of them. The former became evident right away, as sickbay was treating a heavy increase of eyestrain. Fortunately, the treatment was simply to wear sunglasses. To accommodate the latter, uniform regulations were commonly relaxed when under way. Some cutters permitted crewmen to work on deck shirtless and in dungaree shorts, but watchstanders remained in regulation garb.

Food preparation, basic to high morale, fell into the domain of the cooks, who toiled in steamy galleys. When a ship jostled in heavy seas, like a bus driving across badly potholed roads, a good number of crewmen clutched their bunks or station, fighting off seasickness. The cooks had to battle their queasiness trying to put out a meal, and found themselves expending most of their energy just keeping the cookware from falling to the deck. It did not matter how few showed up to eat, the food had to be prepared. Cooks receive infrequent praise. After all, preparing a good repast is their job. On the other hand, griping about the food has always been a mariner's privilege. Sometimes the complaints are merited. Sometimes poor food quality victimizes the cooks. Crew discontent with the food aboard USCGC *Morgenthau* (WHEC-722), a 378, led to the posting of the following notice:

> *It is not necessary to register complaints about the chow by placing the item on the Executive Officer's desk. Every effort will be made to serve the highest quality and best prepared food possible. Eggs are notoriously poor quality in WESTPAC (it's a long way to the nearest chicken ranch). The cooks work like supermen, believe it or not, but do not have X-ray vision. Quite often spoiled eggs will be served with the same frequency in the [Captain's] cabin, wardroom, CPO mess, and, crew's mess. At worst it's still better than powdered eggs or no eggs at all.*

Crews became close-knit through the mission they shared. Pride and pranks also contributed to their bonding, especially through identifying with names and trademarks. Proud of their ship's naval gunfire marksmanship, the men on the USCGC *Minnetonka* (WHEC-67), a 255, painted a 5"/38-gun caricature on the side of the mount shell emblazoned with the name "Iron Hoss" in bold black capital letters next to it. When she concluded her last patrol in September 1968 she had fired 4,684 rounds on *Market Time* duty, more than any other Squadron Three cutter. The USCGC *Duane* (WHEC-33), a 327, used tiger paws for prankishness. Any ship moored alongside her overnight found at daylight black tiger footprints painted on their deck and up the superstructure. There were chuckles aplenty when USCGC *Ponchartrain* (WHEC-70), a 255, rested at anchor off Con Son Island, where some crewmen took advantage of the pause to go ashore. However, when time came for the ship to leave, four men were missing. They were searched for, found, and returned to the ship huddled together in the small boat wearing only their chagrin as shipmates lined the rail greeting them with hearty jeers and cheers. Their clothes had been swiped while they were swimming.

Always on the minds of the men were loved ones back home, but for some, Vietnam had become a family war, which resulted in poignant reunions on the cutters. On Father's Day 1967, a U.S. Air Force master sergeant in Vietnam visited his son, a crewman on *Half Moon*. Another *Half Moon* Coast Guardsman caught up with his Navy brother assigned to a landing ship. Not all reunions were joyous. Not for the Coast Guardsman on another HEC, who went ashore to accompany home the body of his brother, killed in action.

At times the cutters became classrooms for South Vietnamese Navy ensigns fresh out of the country's naval academy. One or two would live aboard for a month or more, and their English rapidly improved in the All-American environment. Each was assigned to a Coast Guard officer and stood bridge watches with him, practicing shiphandling and navigation. For two Vietnamese officers aboard *Half Moon,* it was their first time at sea, since the academy provided no shipboard experience. In their debriefing letter after departing the cutter the ensigns stated that they were pleased to put into use what they were taught in school, that accommodations were comfortable, and the food was okay—except for the hot dogs.

Through the blackness of night two ships glide in parallel, with only the dim red flush of light bulbs from their facing sides betraying their presence. The quiet is almost as complete as the darkness, but random sounds quiver in the air: the rude shrill of a whistle, a hoarse voice command, and the begging moans of pulley wheels ridden hard by coarse manila line. Between the vessels dangles a chair that appears to have been made with slices of aluminum Swiss cheese. The man in it clutches at his lifejacket, praying that he does not have to test it. The wind slapping his face stings his eyes, causing tears to well at their corners. The ship ahead appears far off, a trick of his mind, no doubt, because the loudness of water lapping past the hull tells him he is getting closer to the end of this uneasy journey. In epileptic lurches the chair moves across space until, thankfully, groping hands pull him aboard. The parson has arrived.

As small a group as Squadron Three was, it had the distinction of having a full-time U.S. Navy chaplain. For a newly assigned chaplain, revelation that his flock spent little time in the Philippines came quickly. If he were to tend his sheep he would have to join them in pastures off the South Vietnamese coast. Hence the chaplain, during his year's duty, spent only ten percent of his tour in Subic Bay. As a circuit riding preacher he hitchhiked across the South China Sea on any ship that took him to his parishioners, and logged many miles riding a boatswain's chair along the highline highway. Lieutenant Robert R. Mitchell, who graduated from high school in 1943, was the squadron's first chaplain. He was a man who left his comfortable pastoral post in West Danby, New York, when he felt a calling to help his countrymen fighting in Southeast Asia. "Our servicemen need more than food and bullets in this business. They also need God, and that's where the chaplain comes in," said Mitchell.[1] He applied for and received a commission in the Navy Chaplain Corps and, after two months of military orientation, joined Squadron Three. He would spend a week at a time aboard each cutter, holding services and Bible study. Moreover, he was an important source for helping Coast Guardsmen maintain focus on the importance of what each was doing, which in the daily routine is easily forgotten. He provided a perspective distinct from what they expected to hear from their officers. He also held group discussions on practical matters, such as marriage, covering finances, sex, in-laws, children, and working-wife relations. These sessions carried their influence in the years beyond the battle zone. When the chaplain visited, evening prayer over the public address system was a regular occurrence. Mitchell left with each ship an audiotape of recorded religious music for use during services, including sacred songs sung and recorded by his wife.

The chaplains were fountains of reassurance to the men. When one was seen swinging aboard they felt an internal calm that revived their spirit of self-worth. Commander Harry J. Oldford Jr., executive officer of *Duane,* said of Mitchell that he was a wonderful person. Not a fire and brimstone type, but a great father figure for the guys; he would have lunch and dinner with the crew and always be available to listen. That the *Duane*'s crew held Mitchell in high regard is revealed in her cruisebook, where a page is devoted to Mitchell with three photographs, one of him riding the boatswain's chair, another of him giving a sermon, and the third of the crew at services. Part of the accompanying text reads "...he added something special to the Sunday morning church services and was an inspiration and help to many of us."[2]

Along with their spiritual well-being, the Coast Guard cared for the men's physical health by having every HEC deploy to Vietnam with a U.S. Public Health Service doctor aboard. Some Navy officials questioned the need for a physician on each ship, but Coast Guard leadership strongly felt it prudent, a decision appreciated not only by Coast Guardsmen, but by other American servicemen, South Vietnamese soldiers, sailors, and civilians, and even enemy troops. At least four times at sea, in the pants pocket–size sick bays doctors performed emergency appendectomies on Coast Guardsmen. Another time a Swift boat hurried out to a cutter with two South Vietnamese irregular soldiers who had been ripped open in a grenade booby trap. The doctor on *Androscoggin* operated four hours on the most serious casualty, who had fourteen intestinal perforations along with five other wounds. When the man left for home his survival chances were good.

The doctors made visits to coastal hamlets, where people by the hundreds crowded for attention. Many villagers had never seen a doctor before. Doctors did not shun danger. When five South Vietnamese soldiers were ambushed on Phu Quoc Island, with one killed and another wounded, the landing party from USCGC *Sebago* (WHEC-

42), a 255, sent in to pull them out, carried the ship's doctor. An hour later, the landing party returned to the same location to evacuate the pilot whose airplane was downed by groundfire while assisting in the rescue.

The squadron existed, of course, expressly for patrolling a watery carpet laid down to 40 miles from shore and outlined into nine sections from the DMZ to the Cambodian border. These elongated zones ranged in length from 61 to 122 miles. A ship could spend an entire patrol in one sector or in halves of adjoining ones. Patrolling might be random, or running a barrier line back and forth, casting out radar signals to net traffickers. Ships adjusted tactics for whatever the current military situation required. Cruising in straight lines, circles, or zigzags, it mattered little. This was all familiar to the Squadron Three cutters, which had spent years on Ocean Station duty, where they loitered inside a ten-mile-by-ten-mile patch of ocean for four weeks, sending up navigational information to aircraft and collecting weather and hydrographic data. For these Coast Guardsmen, used to those month-long cruises to nowhere, *Market Time* was Ocean Station with spicy seasoning. During the day the enemy stayed relatively inactive on the water, but at night, wearing the uniform of darkness, he was on the move. To counter this the HECs usually worked 10 to 15 miles off the coast, inspecting any radar contact within 5 miles of them. Contacts more than 5 miles landward were referred to inner barrier boats. The HECs, operating without lights to maintain invisibility, prowled for junks more than 20 miles to sea, and for vessels on a course into the beach or making coastal approaches at other than normal entry points. Erratic maneuvering, running without lights, and the absence of hull markings or a flag also aroused suspicion.

The cutters operated under rules that in the CZ they could stop and search only South Vietnamese vessels, Nationalist Chinese fishing vessels, and hostile craft. From any others they could demand identification and intention. Beyond 12 miles they could only halt South Vietnamese craft and the ambiguously named "vessels evaluated as hostile," which curiously did not happen even when a detected North Vietnamese arms carrier stayed on the safe side of the 12-mile line. In some patrol zones, junks fished out to 16 miles and anchored for the night unlighted or showing a light so faint that it was only visible within a few feet. The wood construction of the junks, as well as the stakes marking their fishing nets, made poor radar reflectors, and it required extra vigilance to keep from running them down. As might be expected, the HECs, cruising farther offshore where traffic is thin, only made a half dozen boardings each patrol. However, surveillance was their main concern and they did that well, detecting an average of 600 craft an outing.

A warship is foremost a waterborne artillery unit; yet this capability did not figure into the original *Market Time* concept. Naval gunfire action was permitted sparingly, and usually limited to emergency situations. However, it must be said that, until the arrival of the HECs armed with a 5"/38-gun that could range more than nine miles, *Market Time*'s smaller-gunned DERs and MSOs lacked sufficient punch. Nevertheless, the first five Squadron Three ships averaged only ten Naval Gunfire Support (NGFS) missions, with an average total of 600 rounds expended. In 1968, with the arrival of Vice Admiral Elmo Zumwalt as COMNAVFORV and Captain Roy Hoffman as the new *Market Time* commander, there came a philosophy change that sent all naval craft on the offensive. The new approach is told in the final statistics from the

1969–1970 tour of USCGC *Dallas* (WHEC-716), a 378: 163 gunfire missions, 6,640 rounds discharged.[3]

Targets were plentiful: ammunition dumps, troop concentrations, and bunker complexes. A cutter would crowd as close as possible against the shore, sometimes with as little as five feet under the keel, to achieve maximum range. Where an inshore area was uncharted or the reported depths suspect, the small boat was lowered with a leadlinesman guiding the cutter to the closest point from which she could "squat and shoot."

The Viet Cong came and went with little dread on the land cupped around the Gulf of Thailand—until the HECs took roost there. Beneficiaries of their presence were isolated friendly villages, with their tiny forces of U.S. Army advisors. Such a place was Song Ong Doc, which one Coast Guardsman described as a village huddling nervously on the north bank of the river. Open on three sides to the enemy, the safety of 3,000 villagers was entrusted to a half dozen American soldiers, 120 regional troops, and a white cutter with a long reach. On 12 September 1967, *Half Moon* rushed to Song Ong Doc, breaking up the attack plans of 200 Viet Cong closing in on the village. In December 1969, USCGC *Chase* (WHEC-718), a 378, received reports feedback from the Army advisors that the cutter's highly accurate gunfire so discouraged the Viet Cong that they were breaking up into smaller, harder-to-hit units and taking greater measures to protect their munitions. From April to December 1970, a cutter was continuously stationed in the vicinity of the village when notice of an increase in junk traffic bringing in men and equipment stirred concern that a major attempt might be made to overrun it.

The cutters were accustomed to performing gunfire missions alone, but on 16 July 1968, off the Ca Mau Peninsula, and separated by 1,000 yards, *Androscoggin* and *Winona* excavated Viet Cong positions with 414 rounds that sent black petroleum smoke billowing above the targets and left the ground shuddering from the secondary explosions coming from ammunition caches. Afterward, the pilot of the airplane spotting this mission—who had spotted on previous shoots for *Androscoggin,* and who knew that this was the cutter's final *Market Time* patrol—made a low pass in salute. He dropped her a flare container, inside which was a Viet Cong battle flag.

As guns drained the magazines, engines dried up fuel tanks, and men emptied cupboards, a ship moved closer to becoming as useful as driftwood unless regularly replenished. Just in meandering on station for a month a cutter traveled 10,000 miles, and, with a Task Unit policy that no ship was to drop below 60 percent of her fuel capacity, this meant frequent refueling.

Naval power is effective only when ships are under way. The U.S. Navy, with vessels from aircraft carriers to patrol boats strung out along North and South Vietnam, remained a powerful force because it kept them at sea through large supply vessels, their sides bulging with stores, fuel, and ammunition, plodding the South China Sea like ubiquitous guardian angels.

Underway replenishment (UNREP), the well-developed evolution for getting supplies from one vessel to another, took place day or night under all but the most severe sea states. Time-consuming, exhaustive, and dangerous, it also demanded skillful shiphandling. A typical UNREP scenario begins a day or two before rendezvous when the cutter radios in a shopping list. As the supply ship comes into sight, all hands are dispatched to UNREP stations. The cutter draws alongside until less than 100 feet separate the ships, pushing through the water at 10 to 12 knots. A Coast Guard gunner's mate snugs into his shoulder the stock of a line-throwing gun, a .30-caliber, bolt-action, 1903 Springfield rifle, loaded with a blank cartridge. Protruding from the barrel is a long metal rod with a weighted tip. A red-orange nylon line is tied to a ring on the rod, and the rest of it is coiled inside a metal cannister under the barrel. When the trigger is pulled, the rod with trailing line arcs over to the other ship. It is grabbed by sailors, who pop out from cover after the projectile concludes its dangerous ricocheting off various parts of the ship.

Next, the small line is connected to a heavier messenger line and pulled across. The stronger lines needed to make the connections for passing freight and fluids are attached to it. When stores and fuel are being transferred, two receiving stations are set up—one forward, one aft. Along the freight lines arrive the all-important mailbags and anyone coming aboard by riding the swaying boatswain's chair. Files of men haul on the lines to bring over supplies and tighten or relax the connections as the intervening distance between ships opens or closes.

The rest of the crew, often naked to the waist, stores everything below. The 54-pound 5"/38-projectiles, coming across in clusters 12 to a rack, must be individually passed below into the magazine. The whole task is strenuous and slow. Vertical replenishment (VERTREP) is faster, but not as common. Helicopters can deliver ten tons in a half hour. However, on the older cutters open deck space is limited and the men are hard pressed to remove the cargo before the next load is overhead. There is also the hazard of flying debris caused by the powerful rotor wash of the helicopters. Only seven percent of all Squadron Three replenishments were by air. Meanwhile, on the bridge the watch remains alert for the unexpected. During a night refueling with the USS *Mattaponi* (AO-41) off to starboard, *Campbell*'s observant watchstanders avoided a catastrophe when they picked up a radar contact 2,000 yards away, approaching the oiler's starboard beam. For an unknown reason, perhaps startled by the looming presence of the ships in the dark, the small South Vietnamese cargo vessel made a sharp course change to the right that would bring her across their bows. An immediate emergency breakaway was executed so both ships could independently cut to their right. To everyone's relief, the freighter safely passed, albeit less than 250 yards down the *Campbell*'s port side. A short while later the ships rejoined and finished the refueling.

For the cargo ships these provision runs became tedious, leaving officers challenged to spice up the labor for their ship's morale and their customers as well. *Androscoggin* observed one such attempt. When she pulled away from the USS *Guadalupe* (AO-32) the oiler's officers donned sombreros and serapes, and brassy Mexican music blared over the loudspeakers for a musical "*Adiós!*"

When Coast Guardsmen first learned that their ship was ordered to Vietnam, the customary uneasiness had for a companion the excitement of a new adventure that manifested itself in a friskiness, especially among the younger men. One cutter had to admonish the crew for unnecessarily running about the ship because of the injuries it was causing. In time, as the patrols added up, the excitement seeped away like air from a worn tire, leaving only the sag of fatigue under duty's weight. An underway ammunition replenishment that began at 2300 would not conclude until 0400, when the last round was stowed. A patrol day could include a gunfire mission, medical aid to an injured man off an inshore boat, replenishing with three different Navy ships, and scratching the night to uncover a furtive enemy. On other occasions, small U.S. Army reconnaissance teams were inserted ashore by small boat and South Vietnamese Army amphibious landings were supported with radar navigation guidance and gunfire. Coast Guardsmen spent many tense hours at battle stations, bearing the weight of steel crab-shell telephone talker helmets and flak jackets. Those below decks in sealed, stuffy compartments waited and wondered. To be sure, not every moment was action-filled, but even those infrequent idle spans siphoned energy. To ward off creeping moodiness that dragged down performance, officers worked hard at keeping up the crew's spirits. To keep the men close to the mission, they passed on information about what the ship was doing and increased interest in other ways. Most of the men were not involved in boardings because the station bill had them elsewhere. Therefore, some cutters rotated them in and out of the boarding teams.

Another way of creating participation was putting a man aboard a PCF for a twenty-four hour patrol. Off-duty tedium was an area that needed particular attention. Aboard *Gresham,* officers taught classes in Intermediate Algebra and English Composition. The theatrical movies distributed by the Navy were run over and over, so much so that their best entertainment value came from ribald and skeptic comments yelled from the audience, addressing what was happening on the screen. Within moments after the opening credits, the most serious drama became a hysterical comedy. Other morale diversions included swim call, weekly bingo games with prizes purchased from profits made in the ship's store, and Saturday night happy hours with pizza, snacks, and soda. Crew members who played musical instruments formed a ship's band, and on "Hump Day"—the halfway point in a deployment—entertained at the ship's party. Still, the most successful morale builder was just getting away from the deafening blast of the deck gun and the ceaseless rolling of the ship. This came in the form of port call liberty. Kaohsiung, Taiwan; Sasebo, Japan; Bangkok and Sattahip, Thailand; and Singapore were some of the places where the men soaked in the scenery, drank the beer, ogled the girls, and spent a lot of money. In Singapore, a frugal seaman used his small savings to buy a rug, a flute, smoking jackets, and chess sets. Others went for bronzeware, wood carvings, silk, and tailored suits.

Central to world traveling is meeting people, seeing how they live, and learning their customs. Many were surprised to learn that in Thailand, driving is done on the left side of the road as in Great Britain. There were other do's and don'ts to know before going ashore. In Thailand, they were informed to stand at attention when the King's Anthem is played. When someone makes the "wai" gesture, putting the hands together in a praying position before your face and slightly nodding the head, you should return the greeting. The normal act of crossing your legs, if done in a position that places your foot higher than a Thai's foot, could be offensive. A Thai considers the top of the head to be the most sacred part of the body and the bottom of the foot to be the lowest. If you raise your foot to any level above a Thai's foot you are indicating that you consider your foot better than another part of his body.[4]

Local bars were not bashful in advertising for patronage. As *Androscoggin* was tieing up in Yokosuka, Japan, a bevy of Japanese girls waited on the stern of the U.S. Navy destroyer to which she was making fast. The girls, each representing a different bar and holding a large bouquet of flowers, swarmed aboard the cutter. Before long the wardroom, chief's quarters, and crew's mess were choked with flowers, causing the commanding officer to observe that his ship looked like a funeral parlor. Afterward, the flowers were given to the wards in the naval hospital.

Besides studying Oriental saloons, the men took part in outdoor recreation like playing basketball. In Kaohsiung games were played against teams composed of Chinese working for local petroleum companies. These liberty bursts, though brief, refreshed a crew as does a splash of cold water in the face of a groggy man. When on the beach the men existed in a quickened time sphere, living two minutes for every actual minute. Although they often returned to the ship with their wallets empty, their minds were flush with fresh memories to carry them through the next war patrol.

While the war seemed to impatient and opposed civilians an endless treadmill, accomplishing little but the killing of hearty Americans, North Vietnam knew it was near defeat. Their casualties well exceeded those of all their opponents, with no perceptible gain. The goal of conquering South Vietnam had fallen from the horizon. Therefore, in mid-1967, the Hanoi government approved a countrywide offensive on South Vietnam's major cities and towns, with visions of the south's population coming over to their liberators in reckless euphoria to join in the overthrow of the Saigon government. Whether or not Hanoi truly believed this would happen, this is what the soldiers were led to believe. That the coordinated assault was to take place during Tet—a revered holiday time for all Vietnamese people that welcomed in the Chinese Lunar New Year with week-long gaiety—showed North Vietnam's desperation. In the months before, through deliberate labor, men and equipment were moved into attack positions and political and military deceptions were employed to cloak what was forthcoming.

To cause disenchantment among the South Vietnamese, the Viet Cong started a rumor that the Americans were going to arrange a coalition government with them and leave the country. At diplomatic posts the North Vietnamese left clues that their government might hold peace talks if the United States halted bombing in the north. Moreover, forays continued on outposts, and enemy units shifted positions, with the dual intent to lure American troops into the country, away from populated areas, and to disguise the pending offensive. The American military was not misled. From studying captured documents and analyzing troop movements, it suspected something big was going to happen soon. On 22 January 1968, General Westmoreland said in an NBC television interview, "I think his [the enemy's] plans concern a major effort to win a spectacular battlefield success on the eve of the Tet festival next Monday."[5]

During Tet it was usual for a ceasefire to be observed for the first day or two, and many South Vietnamese soldiers were allowed leave to go home to celebrate with their families. A concerned Westmoreland asked President Nguyen Van Thieu to cancel the ceasefire. Thieu compromised by reducing the ceasefire from 48 to 36 hours, limiting Tet leaves for military personnel, and ordering a minimum of 50 percent of the troops at all units placed on full alert.

The Tet Offensive began with premature attacks on 29 January, and most of it was over by 11 February. Instead of a spectacular combat success, for Hanoi it was a military fiasco. Half of its actively committed forces were erased, with 32,000 communist troops killed and 5,800 captured. Furthermore, no South Vietnamese rallied in support. By the end of the month, when all the target communities were swept clean, another 5,000 enemy soldiers died. The Americans had 1,001 killed and South Vietnamese and allied forces suffered 2,082 dead.[6] Because this had been a land operation, naval forces had only the peripheral involvement of performing illumination over suspected enemy positions and some shelling, but confirmation of the gravity of the defeat would be dramatized at sea.

Operation Market Time had shown Hanoi that running supplies into South Vietnam by trawler had become foolhardy. Already, seven trawler incursions had resulted in two abandoned attempts and five vessels destroyed or captured. The last try, in July, ended with the trawler captured and her cargo put on public display in Danang to further embarrass Hanoi. Consequently, these bold efforts were abandoned for the more reliable, if slower, land passages, until the disastrous Tet Offensive left the Viet Cong ravaged. The countless wounded faced certain death unless medical supplies were replenished, particularly blood plasma. Stocks of weapons, ammunition, and explosives had been severely depleted. It was time to be reckless. Hanoi ordered five trawlers to sea to get through the blockade with the critically needed materials.

For all those hapless 255s, which lost 61 feet of their posture to the political cleaver and the chance to enter the Coast Guard's World War II annals, it was fitting that as the intruders hastened south three of these HECs were on patrol. In a becoming twist, the squadron's other two cutters back in port were the World War II glory-wreathed 327s.

The *Androscoggin* had been out of town on business. Specifically, she was in Hong Kong as station ship, where the skipper, Commander William H. Stewart, and his crew had witnessed the Chinese Lunar New Year being celebrated by rambling garish street bands and gatherings of laughing, friendly people, many making wishful toasts to the Year of the Monkey, while South Vietnamese communities were having their festivals transformed into funerals.

When the cutter backed off from the mooring buoy on 12 February the Tet Offensive was all but over. Back on patrol two days later off Quang Nai Province, between Danang and Qui Nhon, the grisly accounts started filtering down among the men. They would eventually learn how in Hue, the country's third most populated city, the Viet Cong executed or buried alive more than 2,800 citizens, a blunt contrast to the joy the crew had experienced in Hong Kong. These Coast Guardsmen, brought up with the values of fair play, could not understand the heartless murder of civilians as a war tactic, and longed for some opportunity to punish the enemy.

However, stuck out on lonesome outer barrier duty, that seemed improbable. That was until 21 February, when a *Market Time* airplane sighted a North Vietnamese trawler. But the next day high expectation soured into disappointment when something scared the trawler and she scampered off to the security of Chinese waters. A week later the excitement returned as the crew listened in wonder to the sighting reports from sharp-eyed *Market Time* air crewmen: 28 February, 1830, trawler 150 miles east-southeast of Vung Tau; 29 February, 1000, trawler 120 miles northeast of Qui Nhon; 1541, trawler 103 miles east of Cape Batangan; and 1714, trawler 91 miles east northeast of Nha Trang.

At 2047 on 29 February, more than 40 miles from land, east of Cape Batangan, *Free Transit 11*, a *Market Time* aircraft, passed the covert surveillance baton to *Androscoggin*. Stewart's cutter would be the primary attack unit and he was designated officer-in-tactical command and on-scene commander. For the present though, his concern was keeping the trawler ignorant that she was under watch. To do this Stewart turned to the north, then seaward, and back south in a wide loop to drop eight miles off the trawler's starboard quarter, now a luminous blot on radar. Passivity calls for discipline, whereas action unleashes self-control, and as such, waiting can seem more daunting than fighting. Having to leave the trawler unmolested until she sailed inside the 12-mile mark, time passed for the crew slower than a rock eroding indoors. Meanwhile, four miles from the beach waited the restive dog pack, the cutters *Point Welcome* (WPB 82329), *Point Grey,* PCF 18, and PCF 20. On takeoff alert were two helicopter gunships and a flare aircraft.

Androscoggin kept easy pace with the trawler's ten knots over a restful sea lullabied with languid two-foot swells. With the exception of a few scattered clouds, visibility was clear. Shortly before midnight the crew rolled down their sleeves, buttoned their shirts to the top, tucked pants legs into their heavy work boots, and without haste went to their battle stations through passageways inside the ship. Only the topside mortar and machine gun crews were held back from their posts. These precautions were done to keep the light-tight envelope intact.

Everyone was pleased; they would get a chance to avenge Tet after all. Everything went well until, when 20 miles from shore, consternation struck the men on the bridge. The trawler's westerly track crossed the course of USS *Comstock* (LSD-19) northbound to Danang. Oblivious that the unlighted contact ahead was being shadowed into a trap, the *Comstock* dutifully challenged the trawler with flashing light for her identity. The cutter sent off a frantic message to CSC to call the ship off. Only moments before *Comstock* was to fire illumination over the trawler did word reach her to clear out. Unfazed by this bother, the trawler pressed resolutely inland in a weaving trackline like a merchant ship might travel while crossing known submarine waters to avoid being torpedoed. At the 15-mile mark the trawler upped her speed to 12.5 knots, sending her over the fateful 12-mile line at a half hour past midnight. The tactical plan was to confront her when she was six and a half miles from land. With the trap nearly ready to spring, the outside gun crews took their stations. The rules required that a proper attempt be made to identify a vessel, even one clearly hostile, presumably on the wishful chance that she might surrender. So, off to port the quartermaster flashed the light challenge, which of course was ignored. Stewart ordered up the aircraft and commenced firing 5"/38 illumination rounds. When the third star shell blossomed over the target the crew had their first view of a dumpy, harmless-looking craft only two-fifths the cutter's length.

With the spotlight now on the main character, the play commenced. The trawler substituted her opening lines with machine gun fire and closed on the cutter. The gun crew replaced star shells with high-explosive projectiles as a flare aircraft arrived to take over the stage lighting. The gritty trawler laid out dense white smoke to shroud her evasive turns and continued to drive at the cutter, unaware of *Androscoggin*'s size. The automatic weapons fire did little but scar the cutter's port side, but a serious threat came when two shells exploded in the water off her bow and a third whined overhead and hit the sea. These were believed to have come from a 57-mm recoilless rifle. The cutter's machine gunners instinctively hunched lower behind their splinter shields and returned fire. Then the 5"/38 boomed, and the huge fire ring that spewed from the muzzle lighted up the cutter for an instant.

Realizing now what he was attacking, the trawler's captain twisted his vessel away. In those lagging moments she offered a larger target and took a five-inch round in the starboard quarter that staggered her. A North Vietnamese sailor rushed to the rail and tossed a smokepot overboard. It spread a cloud so thick that it showed up on radar measuring 300 yards by 1000 yards. Then, again, a non-player entered the stage when a cargo junk serenely passed between trawler and cutter, forcing the latter to check fire.

Stewart then ordered in *Shark* 5 and *Shark* 6, the helicopter gunships. To one Coast Guardsman watching from one of the WPBs, the dueling helicopters and trawler appeared connected by glowing red-hot wires. He was amazed that they did not destroy each other in such an intense tracer exchange. When the helicopters withdrew, however, there seemed to be fewer muzzle flash points coming from the trawler. At the point where shallow water kept his cutter from getting any further, Stewart unleashed the dogs. The PCFs, like crazed terriers, made fearless dashes, nipping the trawler's sides with their twin .50-caliber incisors. The WPBs, more like German shepherds, ripped the prey with combined mortar and machine gun fangs. Gouged, bitten, bleeding, weakened, and disoriented, the quarry fell against the beach. Showing no mercy, the pack continued its murderous crossfire. Across the sand a figure lurched toward the treeline. He stumbled, then fell. Getting back on his feet, he lunged ahead until the darkness swallowed him.

When the shooting stopped the final act opened on 1 March, at 0210, four miles south of Cap Mia, in an unearthly quiet interrupted only by the periodic soft "plop" of a parachute flare jettisoning its container from the circling airplane. The dog pack, dispersed in an arc about their prey, panted, ready to pounce at the first evidence of breathing. No one approached the grounded trawler. They awaited the inevitable self-detonation. At 0220 a small blast coughed from the bow, resulting in moderate damage and leading the watchers to think that the self-destruction attempt had failed. Six minutes later, as boarding plans were under consideration, the trawler dissolved into a 500-foot fireball.

Aboard *Point Welcome,* the closest craft to the trawler, the bow gun crew was blown off their feet, bridge windows cracked into cobweb patterns, and from the sky it rained metal and wood. A twisted bayonet clanged on the steel deck between two men seeking cover against the small boat. Radar observers on *Androscoggin* saw the inshore boats disappear in fluorescent obliteration and feared that the trawler had taken them to hell with her. After the last of the debris had fallen the two aft machine gunners on *Point Welcome* stood back up. One asked the other "Where's the trawler?" When their bow swung aside, giving them a view of the beach past the deckhouse, they were stunned. All that remained of the infiltrator was a brown stain on the sand.

From the water the *Point Welcome* crew pulled out a blue lifejacket, bits of cloth, and a bamboo beehive fender. The biggest item they found was a piece of wood hatch six inches wide by thirty-six inches long. Follow-up searches on land revealed debris scattered over at least two square miles of beach and water. So complete was the destruction that the only recognizable section found of the vessel was a 40 foot by 50 foot chunk of bottom plating and keel submerged in eight feet of water. Of the North Vietnamese crew all that was found was a head and a full set of teeth on the beach.

At about the time that *Androscoggin* had picked up her foe, Captain Herbert J. Lynch guided *Winona* into radar contact with a trawler near Con Son Island and stalked her into the CZ. Like *Androscoggin,* the *Winona* had inshore boats primed to intercept. Lynch calculated that he had 18 minutes to stop the trawler before shrinking depths took him out of the action. His strategy was to get in on top of the gunrunner, crowd her, and give her little room in which to evade. At nine miles from shore the cutter was 1,110 yards from the trawler and closing. She flashed the fitting challenge three times. Then three times more using the South Vietnamese Navy codes. All this took four minutes. She then blinked out the international letter "K" meaning that the vessel was to stop immediately.

At the same time, *Winona* hit the trawler with a spotlight, to which the enemy responded by heaving cargo overboard. Five minutes later, at 0200, the cutter fired a 5"/38 warning shot. Committed to his mission of getting the supplies through, the trawler's captain kept course for the beach. A couple of minutes later Lynch concluded the amenities. He bore down on the trawler, now only 550 yards away, and gave the command, "Open Fire!" Out of pure self-defense the trawler shot back. The cutter snapped off her spotlight and the sea battle flickered in the dark, but not for long. Five minutes later two explosions tore apart the trawler, sinking her in 25 feet of water. Lynch had accomplished his task with two minutes to spare. The structural hits taken by *Winona* were of little consequence. Her personnel casualties were minor: one man grazed in the arm by a bullet, a second cut on the forehead by flying metal, and a third knocked down by a six inch by six inch chunk of steel plate that smashed into his helmet.

A third trawler was run aground in a cove some ten miles northeast of Nha Trang along the central coast by U.S. Navy Swift boats, South Vietnamese Navy patrol craft, and Junk Force boats. Viet Cong forces trying to defend the vessel from shore were taken under fire by a U.S. Air Force C-47 gunship. The PCFs pounded the trawler with their mortars until, around 0230, she exploded. The blast only partially wrecked the forward and amidship sections, allowing recovery of much of the cargo. Fourteen enemy dead were found in and around the trawler.

The fourth trawler appeared to be en route to the Lo Dien beach area north of Qui Nhon. *Minnetonka,* as did her sisters, covertly stalked her trawler. Thirty miles from shore, at 0015, the vessel abruptly turned around and headed back out to sea. At 0212, after all the other gunrunners had been engaged, *Minnetonka* was ordered to turn the trawler using any method short of taking her under fire. The cutter did her best to draw the trawler's ire, but the absurd engagement policy preventing offensive action must have made *Minnetonka*'s attempts to get the trawler to shoot look silly to the North Vietnamese crew. The fallout of this encounter could have well brought Hanoi to conclude that trawlers had nothing to fear beyond 12 miles because, over the next 4 years, of the 38 trawlers detected, in 33 instances the vessels demurred and did not cross the sanctuary line.

Minnetonka opened her performance first with the flashing light challenge, followed by firing illumination rounds. The trawler's skipper likely stifled a yawn during this scene, but politely gave his applause in the form of turning on his navigation lights. The cutter crossed in front of the olive drab trawler at 300 yards and then dropped astern to follow from less than 2000 yards, while popping mortar flares over her and firing four 5"/38 warning shots spaced at one-minute intervals. There was no reaction from the trawler.

Well, no one likes being ignored. Okay, let's try a flashing light order to stop. Nothing. Okay, fire machine gun bursts across the bow. Hmmm. Maybe everyone aboard is asleep. Okay, get the South Vietnamese Navy liaison up here. We will pull alongside and wake them up with the loudhailer. Maybe they will stop if they hear the order in their own language. This routine went on for hours. At daybreak *Minnetonka*'s audience had dwindled to three armed men atop the trawler's pilothouse. The cutter fired a final deck gun warning shot at 0700, in sort of a last appeal to come out and play. Twenty-five minutes later the cutter fell behind several miles to follow her on radar for the next couple of days, almost all the way to the Chinese mainland.

Undoubtedly, *Minnetonka*'s crew felt embarrassed over the whole business, while the hardened, suicidal North Vietnamese crew laughed over the strange way the Occidental mind wages war. Still, victory that night clearly went to the rule-conscious Americans and their allies. Five trawlers left for South Vietnam with at least 500 tons of cargo and none of it made it through.

Squadron Three cutters would destroy two more trawlers, this time with the Coast Guard's new, sleek 378s. They had twin diesel engines for economical cruising, powerful twin gas turbine engines for get-up-and-go, and variable pitch propellers for splendid maneuverability. They could go from a dead stop to top speed of 29 knots in a minute, and come to a sudden halt within the ship's length.

Feeling safe, the trawler crossed into the CZ not knowing that USCGC *Rush* (WHEC-723) had been tracking her for four days. The USS *Endurance* (MSO-435) challenged the intruder and fighting broke out right away. *Rush* and USS *Tacoma* (PG-92) joined in. The USCGC *Sherman* (WHEC-720) dashed to the scene from another direction and opened fire with her 5"/38 at 0009, 22 November 1970. Using point-detonating fuzes at a range of 5,600 yards, she was now the only one firing on the trawler. When the trawler stopped five minutes later, *Sherman* continued her attack for another ten minutes. A few minutes after she ceased fire the trawler blew up and sank. Salvors found the stern demolished, along with the wheelhouse, where the cutter had concentrated her fire, but the cargo was still intact.

Five months later *Rush* directed another sea battle. This time she, along with *Morgenthau*, USS *Energy* (MSO-436), USS *Antelope* (PG-86), and helicopter gunships, sent another trawler to the bottom at 0145, on 12 April 1971.

This is how it went for ten months in the life of a Squadron Three cutter and crew: a blend of excitement and tedium mixed with a lot of hard labor. Along with the appropriate war statistics, such as rounds fired, structures destroyed, and the like, each cutter also compiled other such interesting figures of the cruise, such as the following: ice cream consumed—900,000 gallons; number of movies shown—733; and money spent on beer—$58,049.25.

A deployment did not end until the cutter reentered her home port, usually to a noisy harbor welcome of circling Coast Guard aircraft, Coast Guard patrol boat escorts accompanied by water-spouting fireboats, and a posse of whistle-tooting civilian small craft. On the pier, where hundreds of people waited, a military band played martial music. Before long, the gangway dropped into place and loved ones rushed to embrace. In this sweet bedlam the tour concluded.

CHAPTER 6

THE NAVIGATION MASTERS

A U.S. ARMY STAFF OFFICER FROM MACV MET with Captain Loforte on 8 February 1966 to find out who was seeing to it that the new channels and ports burgeoning up throughout the country were marked with navigational aids. The query originated from CINCPAC, MACV's boss, and the Coast Guard seemed the place to go for the answer. After all, its Aids to Navigation (ATON) teams and buoy tenders coddled the marine aids back home and the service operated precise electronic navigation stations around the world. Since 1939, when the Coast Guard absorbed the Lighthouse Service and its duties, it had been the country's navigation safety expert. If the staff officer expected to hear that the Coast Guard had this little detail in hand, he had a surprise coming. Loforte told him that over here that responsibility belonged to MACV and the South Vietnamese government, specifically the Bureau of Navigation (BON).

When American marines, ready to do combat, landed in Danang in March 1965 they breached America's advisory-only wall. Through the gap rushed American forces, spreading themselves over the South Vietnamese landscape. Because this rural nation had such a meager road and rail network, supplies had to reach the dispersed units largely by air or water. From the ports, where most war materials came into the country, cargo moved out either by truck for transfer to aircraft, or by shallow-draft vessels via the waterway tendrils crossing the Southeast Asian geography.

Despite a coastline that made up 60 percent of it boundaries, South Vietnam had few commercial ports. What existed were adequate for a non-industrialized nation where the ox-drawn wagon was common transportation, but not for processing millions of tons of goods each day. Danang, the country's second largest city, typified the situation. Oceangoing ships could not approach its limited pier space because the water depth was a mere 15 feet. To get cargo to docks it had to be shifted into smaller vessels. Moreover, the anchorages faced the open sea. During monsoon season high winds and deep swells halted lightering and caused ships to drag anchor; therefore, the Americans had to overhaul existing ports and build new ones.

Early in 1966, when new port sites were still being picked and accelerated port construction was in progress, disorder was understandable, which included taking for granted that somebody had been assigned to marking channels for safe navigation. Once port managers realized no one was doing so, they took independent action and ATON installation became an uncoordinated effort. The U.S. Navy base at Cat Lo, having the Coast Guard handy, asked it to help mark its approaches. Division Thirteen, still outfitting at Subic Bay, responded by sending over three men with ATON backgrounds. The trio used oil drums, wire, and whatever other materials they could scrape up to create makeshift buoys until permanent ones could be acquired.

Loforte believed the sensible thing to do was to have the Coast Guard assume the entire responsibility for ATON in Vietnam. Although enthusiastic about the idea, he knew it was premature until the appropriate South Vietnamese government agency was consulted, something no one in the American military hierarchy seemed to have done yet. This was confirmed three days later when he met with the United States Agency for International Development (USAID) advisor to the BON and was told that no relationship existed between the Bureau and MACV.

More than a month later, the matter again intervened in Loforte's squadron business with a telephone call while he was out of his office. An unidentified MACV officer wanted to know when the Coast Guard buoy tender was arriving. This was news to Loforte. Two days later he received a copy of a message that the buoy tender USCGC *Planetree* (WLB-307) was coming to South Vietnam. He chased around the MACV compound to find out what was going on until he found a Navy captain who vaguely recollected initiating a request for a cutter to install 25 mooring buoys at various locations, but the officer was unaware that it was on the way.

Around this time, a group of MACV officers came to Loforte to discuss the planning, setting, and maintaining of navigational aids in the developing ports. He was astonished at their presumption that they could just order up a bunch of buoys and plop them down in a foreign country. He tried impressing upon them that a navigation director existed and it would be wise to get with him and work out an agreement. It baffled Loforte that nobody was talking to the South Vietnamese government about ATON. Were they waiting for the Coast Guard to take charge of this unfamiliar matter? On 15 April, at another meeting with MACV representatives, after reiterating for the umpteenth time that someone needed to coordinate the United States requirements as they develop, determine the types and quantities of equipment needed, and negotiate with the South Vietnamese government, an exasperated Loforte concluded by saying that he would pursue the matter with the South Vietnamese. A relieved group left that meeting, and in their collective minds there was no doubt that the Coast Guard was handling ATON matters from this point on.

The *Planetree* arrived at Division Thirteen's Cat Lo moorings on 24 April for a briefing on the dangerous environment in which she would be working. Forty-eight hours later the buoy tender and crew were inspected by Westmoreland and Rear Admiral Norvell G. Ward, COMNAVFORV. They liked what they saw, no doubt convinced that the ATON role belonged to the Coast Guard. Later that day, *Planetree* proceeded to set mooring buoys.

There was still the issue of dealing with South Vietnam. Before seeing the navigation director Loforte once more met with the USAID advisor, who, with unrestrained

Crewmen on the buoy tender *Planetree* line up ponderous chain in preparation to setting a mooring buoy in an anchorage where tankers offload fuel.
(Courtesy of U.S. Coast Guard)

enthusiasm, assured him that Coast Guard coordination of ATON needs would be welcome, and that the South Vietnamese could handle the additional load. Consequently, Loforte entered the director's office filled with an optimism that shortly dissolved into gloom when the man repeatedly stated that his agency could not handle any more work. Loforte left with the impression that the Americans could place buoys all over the country and this man could not care less. Before leaving the building he decided to talk to the assistant director, whom he had met before. His reaction was more like what he expected from the director—if the Coast Guard supplied the materials they could do the job. Regardless of which viewpoint prevailed, MACV headquarters was drawing up an order tasking the Coast Guard with ATON liaison with the South Vietnamese government.

Loforte assigned Lieutenant Richard J. Clements of his meager staff the collateral duty of ATON Officer. Clements immediately set out to round up the hodgepodge of small buoys, chains, and swivels that nobody was certain who had ordered but had been strewn in staging areas throughout the Saigon waterfront. What he amassed he dropped in the South Vietnamese buoy depot in the city. Meanwhile, in subsequent meetings with the director Loforte saw a turnaround in the man's willingness to cooperate. This led Loforte to conclude that the Vietnamese were not frivolous with their trust at the outset, especially if that first meeting is with a group. Their approval had to be nurtured on an individual basis.

Although American–Vietnamese relationships improved and discussions followed, there was still no written agreement defining each country's role. Sometimes all the effort in creating the goodwill that brought about the cooperation fell apart overnight. Loforte had gained a great harmony with the Director, Ports, Harbors, and Waterways, a civilian, when the man was abruptly yanked from that post by the prime minister for an unrelated reason and replaced with a military officer. This meant starting over again to establish a mutual respect.

Whether it was surveying waterways, verifying charts, or installing aids, the South Vietnamese needed nursemaiding. By American standards their pace was sluggish. When the Americans decided to move their ammunition offloading site from congested Nha Be a short way upriver to Cat Lai, the South Vietnamese agreed to clear the channel and put in three buoys. Following much prompting by the Coast Guard the day came to set the buoys. Loforte and Clements rode the barge to check positioning and were surprised that the trip had become a departmental event. Also along were the Director, Chief of Inland Navigation, the Chief, Hydrographic Survey, and their USAID advisor. Happily, the buoys went in without a hitch, but the channel remained obstructed for 150 yards across with fish traps—50-foot-long coconut palm logs—which were to have been already hauled away. Once back on shore, Loforte learned that the army sector advisor had sent the removal paperwork to the province chief, who had passed it up to the district chief, which meant weeks would pass before any action would happen.

Not abiding further delays, Loforte persuaded the BON to send out the barge and crew the next morning with Clements to clear the channel. Significantly, this time agency officials were not along. By the time three traps had been pulled dripping from the water, a flotilla of sampans, paddled by angry, yelling people, came scurrying from land. The South Vietnamese barge crew at this juncture would have quit, but Clements kept them to their task; nonetheless, subtle gestures from the crew made it plain to the upset fishermen that it was all the Americans' fault.

With navigational aids already planned for Danang, Chu Lai, Qui Nhon, and Cam Ranh Bay, Loforte found that the entire ATON affair called for the full-time attention of at least three people to advise and assist the Vietnamese, so he solicited Headquarters for temporary help. In mid-December Lieutenant Commander Everett G. Walters and two petty officers, all masterful in ATON matters and tireless workers, arrived for five-month duty. Loforte explained that their task was to make the Vietnamese responsive to the navigation needs of the United States, but it would have to be done through subtle and diplomatic incentives, not through harangue and hardheadness. Loforte truly believed that although the work must get done, it must be accomplished in a way that it developed capability, enthusiasm, and interest in the South Vietnamese people helping themselves, because this was the essence of United States involvement in the country. Nevertheless, it did not take long for the newcomers' zeal to slam up against the casual Southeast Asian perspective, as attested in Walters's 20 December entry in the squadron diary:

> *Today I learned about Vietnamese working hours. Apparently they observe 17 national holidays, take 2 hours for lunch, and aren't shy about extending it for another half hour or so, and are generally happy to let Mañana take care of everything. This may not be a national characteristic, but at least at the Vietnamese equivalent of a buoy depot, that attitude prevails. Between the hours of 1130 and 1430, everything stops. This is going to make the advise business a little tedious, I fear. I am doing my best to arrange 22 years of gung-ho, do it now Coast Guard thinking, and Allen, BM1, and Zimmer, EM1, are starting to bite their nails. This job would best be filled by a person with very, very, low blood pressure, but I believe I can qualify after recovering from the initial shock.*

The languor at the Phu An buoy yard had been Walters's second shock. The day before he was stunned to see that the country's sole buoy tender, the *Cuu Long*, was a decrepit, World War II, U.S. Army castoff freighter, vintage 1943. What was generously called the buoy deck was a five-foot-wide strip down each side of the hatch cover. The raised hatch coamings were a guaranteed safety hazard, to be tripped over during distracting buoy operations. The vessel's high center of gravity also meant she could not carry the heavier buoys and sinkers. Her ancient electrical system was more than just a potential fire hazard—it *was* one! Her many other ailments were to be expected of an aged vessel given poor maintenance, and so she was not hard to locate, if you looked first in the repair yard. When Walters toured her she had no fathometer, no radar, and the gyrocompass was out of order. These were all critical in setting buoys. When the *Cuu Long* did sail that month she spent 42 days in the Bassac River, installing eight buoys. When the USCGC *Ironwood* (WLB-297) arrived to reposition mooring buoys she pulled out those same eight buoys, resetting them with replacements in only four days.

During the succeeding months Allen and Zimmer hunted down shackles, flashers, power clamps, and other ATON shipments invoiced into the country. They toiled in the buoy yard alongside the Vietnamese, repairing, welding, painting, and constructing aids. Walters inspected channels, studied dredging plans, reviewed buoy laying outlines, made recommendations, and coordinated final installations. If the *Cuu Long* was unavailable he arranged for a tug and barge to move buoys to a port where he had sinkers (concrete blocks) formed on site using local construction forces. Then, using any craft he could get that floated, they loaded aboard the buoys and dropped them into place. Despite the hard work put in, the effort was not enough to meet the demand, prompting Captain William N. Banks, Loforte's successor, to order a staff study documenting the state of things. With ATON tacked onto other new duties (PSWD, ELD) the Squadron One command title no longer fit. Accordingly, a few weeks after Banks took command, his title became Commander, Coast Guard Activities, Vietnam (COMCOGARDACTV).

In April 1967, MACV, NAVFORV, and the Directorate of Navigation endorsed the completed staff report, sending it climbing the chain of command for approval and funding. The core finding of the study was that the requirements of the United States exceeded the capabilities of South Vietnam. The country had 9 manned lighthouses, 17 buoys, and 70 unmanned light structures. To these the United States had already added 42 buoys and had programmed another 30 by the end of the year. South Vietnam's minimal resources barely took care of its own, with some aids extinguished for long periods. The Directorate of Navigation lost its most capable young men to the draft. Moreover, the agency paid low salaries in comparison to wages in the general economy, and extremely low when matched against what American contractors were paying employees. The *Cuu Long* had lost her captain and chief engineer to higher-paying jobs.

The buoy depot in Saigon was adequate but poorly located. To keep buoy tender running times to a minimum the vessel needed to be in the center of the area it serviced. Having summarized the problem, the study stated that the solution was to turn over the servicing of American aids completely to the Coast Guard. This would require assigning a permanent ATON Detail in Vietnam headed up by an officer to serve as ATON Coordinator; regular deployments to Vietnam by a buoy tender; and establishing a buoy depot with tender dock space at Cam Ranh Bay. To bolster South Vietnam's ATON infrastructure the study recommended that USAID continue developing its capability so that it could ultimately take over serving Vietnamese and American navigational aids.

The remedy fit the ailment. Supported by United States law, which provides that the Coast Guard may establish ATON for the Armed Forces beyond the territorial jurisdiction of the United States, the action was approved without bureaucratic delay.

The mission filled out in stages. In July, planning began for putting in a buoy depot at Cam Ranh Bay. In September, the ATON Detail officially went into business, with the arrival of a Coast Guard officer and petty officer to be added to the staff of COMCOGARDACTV. And in February 1968, the buoy tender USCGC *Blackhaw* (WLB-390) changed home port from Honolulu, Hawaii to Sangley Point in the Philippines for the sole purpose of serving navigational aids in Vietnam.

Four Coast Guard buoy tenders saw duty in Vietnam, with *Blackhaw* carrying out 64 percent of the deployments. This class of cutter is one of those specialty vessels that inspires curiosity as to her purpose at first sight. Her appearance is unprepossessing—some would say downright ugly—with a black hull often rippled with dents and mottled with scabs of rust, the results of heaving around concrete sinker blocks, thick chains, and hefty buoys. She is hardworking, blue collar all the way. A deckhouse sits in the middle of her 180-foot length, and between the forecastle and it is a gap that looks as if a huge blade has carved away a portion of the ship to make the buoy deck, which is the intense work zone of buoy operations. The rake of her blunt bow is almost perpendicular, her stern is plumply rounded, and with a top speed of 13.5 knots she is not going anyplace in a hurry. In spite of her ungainly looks she is a stalwart ocean vessel, a fact underscored when *Blackhaw* rode out five typhoons in a six-week span. If the Coast Guard's sleek 378-foot HEC is likened to a thoroughbred racehorse, then the chunky

Of the four Coast Guard buoy tenders to service navigational aids in South Vietnam, *Blackhaw* performed most of those duties. For more than three years— March 1968 to May 1971—the cutter made regular deployments to South Vietnam. (Courtesy of U.S. Coast Guard)

WLB is a draft horse, a vessel built for muscle, not quickness. Her crew works in hard hat, canvas gloves, and steel-toed boots. They perspire even when it is cold outside and there is no way to keep their clothes free of grime and grease. Some shrug off tender duty as mundane, but among seagoing assignments buoy tender crews consistently have the highest morale.

Between March 1968 and May 1971 *Blackhaw* made 14 trips to South Vietnam. From these deployments, which ranged from two weeks to two months duration, she accumulated more than a year in the war zone. Hostile fire was not unknown to these vessels, which saw action in World War II. The theatrical movie "Onionhead" (1958), featuring actor Andy Griffith as a Coast Guard cook on a buoy tender, portrayed this, where in the climax the buoy tender battles an enemy submarine. Therefore, the assortment of machine guns, rifles, pistols, and hand grenades on board was not out of character.

Without the buoy tender the Coast Guard's ATON chore in Vietnam would have been as effective as a gun without ammunition. Typically, the tender arrived in-country with a work list for new installations, inspections, and servicings. An inspection meant checking that an aid was correctly positioned and in satisfactory condition, while servicing frequently meant that a buoy had to be hauled out of the water for repair, painting, or replacement. Because they traveled regularly to and from South Vietnam, the tenders were asked to haul things. On one trip it was 25 tons of furniture to the Navy at Cam Ranh Bay, on other occasions they brought a skimmer to a naval ship and a telephone pole to a unit on Con Son Island. One tender just arriving from the United States collected up a WPB skipper in Danang. The officer had just returned from a respite in Thailand and the tender took him to his cutter on patrol near the DMZ. The buoy tender sent the officer over with a complimentary case of beer for the next party. What so pleased the WPB crew was that the beer had been purchased in the United States and, therefore, contained no formaldehyde, the flavor-corrupting preservative used in American beer supplied to the forces in Vietnam.

An impromptu delivery could be perplexing. *Blackhaw* had left Sangley Point for South Vietnam by way of Subic Bay, where she took on ATON materials, a ton of ceiling tile to go to Con Son Island, and two watertight doors marked for Squadron One but lacking shipping documents. When she brought the doors to the squadron she was told they did not belong there. She then tried the divisions. All three denied ordering them. Thinking they must belong to Squadron Three, she took them back to Subic Bay where once again ownership was disclaimed. Having run out of units to give them to, the tender sent a message to the Fourteenth Coast Guard District in Hawaii seeking the owner's identity. Finally, after hauling them for 6,000 miles, delivery was accomplished, and they were installed—on the bridge wings of *Blackhaw*.

Buoy tenders have in their nature an inherent will to be helpful and, if at all possible, try to honor requests. *Blackhaw* received an appreciative letter for her magnanimity during a one-day scheduled stop in Qui Nhon. In addition to finishing her job of servicing the buoys, at the MSTS unit's request she ran a channel survey of the area where one of its ship's had gone aground and assisted in the recovery attempt of an anchor lost by another of its ships.

The buoy tender may have been in Vietnam to work, not fight, but she knew there was a war going on, underscored by the routine of crews working buoys wearing flak jackets and standing by machine guns. During a 57-day deployment *Blackhaw* went to battle alert 56 times. Her commanding officer, Lieutenant Commander Carl W. Snyder Jr., having become so familiar with the presence of enemy fire, wryly put down in a trip report, "Proceeded to Cat Lo where our usual welcome greeted us. As we proceeded up the river, Vung Tau came under rocket attack. They hit the LST *Tom Green County,* 40 yards off our starboard quarter, the beach and airfield on our starboard hand."

Then there was the time she was putting in buoys near the DMZ to warn coastal craft that they were about to stray into North Vietnamese waters when *Blackhaw* found herself skipping around the battleship USS *New Jersey* (BB-62) firing her massive 16" guns inland. As the tender would make a buoy drop approach she would be chased out of the line of fire by the battleship responding to another gunfire request. Eventually, they came up with an arrangement whereby the big ship would blink the tender when it was clear. The *Blackhaw* then scampered in, splashed down a buoy, and scampered out, awaiting the next all clear signal.

On other occasions in that same area two rounds from a U.S. Navy ship firing shoreward fell far short and straddled *Blackhaw,* and rifle shots from the beach hit her stack. A chance to get in some blows of her own seemed to present itself when, nearing a river mouth, the crew was startled by the sounds of extended machine gun bursts. From the splashes in the water up ahead a small boat appeared under attack. The crew raced to battle stations as the cutter closed the distance. Upon drawing near the boat they felt both anger and chagrin when they saw a soldier firing off to one side and then the other—while his buddy took movies.

Blackhaw's dangerous and hard work did not go unnoticed. For her accomplishments she received the Navy Meritorious Unit Commendation, the Combat Action Ribbon, and the National Defense Transportation Association Award. Her citations mentioned how her landing parties packed heavy equipment into unsecure jungle terrain, where they sometimes spent days away from the ship's protection. Other times the tender had to sit inside shallow inlets adjacent to Viet Cong–controlled territory until the tide rose for her to leave.

Buoy tenders worked closely with the ATON Detail. It was the ATON officer's job to make up the work list for her next trip. The status of navigational aids came from the detail's personal observations and from other sources, which could be contradictory. A mariner reported that Buoy Number 4 in the Bassac River was missing and presumably sunk. A Division Thirteen WPB checked it out and reported that the buoy was where it was supposed to be, or "watching properly." This was followed shortly by a message from another WPB that Buoy Number 4 and Buoy Number 6 were out of position. Another WPB was asked about it and she came back saying both were on station. Finally, in an effort to get a report that he trusted, the exasperated ATON Coordinator intended to send out a WPB whose skipper had served on buoy tender duty.

The ATON officer hurried to each port just ahead of the buoy tender to confer with port officials, making certain all was in readiness. Snyder praised one such coordinator: "My awe continues to expand in regard to LCdr [Jack A.] O'Donnell.... He is required to precede us from area to area and obtain chain where there is none. Make sinkers where it can't be done and obtain the unobtainable.... He has never let us down."[1]

This same officer used quick thinking to get the always troublesome transportation to beat a tender to port when he presented his papers at a flight terminal only to be advised everything was booked. As he stood at the counter pondering his options the airman glancing over his orders saw the abbreviation "ATON" and asked what it meant. The officer answered, "Atomic Nuclear." He got his flight.

Between buoy tender visits it was left to the ATON Detail to traverse the country making what repairs it could. Like a country doctor from a bygone era, Electrician's Mate First Class Candido Rosado snatched up a big black leather bag and set off to visit his "sick patients"—his navigational aids. His colleagues called him "the phantom ghost of the Vietnam coast," as he logged between 2,000 and 5,000 miles a month. Common ailments were battery failures and sensors not turning on lights. Unfamiliarity with buoys caused at least one service call when an army explosive ordnance disposal team investigated a report of a booby trap lashed to a buoy. They carefully removed the suspicious object and sank what was only a temporary battery pack. Nevertheless, booby-trapped buoys were a real concern, the reason tenders took along Navy divers to inspect them first. Another practice before going alongside a buoy was throwing concussion grenades to detonate any explosives attached below the surface.

Coast Guardsman from the Aids to Navigation Detail has an audience
while he repairs a range light for the Tan My harbor channel.
(Courtesy of U.S. Coast Guard)

Getting to ATON ashore exposed the detail to enemy assault. When an isolated military camp came under mortar fire one Coast Guardsman, judging that he would not reach the safety of a bunker alive, took refuge in the river. Reaching the range structures built on a high point of land outside the security area of Tan My was no casual hike. First the ATON Detail checked with the port commander for current intelligence on enemy activity, then picked up an armed patrol and four-wheel drive vehicle, loading all into a landing craft, which dropped them off at the end of a spit. From there they drove to within 100 yards of the structures and climbed the rest of the way on foot. A couple of hamlets nearby provided a clue that it was safe to continue. If children were playing on the sand dunes it was likely the Viet Cong were not about. No children, watch out! Oh yes, and be careful not to step on the graves in the cemetery. That upsets the locals.

Coast Guardsmen concerned with ATON in Vietnam knew of its importance, yet their arduous labors were frequently thwarted not by the enemy—who probably found the aids useful as artillery reference marks—but by their own side. The USCGC *Basswood* (WLB-388) received an inkling of the difficulties ahead on her first trip to Vietnam when she found herself idle in An Thoi harbor because it was Sunday and the Vietnamese crane operator needed to move equipment did not work Sunday, nor did he work on payday, which was the next day. Some of the crew took part in swim call, and others relaxing along the rail witnessed the landing craft ferrying a liberty party ram and sink a buoy, to which the *Basswood* crew responded with a derisive cheer.

As *Blackhaw* was leaving a river after servicing buoys, she watched a U.S. Navy harbor utility craft run over a buoy and then go aground. With stoic reserve the tender turned around to repair the buoy.

In the Vung Tau inner harbor channel, barges not in use, or those used for storage, were secured to mooring buoys close to the channel line. Because of silting on that side, several barges were tied in a line or nested. This was okay unless they were haphazardly tied, as they often were, and as a result swung into the channel with the tide, hitting the channel buoys and breaking the lanterns or dragging the buoys under them. Some civilian contract tug and barge operators thought nothing of tying onto a buoy and dragging it off if it was in their way.

Marine aids attracted irresponsible adults as windows in an abandoned building draw naughty kids with rocks. The unrelenting vandalism ran up repair time and expense. Deterrents met with mixed success. Concertina wire wrapped around a Chu Lai rear range did stop its destruction, but when it came time to service it, the ATON Detail had to remember to bring a long ladder to lay over the wire.

But nothing could prevent the ruin from gunfire. In a December 1968 summary it was noted that two buoys were sunk by gunfire, three were hit by gunfire, and four lanterns were shot out. It was not out of place to find more than 20 bullet holes in buoys. As disheartening as all this was, the Coast Guard did sustain a navigation system that guided marine traffic to safe water. The Coast Guard also operated an electronic navigation system to primarily assist aircraft.

When the North Vietnamese delegation walked out on peace agreement negotiations on 13 December 1972, United States intermediaries felt a settlement was merely a nudge away, and that this contrariness was a ploy to see what advantage it might bring, such as an impatient American Congress cutting off funds for the war. President Richard M. Nixon, deciding that the prod would be a thumping, ordered *Operation Linebacker II*. Beginning 18 December continual night and day aerial attacks gutted the economic and military vitals of Hanoi and Haiphong. Targets heretofore off limits were pummeled. The B-52s, the heavy bombers, joined the tactical fighter-bombers—wave after wave of them. The onslaught was well into its second week with no letup apparent when the North Vietnamese, seeing their country's industrial capabilities being reduced to junk, returned to the discussions, and within two weeks a peace settlement was signed.

One would have thought that the air offensive had been ordered at a bad time for the U.S. Air Force, because it was northeast monsoon season. Visibility over the objectives would be poor, and if aircraft had to drop below the 3,000- to 1,000-foot ceilings they would be erased by air defense weaponry like chalk on a blackboard. But, thanks to a Coast Guard electronic navigation network, the airplanes could strike blind targets with accuracy in all weather.

Without argument air power took the lead in crippling the enemy's supply flow, with thrusts into North Vietnam, against infiltration routes through Laos, and on staging points in South Vietnam. The targets varied from fixed, like bridges, to elusive, like men treading through jungles carrying munitions in an A-frame strapped to their back. But the visual, radar, and air navigation plotting methods used to strike the enemy had major flaws. Darkness, poor weather, and dense foliage hampered visual sightings. Although radar overcame some of these obstacles, it required a lengthy precise target approach, which increased the chances of being shot down. The air navigation equipment in use so lacked consistent accuracy that aviators could not be certain they were returning to the same target, or more critical, to the location of a downed crewman. This was the Air Force's predicament in March 1965 when officers in Washington, DC representing each of the armed forces met for a periodic luncheon to discuss the state of military affairs. An Air Force officer relating this problem emphasized that Southeast Asia even lacked adequate geographical maps for reference. One of his listeners, a Coast Guard electronic engineering officer, told him they needed an electronic grid of the region, which a Coast Guard LORAN (Long Range Navigation) chain could provide. With LORAN-C an aircraft could return within 50 feet of anyplace, under all weather conditions.

The system had been around since World War II, when LORAN-A had been designed for military use. Following the war it became a common navigation implement for aviators and mariners. A LORAN receiver obtained a two-point reading. Each point was determined by the time difference of pulsed radio signals from two LORAN stations. Where the lines from these points intersected on a LORAN chart was the receiver's location. Once a LORAN reading for a spot was known it became a reference. On the water, where there are no seamarks, commercial fishermen rely on this constant to take them back to bountiful fishing grounds. In 1958, LORAN-C replaced LORAN-A for military use, not only because of greater accuracy, but also because it was not disturbed by atmospherics, as was LORAN-A.

Excited over what he had learned, the Air Force officer returned to the Pentagon and passed it along. Shortly thereafter, the Air Force called for a conference with the Coast Guard about the prospect of installing a LORAN-C chain in Southeast Asia. Representatives from the Department of the Army, Department of Defense, and Office of the Secretary of Defense were present to hear the system explained. The Air Force really wanted to know just one thing. Could the Coast Guard have the system working by August 1966? Generally, assembling a LORAN network in the United States took 10 to 12 months. If one added to that an estimated number of weeks for the logistics of getting men and materials to remote sites halfway around the world, it could be done, if they started now. The Coast Guard agreed to provide the sweat. All the Air Force had to do was provide the funds—14 million dollars. The euphoria evaporated. The Air Force did not have the money.

Months passed as the Air Force and Department of Defense tried to jiggle money loose from the Federal government piggy bank. Meanwhile the Coast Guard, believing that construction would eventually get funded, formulated plans, which started with naming Captain Thomas R. Sargent III, who was in charge of the Civil Engineering

Division at Headquarters, project officer on 22 September 1965. This methodical but flexible leader, with a thorough knowledge of LORAN, now had the sole responsibility for completing a LORAN chain that at that time only existed in the mind. No one even had an idea where the stations would be put.

Looking for money to pay for the preliminary work, Sargent suggested at a strategy meeting that Navy funds already appropriated for a defunct LORAN installation at the entrance to Gibraltar be used. Approval, however, would have to clear the Navy, Department of Defense, and the General Accounting Office, and this would take time. Sargent, anxious to progress beyond the desk and telephone stage, on 1 November recommended that Coast Guard LORAN administrative funds be used to get a head start. A month later he was en route to Southeast Asia on a site survey and to establish contact with the many individuals whose cooperation had to be secured to move the project along with as few obstacles as possible.

The name first given to the construction project by the Department of Defense was *Red Horse*. But when confusion occurred later when that name was also given to a U.S. Army operation the code words were changed to *Tight Reign*. Why *Tight Reign*? Sargent said it had no basic meaning unless it was originated to indicate a top secret priority installation (*Tight*) by an autonomous group (*Reign*). Another source contends it stood for the extremely close microsecond transmission tolerances, tighter than any other LORAN-C chain at the time.

Sargent made his first visit to Vietnam on 8 December, arriving in Saigon from Bangkok. Although the Continental Palace Annex hotel where he and his staff stayed had an elevator, air conditioning, and ceiling fans, they got little use from them because the electricity was shut off during the afternoon until 2200. The hotel may have lacked hot water and soap, but towels were plentiful. But they did not complain; they felt fortunate to have quarters in the crowded city where visitors were lodging in tents.

Army staff officers at MACV told them that acquiring real estate was no problem if it was government land. After briefing key officers of the Air Force's 2nd Air Division, whose airplanes would have the LORAN receivers, Sargent and company flew to Con Son Island, 45 nautical miles southeast from the coast of the Mekong Delta. Before landing they made an aerial scout for a place to put in a station. At the residence of the province chief they gathered with the deputy province chief and a South Vietnamese army officer with the title of Deputy Commander, Special Sector. What made it a special sector was a prison holding 4,000 inmates—a mix of political, Viet Cong, and standard criminal prisoners. Sargent asked for acreage on the island's north end. Without any mention of a formal lease, transfer, or purchase, his amiable hosts told him he could have it and toasted the agreement with local beer. When Sargent mentioned this back at MACV he was told that was fine, they would get confirmation from Con Son in writing and forward a request letter to the South Vietnamese Armed Forces logistics office, a routine process solely for recordkeeping. As simple as that, the first station was acquired.

Awaiting Sargent in Bangkok was a telegram from Headquarters with more good news: the use of the Navy funds had been approved and construction could begin. Somewhat tempering this cheer was the fact that the deadline imposed by the Air Force nine months earlier remained unchanged, leaving them with only eight and a half months to complete the job.

Up to this point all plans had been tentative. To get at least a warm engine start everyone involved did what could be done short of spending money. When the approval came people scattered in different directions like a billiard ball break. The Coast Guard Supply Center, Brooklyn, New York, as the equipment staging site, hurried to increase its complement to handle the swelling workload. Engineers rushed to finalize station designs. Contracting officers grabbed up telephones to close out negotiations with suppliers and construction firms. Personnel staffs scrambled to find volunteers for the rest of the Construction Detachment and crews to run the stations.

Sargent and a handful of men arrived in Bangkok on 15 January 1966 to set up shop. In that advance group traveled Baker W. Herbert, a highly self-motivated chief warrant officer who—having already completed 20 years of active service—instead of requesting retirement, submitted a letter volunteering for Vietnam duty. A day or so after Christmas a personnel officer at Headquarters reached for his telephone. Before him on his desk sat a mute yet expectant traveler conveying a request: this was Herbert's letter. Herbert, on leave with relatives in Ohio, answered the telephone and heard the voice ask if he still wanted to go to Southeast Asia. When Herbert said he did the voice turned secretive, saying only that the Coast Guard had a project that could not be discussed over the telephone and orders would be processed within 15 minutes, and for him to report to Washington, DC for a briefing a few days from then. So it happened that less than three weeks later—having had scant time to relocate his family and household for his year's absence—he found himself in a group meeting with the commanding general and his staff of the United States Military Assistance Command, Thailand (MACTHAI). In spite of the lofty high priority given *Operation Tight Reign,* they were told that office space was virtually impossible to come by and that they could not provide a vehicle for their transportation. These were scarce items in an overly packed city that MACTHAI itself was barely wedged into. Regardless of the size of a task, roadblocks will arise that deaden inertia and threaten its timely completion. For *Tight Reign,* these hindrances were only beginning.

Herbert's assignment to the Construction Detachment came with a box of titles: contracting officer, supply officer, administrative officer, and agent cashier. All mundane rubrics, none of which arouse youth to rush into a recruiting office and take up arms for their country. Yet the fulfillment of missions is made possible by men in such roles who have the steadfast qualities to treat roadblocks as nuisances rather than obstacles. Herbert was such a person. He had that patient understanding that brings a young man to confide his troubles to a grandfather. His leadership commanded trust. But his patience did not apply to people who shirked their jobs, and if he could not go around you he would go through you. For the Coast Guard his finest asset had always been simply getting the job done. So Herbert set out into the city to solve their first problem, carrying his resolve and a briefcase holding $25,000 in United States Government Treasurer's checks. These would be used, in part, to expedite transactions that would otherwise be delayed through bureaucratic processes.

Inquiries brought him and his associates to 300 Silom Road, where the new Bangkok Bank building was being finished. The friendly bank president showed them offices on the third floor that would be ideal for their base of operation, and after, for the LORAN chain's headquarters. But the banker, as the proper manager of others' money, regretfully declined to rent to the Americans because it took too long for the bank to get paid through intergovernmental channels. Herbert leaned toward the man, tapped his briefcase on the table, and said the words that will capture any financial officer's immediate attention, "I have cash." Herbert paid a year's advance rent on two adjoining offices. That same day, after telephones were installed, astonished MACTHAI staff members were given the Construction Detachment's new address and telephone numbers.

The matter of local transportation was similarly resolved. Herbert paid cash for a new Volkswagen van and hired a reliable Thai, outfitting him with a representative uniform. They now had a vehicle and a driver.

Money could not solve all of the problems. As it turned out, foreign nationals were more cooperative than Americans. Herbert lamented that it was a hard sell to get anybody in the other armed forces to do anything for them. The Army promised railroad cars for moving equipment to the sites, but failed to deliver. When airplanes were needed from the Air Force it took threats of going as high as the Secretary of Defense to shake loose flights. Just to avoid further hassle, the Coast Guard used its own cargo aircraft to bring in materials. To be sure, demands for service during the military buildup overwhelmed respective units, and the Construction Detachment's requirements were not the only ones boiling in the priority cooking pot. But each impediment whittled away precious time. When the chartered freighter arrived with practically everything to erect the LORAN stations, Herbert was informed by a U.S. Navy commander—whose view was that bombs were more important than buildings—that 16 other ships would be offloaded before the Coast Guard's, regardless of its priority. Undeterred, Herbert traipsed along the waterfront for a solution. He came upon a U.S. Army dockmaster and explained the situation to the non-commissioned officer-in-charge (NCOIC), with the result that Herbert's ship moved ahead in line. Herbert found Army NCOICs indispensable: "These guys can do more for you than a general."

Along with Herbert, the Construction Detachment had other men who could surmount hurdles. There was Commander Harold R. Brock, regarded by some as "an absolute genius" in building overseas LORAN stations, and Lieutenant Commander Maynard J. Fontaine, whose electronics know-how was indispensable in selecting transmission points and then calibrating the system to its peak effectiveness.

The search for LORAN sites continued in February and March. Danang, a choice location, had been chosen for a monitoring station, but this was a perilous stage. Intelligence reported large increases of North Vietnamese troops moving across the DMZ and spreading into the northern provinces. At the same time, serious anti-government civil turmoil erupted in Danang and Hue as large-scale student and Buddhist demonstrations became violent.

The trouble turned bizarre when South Vietnamese Army units began training weapons upon each other after the popular I-Corps commanding general, a political rival of the prime minister, was relieved of command but refused to step down. The uncertain outcome of these external and internal threats forced the elimination of Danang as a LORAN site and, instead, places were found in secure and tranquil Thailand for the three other LORAN stations.

Along the Gulf of Thailand, in a small valley on what had been a tapioca and coconut field at Sattahip, 109 miles below Bangkok, would go the master station. Up north, on farmland at Lampang, 80 miles south of Burma and about the same distance west of Laos, would go a signal station. To the northeast, on Udorn Royal Thai Air Force Base, some 50 miles south of Vientiane, the capital of Laos, would go the monitoring station.

Following land acquisition came site development. As many as 200 contractors and laborers, guided by Coast Guardsmen, cleared ground, set up construction camps, laid down concrete, and installed underground utilities. By July, with the stations close to their final form, some operating crewmen reported for duty, primarily the technicians to install and calibrate the electronics.

The task for Sargent and his 19-man detachment had been formidable: carry out topographical surveys, acquire land in foreign countries, construct a four-station LORAN-C chain in tropical heat in isolated terrain under primitive living conditions across the world from the supply source, and do it right and promptly. The men could feel pleased with themselves on 8 August when the chain went on the air, beating the Air Force's deadline. From this point came the normal period of testing, monitoring, and stabilizing the signals.

On 15 August, U.S. Coast Guard Southeast Section (SEASEC), the command office for the chain, was established in Bangkok. Then, in file, each LORAN station went into commission: Lampang, 18 August; Sattahip, 29 August; Con Son, 2 September; and Udorn, 15 September. At 0400, 28 October, the entire system went fully operational.

A lieutenant commanded each station, with a chief warrant officer next in charge of the two dozen or more enlisted men assigned. Designed for function rather than appearance, the stations did not interrupt the landscape with ornateness. Each clearing was home to a compact collection of long single-story buildings with outside walls of corrugated steel and mildly sloped rippled metal roofs. The cylindrical water and fuel storage tanks offered the only contrasting geometric shape. The sole distinctive, but undramatic, landmark was a slender, nearly unnoticeable, 625-foot-tall transmitting antenna held taut by encircling guy wires. The solitary reason for a station's existence is continuous transmission. Although the accepted standard of usable signal time of any LORAN chain during this period was 98 percent, the SEASEC chain steadily performed above 99.7 percent. This meant that in a 30-day month of 43,200 minutes the system was unusable for only 130 minutes, and these pauses were generally under five-minute durations.

Life at the Thailand stations was much the same as any overseas LORAN unit, with its hazards and routine. Disease was a threat. Here it was malaria, cholera, plague, and, as is common near military installations, venereal diseases (VD). The Sattahip LORAN Station crew information book of 1 September 1967 warned that among the inspected prostitutes employed by bars and clubs within the area VD was found in 452 of every thousand girls.

As expected in the tropics, poisonous snakes thrived. Here slithered the deadly Maylasian pit viper, bamboo viper, banded krait, and cobras. Banditry was a danger. Bandits, or camoys, had stolen 31 miles of copper ground wire from Lampang and a number of times they had attempted to stop station personnel returning at night by taxi or government vehicle.

But mostly, a crew member's day, which began with reveille and ended with taps, unless standing watch, passed without event. The days were plugged with keeping up

The locations of the five Coast Guard LORAN Stations in Southeast Asia that provided all-weather electronic navigation for American aircraft attacking enemy targets.

the equipment and grounds. Off-time diversions included mingling about the Thai culture, reading, playing sports, and studying correspondence courses. Security fell to Thai guards trained by the Thai army, but paid by the United States government. The guards, barracked on the station, came under authority of the commanding officer.

Con Son Island, because of its distance from the South Vietnamese mainland, was spared from the war's bloodletting. An island of rocky cliffs and broad sandy beaches gently massaged by the sea, its verdant hills were alive with the happy chitterings of birds and monkeys. This idyllic setting allowed Coast Guardsmen to hike, bicycle, swim, and skin-dive without fear of the enemy. The Coast Guard shared the island with a seven-man U.S. Navy radar station, a U.S. Army DECCA (navigation) station run by four civilians, and a U.S. Army sergeant advisor to a South Vietnamese signal post. Along the more populated eastern shore a peninsula divided the coast into north and south bays. Off the larger southern bay sat Con Son, a town of 1,500 people.

Just above it sprawled the seven-building prison complex. Not all the prisoners lived in total confinement. Up in the northern bay near the LORAN station resided the trustee compound, from where some of these almost reformed individuals were hired to help out around the station and sometimes provided lighthearted moments. One such houseboy, while doing the laundry of the officers and chiefs, could not tell the difference between the white powdered soap in one barrel from the white powdered bleach in the other. In making the wrong selection he transformed plain khaki into a mottled camouflage. The same person mistook a spray can of aluminum paint for insecticide, with the result of leaving the living quarters with shiny bugs as well as shiny furnishings.

Most travel to and from Con Son took place by air, with U.S. Navy *Market Time* and U.S. Air Force aircraft landing supplies during the week. So a Coast Guardsman assigned to Con Son LORAN Station arrived first in Bangkok for a briefing, then caught a plane to Saigon, where he dawdled until a flight came up to carry him to his new duty station.

More than two years after the chain went on line, the unabating North Vietnamese aggression prompted the Air Force to ask the Coast Guard for further coverage over North Vietnam. And so, into Tan My, less than 40 miles from the DMZ, went another LORAN station. Because of its imperiled location, security was provided by a cadre of U.S. Air Force air police with guard dogs, bolstered when necessary by a U.S. Army platoon and mortar squad. In addition to the standard issue weapons, Coast Guardsmen were trained to fire the station's anti-tank weapons for use against North Vietnamese armor. From the sea they could expect naval gunfire protection. When fighting swirled nearby, the Coast Guard medic found himself treating battlefield casualties.

Site development for Tan My had begun March 1969, with an imperative to get the station up quickly. To comply, the Coast Guard sent in an air-transportable LORAN station—essentially one plucked off the warehouse shelf. In June, cargo planes delivered the components into the country, where a U.S. Navy ship carried them to the LST ramp at Naval Support Detachment, Tan My, adjacent to the LORAN site. Within three weeks four dozen flat-roofed, boxy, white trailers were interconnected in rows. The antenna went up and testing began in July. On 15 August Tan My LORAN Station was commissioned and ready.

Tan My LORAN Station, near Hue, in the far northern part of South Vietnam, sits on a point of land along a bay that is separated from the South China Sea by a thin strip of land. (Courtesy of Lt. Ernest R. Riutta, USCG)

Tan My LORAN Station rested on flatland at the edge of a bay that, during a tide higher than normal, stole through the outer fence. Viewed from the air, the encircling perimeter road gave the station the appearance of an enormous pizza pie with dappled grass, white sand, and water puddles for toppings. The white squares covering a tiny portion near the northeastern "crust," close to the water, were not mozzarella cheese cubes, but the unit's buildings. From the top of the antenna, located dead center, wire spokes radiated down like a partially opened umbrella without its fabric to clutch concrete blocks holding the signal tower in place along the surrounding road. Beyond the road, evenly spaced, three blockhouse guard towers stood sentinel, while sandbagged fighting bunkers squatted along the perimeter road, waiting in silent readiness. A barbed wire–topped hexagon fence enhanced with electronic sensors defined the outer boundary. A hundred yards beyond the southwest corner began the small fishing village of Tan My. Toward the western horizon the flatlands reached out for miles before touching the nearest hills.

Lieutenant Ernest R. Riutta commanded Tan My LORAN Station from the fall of 1971 to the fall of 1972, which took in that insecure period of the Easter Offensive when North Vietnamese Army divisions backed with tanks poured into the northern provinces.

When U.S. Army helicopter gunships needed a refueling station closer to the fighting, the LORAN station added a fuel farm. Although the huge, billowy fuel bladders were outside the fence, helicopter crews still discovered that the station's galley served not only hot, but delicious, food, and refueling became an excuse to drop in for dinner.

Before the enemy cut the road to the south, forcing supplies to come in solely by helicopter, Riutta would run convoys of six to eight trucks down to Danang and back. Getting by Hai Van Pass, a popular Viet Cong ambush spot, was the most nervous part of the trip. Riutta declined marrying up with 100-truck convoys, which, while heavily armed, took longer to snake clear of the narrow gap. He reasoned that his small convoys squirting through as fast as they could improved their survival chances—a tactic that did not cost him a man or any equipment.

Between 30 March and 30 June 1972, B-52's flew 2,724 sorties to stop the North Vietnamese drive.[2] Whenever Riutta saw the contrails of these bombers high above the station he alerted his men that Quang Tri Province was about to get pounded and sent them to stand by the servos and reset the timers if necessary so the planes would not lose LORAN transmissions. Experience had shown that the terrific ground shock of saturation bombing knocked their signals off the air.

Aviators came to trust this pinpoint navigation system. In April 1972, when flying as a forward air controller (FAC), the pilot of an OV-10 Bronco was attacked by surface-to-air missiles (SAMs). Seeing where they came from, he called for air strikes to knock out the launchers, but no aircraft were available. Low fuel forced him to leave the area. Back at Nakhon Phanom, Thailand, he studied a roll of reconnaissance film taken that morning and located the SAM site. From the Task Force Alpha computer he plucked accurate coordinates and the LORAN bombing data. Heavy clouds had moved over the area, but in a LORAN strike that did not matter, so he telephoned Seventh Air Force, saying, "This is *Nail*—and I've got a SAM site just south of the DMZ, do you have a LORAN aircraft available to hit?" The man at Seventh Air Force replied, "I have *Greaser* flight hanging over the Danang VORTAC.... I'll give him to you." The young FAC went over to one of the controller consoles, and the duty controller let him use the radio to call *Greaser* flight. The FAC gave the LORAN target data and the run-in heading, and cleared the flight for the strike. *Greaser* flight thought he was talking to an airborne FAC, not one sipping coffee over a controller console in Thailand. *Greaser* flight went in, released, and reported back, "I have secondary explosions through three layers of clouds."[3]

The application of LORAN saved lives too. Its priceless value in lifesaving became known in the well-publicized rescue of Lieutenant Colonel Iceal E. Hambleton, USAF, a navigator in *Bat-21,* an EB-66, shot down near the DMZ on the afternoon of 2 April 1972. By using radio bearings from Hambleton's survival radio and LORAN the OV-10 pilot established the downed aviator's exact position in a few minutes. Hambleton's misfortune was landing in the midst of North Vietnamese troops and material pouring into the south. Hambleton's LORAN position was passed to the Task Force Alpha targeting center at Nakhon Phanom for analysis. Personnel there checked recent photography of the region, corrected the target coordinates for mapping errors, and put together the information for LORAN strikes. The FACs, using LORAN guidance, made area-denial ordnance drops to create a safe zone around Hambleton. The miniature mines, about racquetball size, were intended to keep the enemy away until rescue could be made. This seeding had to be repeated and repeated to stay ahead of the enemy's mine-clearing efforts. Because of his hostile location, it took 12 days to safely extricate Hambleton, and without LORAN to keep him pinpointed he would have most surely been captured or killed.

Little public notice shines on non-glamorous missions. All the same, the industrious ATON teams, indefatigable buoy tenders, and alert LORAN stations earned the Coast Guard the title of Navigation Masters of the Vietnam War.

CHAPTER 7

ATTACK ON *POINT WELCOME*

IN THE DARK MORNING HOURS OF 11 AUGUST 1966, off the coast where the two hostile Vietnams leaned against one another in a no-man's land called the DMZ, a friendly fire tragedy was evolving.

Sometime before 0300 a U.S. Army OV-1B Mohawk spotter plane, call sign *Spud-13*, swung north making a final pass over the DMZ before being relieved. Inside the cockpit the Side-Looking-Airborne-Radar (SLAR) etched an image that appeared to the pilot to be in the mouth of the Ben Hai River. According to his briefings it should not have been there, and he passed the sighting along to his relief, *Spud-14*, as a potential target.[1]

Down on the surface, the *Point Welcome* loitered just below the 17th Parallel, the top of her patrol boundary.

The line that divided North and South Vietnam was nominally called the 17th Parallel, a misleading term because the provisional demarcation actually ran down the center of the Ben Hai River from its mouth at the South China Sea, on a tortuous southwesterly course into the mountains, where it became the Rao Thanh continuing on to the Laotian border. At the coast the dividing line was a little more than a mile above the 17th Parallel, and for most of its length to the border it was well below it. The three miles on either side of the serpentine border was the DMZ, a buffer zone declared exempt of military presence. The territorial waters of the two countries were separated by the division line extending seaward perpendicularly from the coast. Since the land here slanted northwest to southeast, South Vietnam's waters in fact reached well above the 17th Parallel. For all that, *Market Time* inshore patrol craft were ordered not to go beyond the 17th Parallel. A couple of likely reasons for this were, first, a straight boundary simplified navigation, reducing the chance of boats straying into trouble, and second, it kept them out of range of North Vietnam coastal artillery. On this night, as normal, *Point Welcome* roamed below the 17th Parallel, but still well within the DMZ.

The DMZ concept may give peacemakers contentment, but in the long term it just breeds mischief, because its sanctity has as much chance of remaining inviolate as a platter of shrimp left on a table in a house with a cat. The cats in this circumstance were North Vietnamese troops. In the first half of 1966 divisions of them crossed the DMZ into Quang Tri and Thua Thien provinces.[2] One of the operations to disrupt this large-scale intrusion was *Tally Ho*, in which small reconnaissance aircraft hunted for enemy concentrations on which to sic fighters and bombers. Targets were of two types: predesignated and opportune. In the former, aircraft took off to attack a target already evaluated and declared hostile by earlier overflights. In the latter, a search plane reported a target to a mission control aircraft, which would judge whether it was friend or foe. If foe, an attack would be ordered. The *Tally Ho* hit area included the DMZ and ranged some 30 miles into North Vietnam, marking the first time in the war the United States had begun air strikes into the DMZ.

After *Spud-13* turned surveillance over to *Spud-14* a U.S. Air Force B-57 Canberra winged into the sector prowling for something to shoot at with its 20-mm cannons. This light bomber of British origin had been in the American inventory since the early 1950s and was being phased out of active service into the reserves until its highly accurate interdiction capabilities became desired in Vietnam for night strikes on infiltration routes. During its extended longevity it gained a reputation as the best truck killer around.

The Canberra, call sign *Yellow Bird-18*, fresh from dropping a bomb load on a predesignated mission, radioed *Blind Bat-2*, the C-130 Hercules serving as *Tally Ho* controller and flare ship, asking for a target. Advised there was nothing at present, the two-man bomber crew decided to orbit and wait. Something would turn up; darkness always brought out the enemy.

Point Welcome's small bridge allowed two people to move casually about without bumping into each other. The tall, lanky, officer-of-the deck and executive officer, Lieutenant (j.g.) Ross Bell, and Gunner's Mate Third Class Mark D. McKenney talked about home and about what they would do when they returned to Danang. They speculated on whether mail call would bring any homemade cookies. Under their feet the drifting cutter rocked gently. The late running poker game had broken up quite a while ago; therefore, except for the engineer on watch with them the other ten men aboard slept. While the pervasive quiet induced them to speak in soft tones, it was also out of courtesy to those asleep, who deserved any snatches of rest they could get from this wearisome duty.

Throughout their watch they looked upon the fireworks to the northwest where flares transformed segments of sky from night into a sickly yellow daylight long enough for the enemy to be seen and given their servings of bombs and rockets. They saw brilliant flashes from the explosions, but the faint thuds reaching their hearing belied their destructiveness. It seemed to them that the Air Force was earnest about ridding the North Vietnamese from in and around the DMZ. They also kept a radar eye on some junks that the previous watch had spotted in the mouth of the Ben Hai River. If the craft moved below the 17th Parallel they would go after them. Among the night orders, the captain had written that he was to be called if *X-Ray Alfa*'s boats got within a mile of the 17th Parallel. The Junk Force boats from Coastal Group 11 out of the Cua Viet, the next river mouth down, lacked radar and could easily journey too far north.

Point Welcome on patrol near the demilitarized zone before coming under attack by U.S. Air Force planes. (Courtesy of ENC William H. Wolf, USCG)

At 0315 the cutter sat with her bow facing south and engines shut down while the engineer ran routine checks. A navigational fix placed the WPB three quarters of a mile off the beach and about the same distance below the 17th Parallel.[3] This put her two and a half miles from the southern bank of the Ben Hai River, close enough, considering the slant of the coast and the sharp angle formed where the river emptied into the sea, for *Spud-14* in a flyover minutes later to conclude that the big and small blips showing up on the SLAR were at the river mouth and tell this to *Blind Bat-2*.

The Lockheed C-130, one of the most versatile aircraft ever built, was designed as a heavy transport, but also performed tanker, gunship, reconnaissance, search and rescue, and airborne command and control duty. Tonight, as a forward air controller packed with flares peering to uncover targets of opportunity, the chunky four-engine aircraft banked for a run down the coast to take a look. *Yellow Bird-18*, having overheard the promising conversation with *Spud-14*, followed along.

Blind Bat-2 passed over the cutter at 5,000 feet looking for lights, which it would not see because *Market Time* craft ran dark. At 0330 the big plane scattered four flares off the mouth of the Ben Hai River. Looking down, the air crew saw two junks near shore and a larger vessel south of them.

By the artificial light Bell and McKenney could see the junks they had been watching on radar, but neither was alarmed about the closeness of the flares. Before an attack came they expected the airplane to first make a low pass with its recognition lights on, and thereupon, the cutter would signal back by either turning on her running lights or sending up two red flares.

The C-130 lowered to 4,500 feet and made another pass, this time, however, with lights off because the pilot was fearful of being hit should the vessel open fire. Meanwhile, at 6,000 feet, with dogged patience, the B-57 circled.

The second flare drop aroused no concern, but when the much closer third package fell seaward of the cutter Bell started the engines, sending the *Point Welcome* south at five knots. He ordered McKenney to tell the captain that they were being illuminated.

When Bell headed the WPB southward the C-130 pilot became convinced by the bow movements he was seeing deliberate attempts to evade his flares and showed his inexperience against naval targets when he testified that he estimated her running away at 30 to 35 knots leaving a wake 200 yards long.[4] He reviewed what he knew: *Spud-14* had said the target came out of the river; in his pre-flight briefing he was told that no friendly boats would be in the area; during his passes the craft showed no lights; and it now was taking blatant evasive action. Believing further confirmation unnecessary, *Blind Bat-2* popped four flares in an arc ahead of the cutter and told *Yellow Bird-18* to strike.

McKenney's feet barely touched any rungs of the steep ladder leading from the bridge to the main deck. His heart raced. Dread had taken hold of this 21-year-old by the time he burst into the captain's cabin.

After receiving permission to attack, the B-57 lined up to approach from the north. During an earlier flare drop the pilot had informed *Blind Bat-2* that the target looked like the classic silhouette of a Chinese junk with high stern and big sail, a remark that certainly did not shade the mission controller's mind with doubt. It is noteworthy that throughout the episode no one noticed the American flag on the mast, nor the four large international call sign letters painted on top of the pilothouse.

Chief Boatswain's Mate Richard H. Patterson started for the bridge ladder to relieve Bell, taking little notice of the light around him. He had been used to the moon being up when taking over the watch. From 3,000 feet, *Yellow Bird-18* began its run, with the four wing guns aiming for the stern.

McKenney yelled, "Captain! Captain! Captain!" By the illumination coming through the open door he saw 25-year-old Lieutenant (j.g.) David C. Brostrom roll over and ask, "What's the matter?"

"Were being illuminated!"

Just as Brostrom threw off his blanket and jumped out of his bunk the 20-mm projectiles hit. They ripped aluminum and steel apart like hands tearing a loaf of French bread. Patterson, thrown down hard from the ladder, momentarily blacked out. Before toppling, Bell hit the "General Quarters" alarm. Lying on the deck, his vision beginning to cloud over, he saw that some of his toes were gone, but felt no pain. A chunk of flesh was missing from his broken right arm and he bled in numerous places where metal fragments had raked him.

With the alarm's urgent blare cruelly yanking the crew from their dreams, *Yellow Bird-18* leveled off at 200 feet, banked seaward, then gained altitude to assess the results. Pilot and navigator were pleased to see the vessel's stern afire.

The men spilled out on deck. Some had the impression they had run aground; others had no idea what was happening. The only thing they were sure of was they had a fire to put out. Chief Engineman William H. Wolf made certain the fire mains were primed with water. Patterson took charge and led the firefighting as nozzle man on the portside hose. Lugging the hose behind the chief was Electronics Technician Second Class Virgil G. Williams and after him Engineman Second Class Jerry Phillips. Boatswain's Mate First Class Billy R. Russell and Seaman David E. O'Connor manned the starboard hose. Nearby, Commissaryman Second Class Donald L. Austin and Lieutenant (j.g.) Do Viet Vien, the liaison officer, readied the portable fire pump for use. McKenney and Fireman Houston J. Davidson had gone forward to bring back foam cans. In the doorway of the deckhouse British freelance photographer Timothy J. Page attempted to capture the events with his camera. The fire came from gasoline spilled across the deck out of the destroyed small boat fuel cans.

On the bridge, broken glass and shrapnel crunching under his feet, Brostrom stepped around Bell. He seized a microphone and called CSC, Danang, "*Article,* this is *Article India,* am being illuminated and attacked by what I believe is Vietnamese aircraft. Have received hits."[5] *Article* acknowledged. Eighteen miles to the south USCGC *Point Caution* (WPB 82301) overheard the conversation and radioed the *Point Welcome* asking if she needed assistance. Brostrom replied, "...affirmative. I have taken hits. Request assistance."[6] The *Point Caution* answered that she was on the way.

When *Yellow Bird-18* saw the fire go out it prepared for another strafing, this time intending to knock out the bridge.

At CSC, Danang, a permanent communications layout was still in development. The current setup was fragmented with radios in one location and the telephones and teletype in another. Brostrom's call had been taken by the petty officer monitoring the radios on YR-71, the workshop barge that supported the WPBs and PCFs. More than 400 yards away in the CSC building U.S. Navy watch officer Lieutenant Arthur J. Cote reached for the telephone and listened to the petty officer's report. Cote told his assistant to order other cutters in the area, and a DER, to the scene, then he got busy on the telephone to try to stop whatever was going on. His calls had to go through a Vietnamese switchboard on base, which was an iffy matter; sometimes you had to go through the city switchboard to make a call on base. A few weeks earlier it had taken Cote six hours to get a call through. Oddly, though, on this night there were no delays. Unfortunately, because he did not know the attacking aircraft's identification and the fact that CSC had few dealings with the U.S. Air Force, much time lapsed before the source could be pinpointed.

The *Point Welcome* crew, having extinguished the fire, stood amid the litter of firefighting equipment taking a breather and trying to figure out what had happened. The residual gasoline had been washed overboard, leaving behind paint blisters speckling the burned deck and transom. Patterson suspected that the gasoline can had blown up but he did not know why. While they wondered, they were oblivious of the B-57's portside approach and the fact that they were conveniently grouped in the plane's fire zone.

Brostrom ran out to the starboard side of the narrow platform behind the bridge holding either a Very Pistol or Aldis Lamp—which one he had never became clear. Before he could send an emergency recognition signal the cannons clattered behind him and the lethal rounds nearly cut him in half. Almost opposite of Brostrom on the main deck, Phillips took mortal wounds in the abdomen. Davidson, coming back for a knife to loosen the foam cans from the rack, was starboard of the deckhouse when shrapnel mangled his hands into bloody uselessness. Tim Page, who had expected a relaxing photographic assignment lazing in the sunshine and swimming in the sea, spiced with a few fishing junk boardings, was felled with multiple shrapnel wounds. During the attack his camera was lost overboard. Up forward in the paint locker just below the open hatch, McKenney was stretching to his right for foam when the left side of his exposed back was riddled with shell fragments. A hunk of metal lodged in his thigh and cuts in his forehead made paths of bloods on his face. Down too, with wounds, went the South Vietnamese liaison officer.

When the plane passed over, Patterson got to his feet and ran up to the bridge. Giving little mind to his dead skipper and wounded executive officer he slammed the throttles ahead to get the idling boat from being a sitting target to a moving one. Taking command, he shouted orders to get the wounded below and to stay off the main deck. He told Russell to check on him after each pass and if he was hit Russell was to assume command.

The Canberra was not through. This time it would cut up this enemy presence from bow to stern. *Blind Bat-2* continued hatching flares, each one burning for close to three minutes. Their lazy, drifting descent, along with the short intervals of darkness after they burned out, painted an eerie tableau of shifting shadows, which to the fliers made the target appear as an undefined darkness on the glimmering water.

Back at CSC, Cote made frantic calls to the operation centers of the primary outfits in the region: the U.S. Marine Corps and the South Vietnamese military.

The B-57 strafed the cutter a third time, scattering the crew for cover. Nineteen-year-old O'Connor, reacting out of instinct bred by military comradeship, threw himself over the mortally wounded Phillips, who still lay crumpled where he fell. *Yellow Bird-18* climbed and settled into a watchful orbit, advising *Blind Bat-2* that it had gone "Winchester"—out of ammunition. The bomber's role had ended, leaving the job unfinished.

Patterson ran an erratic southerly course for the Cua Viet, seeking refuge at the junk force base. Bell, who had been fading in and out of consciousness, had informed him that *Article* had been advised of the situation. Crewmen had tried moving Bell below, but when he could not stand they wrapped him in a sheet, gave him a shot of morphine, and tucked him under the chart table in the starboard corner. None of the radios worked, as the second strafing had wrecked the grove of antennas about the deckhouse. Patterson searched for flares in the box near his dead captain. Finding none, he sent Wolf to the cabin to try getting out on the radio there, then turned his attention to the sky and the sinister flare light, which would not go away.

The mess deck, usually the social heart of a small patrol boat where food is shared, games played, books read, music enjoyed, and thoughts exchanged in a congenial atmosphere, had become a medical emergency room crammed with suffering. In this compartment, not much larger than a compact size automobile, bed sheets were torn up for bandages as men tried to stop the life-draining bleeding of their shipmates. The seriously wounded were put on the two tables. To protect them from further harm they were covered with mattresses pulled from bunks.

While outside the night shrouded the human impact of the attacks, inside the mess deck lights emblazoned jagged flaps of skin and exposed flesh and bone. Blood was everywhere. It pulsed from wounds. It was underfoot, causing the men to slip as they worked. It slickened the handrails and steps of the steel ladder entryway. McKenney slumped at the bottom of the ladder, where, refusing to let his wounds keep him from lending a hand, he had aided in getting Phillips into the mess deck. Seeing the engineman's dreadful condition in the light, the young gunner's mate became engulfed in despair. The cries of pain, the helplessness of not being able to strike back, and the mental anguish of being shot by your own side gripped him all at once. Reaching out for the source of life, he folded his hands and prayed, "Dear God, help us."

Yellow Bird-18 was out of it, but a new threat arrived. Two F-4C Phantom jet fighters that had flown to the Laotian border along the DMZ looking for targets were flying back east when *Blind Bat-2* asked them to pick up the assault. *Coyote-91*, the lead F-4C, queried *Blind Bat-2* if he was aware how far south this craft was, although at the time she was still within the DMZ. *Blind Bat-2* answered that the target had been followed from up north. Still skeptical, *Coyote-91* asked if recognition passes had been made. *Blind Bat-2* gave an affirmative.

The second F-4C, *Coyote-92,* seeking further confirmation of this target, turned on its red and green navigation lights and made a 360-degree, 250-knot turn over *Point Welcome* at 1,000 feet. When neither crew saw a responding recognition signal they climbed into attack position.

Spurred by the ruthless presence of the mock lighting overhead, Patterson drove the cutter hard, making reckless zigs and zags. By leaning his thick upper body out of a window he would listen for the telltale pop of a fresh parachute flare kicking free of its container to clue him when to change to a course that kept them on the fringe of darkness. To keep the attackers from anticipating his maneuvers he would at times pull full back on the throttles, stopping the cutter's forward momentum before committing to a new direction. His boat handling was all the more remarkable for he was piloting solely by throttle manipulation because the rudder would not answer the helm. At the sound of an incoming plane Patterson took cover and had likely ducked out of sight when *Coyote-92* came over with its lights on. With his radios gone, no flares, and the power cord to the Aldis Lamp severed, he felt the only way to stop the attack was to reach friendlier forces. He could have turned on his running lights but he considered that would be suicidal. He was not confident that those lights would mean anything to the aircraft other than giving them an easier target to hit.

Coyote-92 dropped to 3,000 feet, going for the *Point Welcome* from astern carrying two cluster bombs (CBUs). During descent the CBU cannister breaks apart, dispersing bomblets to expand its deadly effective range. In order to reach the WPB, the F-4C had to fly outside the flare light. When a CBU was released Patterson had changed direction sharply, causing it to strike where the cutter had been, a miss of only 300 feet.

In the cabin, Wolf found a working radio but could only raise a U.S. Navy minesweeper far offshore, which told him she was without the capability to get the attack called off. Filled with frustration, Wolf dashed out to the starboard waist machine gun, jerked back the breech and let it go, clanging a round into the chamber. He tried aiming on an incoming plane, but the darkness, the WPB's erratic course, and the speed of the aircraft made retaliation futile. He gave up and returned to the radio.

Coyote-92 swooped down again. This time the target stayed under light. But, with uncanny instinct Patterson maneuvered at the right instant. Only two or three bomblets struck the port stern, with the rest missing to seaward. As instructed, after each pass Russell ran up to the bridge to check on the chief.

Cote was operating like a blind man wearing gloves sorting through a stack of keys to find the one to disarm a bomb before it went off. The split-up CSC arrangement ate up precious time because Cote and his assistant had to pause in whatever they were doing to talk by telephone to exchange new information. Cote had already briefed *Market Time* headquarters in Saigon and called for helicopters to be put on medical evacuation alert. At the moment he was on the telephone updating his boss, Commander Joseph D. Nolan, USN, the Northern Area Task Group Commander. He told Nolan that the cutter believed it to be under attack by Vietnamese aircraft, but both South Vietnamese forces and American marines said they had nothing going on. Nolan told Cote to stick with it and keep him posted.

Coyote-92, its ordnance expended, climbed to 12,000 feet and went into spectator orbit, expecting to watch *Coyote-91* with its 500-pound bombs blast the shifty boat into razor blades.

At a compound in Quang Tri city, in the northern province of the same name, Captain Richard P. Pierzchala, USMC, artillery advisor to a South Vietnamese unit, entered a bunker to make a radio call and heard an excited voice coming over the advisor's channel.

From 10,000 feet *Coyote-91* began its bombing dive, while on the water the WPB scurried to avoid the crush of an explosive foot. The jet soared in from land side, released its bomb, and pulled into a steep climb. The bomb evaporated a great deal of saltwater, but had missed the target by 150 feet.

The jet rushed into another dive, but held off releasing the remaining bomb when the alignment was not right. In Quang Tri, Pierzchala heard over the radio, "My playmate is down! My playmate is down!"

Patterson watched the sky, his ears straining to pick up the jet's roar. Here it came again. Using the sixth sense that had kept them alive to this point, he wrenched the throttles to swerve the bow onto a new heading. The next explosion of water caused the cutter to disappear from the aviator's view. The *Point Welcome*'s crew felt the deck heave up at them when the cutter came straight up out of the water. Free of the sea's hold, the 67-ton craft was clobbered by a force that turned her direction 90 degrees. Even though *Coyote-91* had made an accurate bomb drop, the Coast Guard cutter with the American cartoon character Wile E. Coyote painted on the flag locker had lived up to her mascot's resiliency. The sea coyote had eluded the air coyote by a mere 50 feet.

The defanged Phantoms circled overhead until seeing the vessel go dead in the water, then headed back to base, leaving *Blind Bat-2* lingering around like a vulture waiting for its quarry to die. The C-130 kept dropping flares, anticipating the arrival of more attackers as soon as they could get airborne.

When the engines faltered Patterson was puzzled. He could barely coax enough way to keep a heading. Aware that immobility meant doom, he told the men to gather the wounded and abandon ship. He split them into two groups, one under his charge and the other under Wolf's. They would swim for the Cua Viet, now only a few hundred yards away. Launching the small boat would consume too much time, and from her shot-up appearance her usefulness was in doubt, so just the balsa and rubber rafts were dropped overboard. Lifejackets were put on the wounded. Bell, who was conscious, was brought down from the bridge, his right arm limp and useless. Some of the men jumped into the water to assist in lowering the wounded. A couple of men thoughtfully went to get their captain, but any idea of taking him along ended when they turned him and only the top of his body moved. Page and the South Vietnamese officer were pushed into the balsa raft. Bell was placed in the rubber raft, which would only partially inflate. Those in the water held on to the rafts' lines to move them along. McKenney swam, gripping the dying Phillips with one arm and stroking with the other. It was quiet on the sea except for their soft movements through the water. As this ragged formation swam to survive, each man, alone with his thoughts, sought to understand why this was happening to them.

"My playmate is down! My playmate is down!" For minutes Pierzchala had tried to get in touch with the urgent voice and get the caller to tell him in the clear what was the matter. The voice belonged to a U.S. Navy advisor at the Cua Viet Junk Force base who evidently had heard the *Point Welcome*'s radioed distress. Pierzchala finally understood that "playmate," a friendly vessel, was under illumination and attack. He immediately switched to an aircraft frequency and repeatedly called, "If there are any U.S. airplanes strafing a ship underneath illumination, that's an American ship!" He also alerted the field hospital at Hue/Phu Bai for a medical evacuation.

In his quarters, Nolan was restless for an update from his watch officer. He smoked a cigarette. He looked at his watch several times, thinking that the other vessels should have arrived by now. His patience gave out and he called Cote. During their conversation Cote's assistant relayed that *Point Caution* nearing the scene was also getting illuminated. Nolan cut the talk short, but before hanging up told Cote to contact *Panama*, the U.S. Air Force operations center in the area. Finally, Cote had found the key he was groping to find. Nolan, figuring that Cote might not be able to get through to the Air Force right away because of all the units he was dealing with, called *Panama*, who acknowledged their planes were working a target in that area.

Around 0430 *Blind Bat-2* was told that the vessel below was friendly. The flare drops went on, but now to aid in rescue.

Nothing had changed in the minds of the swimmers; the flares were still exposing them, but they drew hope from the sandy coast ahead. Just when it appeared they might make it to safety after all, machine gun and small arms fire poured on them from the beach. Tracers passed a foot over Williams and Davidson swimming together, the latter having little use of his torn hands. The shooting seemed to come from two directions, directly ahead and from a point farther along the shore. Caught in a quandary, some of the men began moving back to the cutter. O'Connor swam on ahead of everyone else, intending give his shipmates covering fire from one of the *Point Welcome*'s machine guns. Bullets plucked the water near him. He started around the bow seeking to put the vessel between him and shore when a spotlight captured him from behind. His fear turned into relief when he saw the *Point Caution*.

McKenney heard a voice from boats ahead cry out that they were Americans and the shooting ceased. Phillips, now dead, was pulled from the gunner's mate's hold. McKenney found himself dragged from the sea, the water and blood from his clothes staining the rough wood deck of the junk force boat. He would feel the full impact of the physical and mental pain soon enough, but for now he felt only joy.

The *Point Welcome*'s crew's ordeal lasted more than an hour. It began when an American plane fired on them and ended shortly after skittish South Vietnamese sailors shot at them. Some of the simultaneous fire that came from the beach, however, was believed to be from the real enemy. The dead and wounded were taken ashore and flown by helicopter to the field hospital at Hue/Phu Bai. Patterson and three shipmates were joined by men from another cutter to take the *Point Welcome* back to Danang. The engines had faltered because they had lost their air supply; after temporary repairs were made to the blowers the cutter traveled under her own power, but at reduced speed. During the ten-hour trip they had plenty of time to ponder the "why's" and "what-if's" of the attack.

The Board of Investigation ordered by COMUSMACV convened in Danang also wanted to find out why this happened and to come up with ways to prevent a repeat of it. The four-member board representing the Army, Navy, Air Force, and Marine Corps heard the first of the 37 witnesses on 15 August and the last on 23 August. The gist of the findings was summed up in the second paragraph of the 9 November 1966 letter from COMUSMACV to the Commandant, U.S. Coast Guard: "It is evident from the record that there was a lack of coordination between different component forces operating in the same area, and that existing orders and instructions pertaining to identification and recognition of friendly forces were not observed."

Put another way, one hand did not know what the other hand was doing. For more than a year Coast Guard cutters, as part of *Market Time,* had patrolled off the DMZ. The Air Force's *Tally Ho* over the DMZ came later. The two operations, which overlapped offshore were, of course, known to COMUSMACV, but because NAVFORV and 7th Air Force did not routinely exchange messages of what the other was doing, the individuals that went on the missions had little, if any, knowledge of the other.

The aviators knew about the periodic clandestine forays by high-speed naval craft into North Vietnam, which they referred to as MAROPS (Maritime Operations); however, they were told none were in progress on 11 August. Of *Market Time,* they knew nothing.

Point Welcome did not come out of the Ben Hai River as thought by *Spud-13* and *Spud-14.* An analysis of the SLAR film showed the cutter never moved over the 17th Parallel, but when *Blind Bat-2* arrived the cutter was near enough to the river to support the spotter plane's judgment. Furthermore, unacquainted with *Market Time*'s operational orders, they could not understand why the bigger vessel did not attack the smaller ones unless they were on the same side.

Under the rules of recognition the attack could have been prevented, except that everything worked against it. The C-130's recognition pass came too high for the crew's notice. When the C-130 illuminated the cutter for the third time, Brostrom would have been able to get off a recognition signal, if not for the pesky B-57 hanging around looking for something to shoot at. Virtually all chance of the cutter communicating with the aircraft was lost in the second strafing, which destroyed the radio and signaling equipment. The only recourse seemed to be dodge and run.

The cutter was fortunate in a couple of ways. The extremely accurate B-57 ran out of ammunition, expending its 1,160 rounds in three passes. Had its attacks gone on, no one would have survived. It was well that the F-4Cs with their bombs had not been the first to attack. They would have taken the WPB unaware and she would have been sunk.

Patterson's performance in command under fire was noted by the Board of Investigation worthy of suitable recognition, which was ultimately the Bronze Star with

Port side of *Point Welcome*'s pilothouse, heavily damaged by U.S. Air Force B-57 20-mm cannon fire. (Courtesy of U.S. Coast Guard)

Combat "V." The *Point Welcome* survivors felt that he deserved no less than the Medal of Honor. Without doubt, his seamanship kept the cutter from being hit by the bombs and his calmness in crisis had a settling influence on the crew.

Steps were taken to avoid a repetition. Aircraft were not to attack vessels off the DMZ without first contacting CSC, Danang, and information flow improved between the Air Force and the Navy.

The peril of troops being killed or wounded by their own side haunts every war. No war gets by without "friendly fire" incidents. This is no consolation to the next of kin, nor to those hurt in them. Grieved too, are those who did the firing and those acquainted with the dead and wounded. Loforte wrote in the squadron diary: "This was a week of sudden death for two of our people, horror for nine others and deep shock to everyone else in Squadron One. With the memory of *Point Welcome* fresh in my mind it is difficult to remember anything else happening."

Brostrom, the son of a retired U.S. Navy commander, was the first Coast Guardsman to die in action in the Vietnam War. A fellow officer said of him, "I liked Dave, he had high ideals. I thought he would go far in the Coast Guard." The nation cannot forget that the young skipper and his engineman gave up their lives for their country, because along with the others who died in the Vietnam War their names are cut into the burnished black stone of the Vietnam Memorial Wall in Washington, DC.

When *Point Welcome* returned to service, her cartoon mascot, Wile E. Coyote, sported a Purple Heart medal and Band-Aids. (Courtesy of ENC William H. Wolf, USCG)

The physical wounds of the crew healed, if not all of the mental ones. Bell went on to have a full and normal career, commanding some of the Coast Guard's major ships. Patterson, Wolf, Russell, Williams, and McKenney completed 20 years or more of active duty and retired. Austin, O'Connor, and Davidson left the service when their enlistments expired. Tim Page recovered and went on photographing the war until wounded by an enemy mine. His career resumed after a lengthy rehabilitation. What befell the Vietnamese liaison officer after the fall of his country is not known.

As for *Point Welcome,* she was repaired and ready for patrol again in mid-October. Humor is that singular human element that helps us endure calamity. When the cutter returned to sea her cartoon mascot, Wile E. Coyote, sported a different appearance. He was repainted with bandaged wounds and wearing a Purple Heart Medal.

CHAPTER 8

MARINER PROBLEMS APLENTY

ABOARD THE AMERICAN MERCHANT SHIP ANCHORED IN VUNG TAU harbor two mariners argued. Their inflamed words carried beyond the hatch covers and cargo booms, reaching the ears of passing South Vietnamese above the clatter of their putt-puttering junks. When one of the sailors turned his back in disgust to walk off, the other, enraged, grabbed an iron pipe and crashed it against the seaman's head with such force that onlookers hearing the crack of bone knew he was dead before he hit the deck. A few suspended moments later the crowd stirred. To their amazement the victim rose, only now he had a hand wrapped around a knife, which he used to carve up his assailant with deft strokes. In the aftermath, the clubber was expected to cling to life, but only for a few days. The knifer, hospitalized with a serious skull fracture, would have to undergo surgery. Yet, at some point before the operation this hard-to-kill sailor walked out of the hospital and was last reported wandering around Saigon.

Incidents like these were on the increase. Some of them delayed ship sailings. Some of them, such as unpunished assaults on Vietnamese citizens, bludgeoned good will. Maritime officials, both management and labor, and the commander, MSTS, were troubled by these damaging personnel problems and strongly believed that it was up to the Coast Guard to bring order, and rightly so. Since 1942, when the Bureau of Marine Inspection and Navigation moved from under the Department of Commerce into the Coast Guard, the Service had administered a commercial vessel program that wrote and enforced regulations; performed shipboard safety inspections and marine casualty investigations; and issued licenses to qualified mariners. With this last duty came intervention powers that could lead to license revocation in cases of negligence or misconduct. And, without papers, a mariner's seagoing employment vanished. Accordingly, it seemed only normal that the Coast Guard should have a merchant marine detail in Vietnam similar to those it had in the United States and major foreign ports.

The Military Sea Transportation Service (MSTS), as an agency of the Department of Defense, had the burden of supplying the American forces with everything necessary to sustain a monumental war apparatus. For the simple reason of economy, waterborne conveyance accounted for 98 percent of the logistical nourishment brought into South Vietnam. A ship could haul more goods for less money. By comparison, the Military Airlift Command estimated in December 1966 that the cost of transporting a short ton of cargo in a C-141 cargo aircraft from Dover, Delaware to Saigon, was $709. The ocean freight rate from an East Coast port of the United States to any port in South Vietnam for a similar quantity of cargo, exclusive of stevedoring costs, was approximately $73.50.[1]

At the outset, however, MSTS had trouble finding ships to match with cargoes and in acquiring enough of them, altogether, to keep up with delivery demands. This happened because its own fleet was required to remain small so that the maritime industry could earn money moving government cargo. The military was assured that sufficient ocean transport would be made available since in war the president of the United States would enact his wartime powers to requisition the civilian ships needed.

But this failed to occur. Not only was the fighting in Southeast Asia unconventional, but so too were some of the related political decisions of President Lyndon B. Johnson. For him, his grand social agenda for the country came first. He was not going to be diverted from that course by exercising wartime prerogatives on overseas fighting that should not last much longer. Such action would not only impose an atmosphere of wartime hardship, but draw monies away from his pet domestic programs. In other words, he tried running the country in a peacetime mode while carrying on a war.

Consequently, MSTS had to rely upon companies volunteering their ships. Although the response was reasonably good, it was not enough. The shortfall forced a search for hulls among the National Defense Reserve Fleet, a disparate collection of nearly 1,500 hard-worn old vessels dying in anchorage. Two hundred and fifty of them, with speeds of fourteen knots or more, made the list for possible usage. Reactivation costs ran somewhat more than a half million dollars per ship and by 1 January 1967, 172 vessels had been returned to sea under contract to shipping firms. Ultimately, 350 ships engaged in the waterborne conveyer belt across the Pacific Ocean.

Finding crews for these ships became a problem. The steady decline in the size of the merchant fleet over the years had people shunning a seagoing career for other more stable and lucrative fields, and thereby shrank the pool of available mariners. Ships, therefore, could not be choosy. They took whoever they could get. Moreover, a ship could not leave the dock without a full crew. A full crew in Coast Guard terms meant the minimum (which it set) needed to safely operate the vessel, while a full crew set by labor union contracts called for another, higher, figure. If, for example, the Coast Guard determined safe operation could be achieved with a master and two mates, the union might call for a master and four mates—its objective being, of course, to keep its membership employed. Under these circumstances, however, the labor unions were not without patriotism and did not fuss over crew numbers. Given the mariner shortage its members had plenty of work.

The Vietnam run gave merchant seamen much to grumble over. They existed in a reclusive world beset with physical discomfort, loneliness, tedium, and fear. With ships often lacking air conditioning, the tropical heat turned these steel envelopes into ovens, broiling crews in their pinched quarters. The slow mail service cut them off from home. The long cruises became lengthier, with inordinate waits for offloading berths. And, it was war. Merchant ships were chronically ambushed and mined. Mariners died, as when the *Baton Victory* hit a mine in the river en route to Saigon, killing seven men in the flooded engine room.

But during adversity the human psyche gets jolted into action, and most mariners adjusted to these employment conditions. Still, it was in this setting that emotional embers smoldered within the mind until, without warning, they flared up into a conflagration of rabid misbehavior in the form of disobedience, drunkenness, desertion, assault, sabotage, suicide, and murder. Officials tried improving hardships as they were identified. Air conditioning was installed in ships returning home, but the living quarters remained confining. Mail deliveries were speeded up, but in some instances letters only intensified loneliness. To dispel some of the boredom the United Seaman's Service provided motion pictures on ships and installed modest-sized mariner recreation centers in South Vietnamese ports. None of this lessened the arduous work or prevalent danger, nor did it solve the unruliness.

In foreign ports the responsibility for American seaman conduct falls to the United States embassy. A staff member designated the shipping consul sought out the facts, then took corrective action, which more often than not merely sent the culprit back to the United States. Over time, the State Department, under which embassies function, realized after some major overseas incidents that consular officers were overburdened in trying to resolve maritime troubles, especially where local authorities refused involvement. Therefore, it became State Department practice to request Coast Guard officers for embassy duty to handle these issues. To the contrary, in South Vietnam, much to the annoyance of MSTS and shipping industry management and labor, the American embassy in Saigon maintained it could do the job without the Coast Guard's help.

No one knew when any delay in the routine supply flow could mean the difference between winning or losing an engagement, only that it is axiomatic that a continuous supply line is critical in war. Although the enemy lacked the capability to seriously disrupt shipping, it received inadvertent help whenever a crew problem aboard a cargo ship kept her from sailing. Crew shortages caused by desertion or hospitalization after brawling kept supplies from moving nearly as effectively as a mine ripping open the hull.

Aboard ship mariners answered to the captain, who could reduce their pay or lock them up, but ashore they could get away with almost anything. It was the American military's position that they were civilians, and therefore not their jurisdiction. The Vietnamese police likewise stayed clear; they saw mariners as Americans working for the American military. This was a practical stance as well, for a surly merchant seaman could outweigh a Vietnamese police officer by at least fifty pounds. From time to time, MPs, intervening to prevent further injury or destruction, dropped a bloodied seaman off with a baffled MSTS representative, who did not know what to do with the surprise guest.

Absent of controls, matters worsened. In Vung Tau the mayor was hit in the face by a drunken merchant sailor. Nothing was done about it. A nighttime fight in Danang that started on ship between two mariners staggered to the dock, where one of them pulled a knife on his unarmed opponent. The master, in a show of gutsy initiative, jumped in and disarmed the knife wielder, gripping him in an armlock until the MPs arrived. Expecting his seaman to be dragged off to jail, the master became disheartened when the MPs told him they could not help him, that this was a civilian matter.

Since the beginning of the massive sealift, shipping interests had been calling for a Coast Guard merchant marine detail in South Vietnam. The caseload was just too great for an embassy staff that did not have the time to travel to other ports to ascertain the facts. Out of frustration they took their argument to Loforte, who chronicled some of their complaints in the unit diary:

> *8 Feb 1966 — Met with Captain Jacques, USN, Chief, Military Sea Transportation Service Office, Saigon. Discussed the personnel/disciplinary problem between master and crews of civilian manned ships. Apparently problems result from long layover periods in port. Explained that Embassy does not want merchant marine detail. I will assist informally if required.*
>
> *25 April 1966 — Met Mr. Frank H. James, representative of Lykes Lines at Tan Son Nhut. He recognized the cap device and came over. Asked about merchant marine detail for Saigon ....Explained that request for merchant marine detail had to come from State.*
>
> *12 May 1966 — Met today with Mr. Frank X. McNerney, Maritime Administration representative to Vietnam. We discussed...unruly behavior of merchant seamen both on board ships in port and while ashore. Mr. McNerney is very strongly in favor of a merchant marine detail in Saigon...*
>
> *19 May 1966 — Attended a meeting...collection of marine interests.... Their biggest and unanimous cry: "When is the Coast Guard going to get a merchant marine detail here?"*

The clamor, annoying and insistent like a mosquito buzzing around one's ear, aroused the State Department to query the embassy for its reaction to assigning a Coast Guard element there. The reply was quick and terse: *No!* This unequivocal reply was in support of the staunch opposition of one of its consuls, a diligent man, earnest in his public service, who felt his office could do as much as any Coast Guard detail. His strong feelings were born in a previous embassy assignment where he felt badly let down by the Coast Guard merchant marine detail, which he saw as doing little to help him with maritime affairs. The rift may have been the result of a clash of personalities. Regardless, Loforte spoke to him on the value of bringing in the Coast Guard, dispatching the consul's prior experience as an anomaly in performance. Loforte sensed the hardness in the consul's objection softening, but the embassy posture remained unchanged and the merchant seaman violence went unchecked, with incidents such as two in July that Loforte passed on to the embassy for action. A U.S. Navy commander was assaulted with fists and knife in one, and two brothers beat up a Vietnamese man in the other.

Irate with the embassy's persistent refusal of Coast Guard assistance and seeing no evidence of a change in attitude, MSTS, pondering alternatives, decided to get its own maritime troubleshooter. In November, MSTS asked the Coast Guard for an officer to fill that role. The officer would have an admiral's clout behind him by serving under the MSTS, Far East Command in Japan, but be posted in Saigon. He would have the unobtrusive title of "shipping advisor," giving him official status and unrestricted travel authority. Once among the merchant marine, it would be up to his wits and the sway of the Coast Guard reputation to meet each crisis. The officer given this task was not to be envied. The marine community expected him to single-handedly, and without the punch of the State Department, rid them of the troublemakers. At the same time his own Service expected him to accomplish his assignment without causing the Coast Guard political embarrassment among the labyrinth of intergovernment agencies, most particularly the U.S. Embassy. The Coast Guard also had expectation that their man could "...promote an area of understanding with Department of State officials from which a State request for a merchant marine detail in Saigon might emanate."[2]

Forty-one-year-old Commander Edward "Frank" Oliver, a man well-acquainted with merchant marine life, drew the dicey chore. He began his sea career in his teens as a tugboat deckhand. Later, upon graduating from the California Maritime Academy in the middle of World War II, he found himself a deck officer in a lumbering but renowned *Liberty* class cargo ship. He took part in several Pacific Theater amphibious assaults and was decorated for his gun crew role in a successful battle against an enemy submarine. He left the merchant marine for a Coast Guard career in 1950. The job now assigned him was a familiar one. Not long ago he had spent three years solving maritime problems for the Consulate General in Naples, Italy.

Oliver relished difficult assignments. A man of medium height with wide shoulders and a sturdy frame, he gave one the impression that this was not a guy with whom to get into a brawl. That he had a sense of humor was evident, because the mouth on his broad bullish face would often crease into an enchanting leprechaun smile. He was a courteous listener. When spoken to he had a manner of leaning forward, his expression intent, as if what one was saying at the moment was supremely important. Ego did not interfere with his mission. While he expected the normal respect due his rank, he was not pompous about his status. That first weekend in December when he arrived in Saigon he was given temporary quarters in the Cholon district, where he was not surprised by the lack of water and the large resident insects, but he did raise a bushy eyebrow when an Army sergeant handed him an M-16 rifle with extra ammunition and told him he had guard duty. Oliver gently apprised the sergeant, "You've got the wrong man. I'm a Coast Guard commander." To which the sergeant answered that here everyone stands duty at night and it was his room's turn. Oliver accepted the explanation without further question. His four-hour watch, which began at midnight, introduced him to a Viet Cong favorite pastime—attacking Tan Son Nhut Air Base. He watched and listened. To the north flares turned portions of the sky a murky yellow, small arms tracers punctuated the air with thousands of red dashes, and mortar shell explosions rocked the city to sleep with a harsh lullaby.

Notwithstanding his guard stint, Oliver was treated as somewhat of a celebrity during his get-acquainted week. With a daily average of 75 ships in anchorages, the potential for merchant marine problems ran high, and a good number of the people introduced to him had been calling for someone in his capacity for a long time. Oliver tempered any great expectations by explaining that he could not revoke or suspend licenses or documents. That could only be done by an administrative law judge back in the United States after a hearing. What he could do is prove misconduct through his investigations.

Oliver was given an austere office in the MSTS building, a huge, white colonial French masonry structure that gazed over the Saigon River on one side and a feeder waterway along another. The office permitted him immediate access to the radio room, which kept in touch with MSTS sub-units throughout the country. His desktop was as cluttered as his office was barren. He had been asked to review the casualty findings in collisions and strandings involving MSTS ships. Along with these, nearly a hundred reports of merchant seaman mischief covered his desk. As he sifted through the paper dunes two MPs brought in his first customer. The belligerent mariner standing between the MPs had just wrecked a bar and stolen a girl's purse. Oliver's questioning uncovered that the culprit had been arrested seven times in the past three weeks. Each time he had been released with no apparent action taken by the embassy. The man had also missed sailing with his ship from Danang. The MPs agreed to hold him in custody while Oliver made arrangements to get him out of the country. The next morning the troublesome sailor was on a vessel headed for sea, and the new shipping advisor had one less problem.

Loforte introduced Oliver to the key people in the military-civilian mix. These visits included a critical one to the embassy, where the Coast Guard had hoped to create rapport. They were cordially met by the maritime consul, who opposed Coast Guard assistance. With diplomatic acumen he stunned the officers by apologizing for not having room at the consulate to set up a desk for the commander. Not a vindictive person, the consul saw no reason to be obstructive if by chance Oliver could relieve him of some of the workload. It entered Loforte's mind that maybe his talks with the consul had, indeed, softened his hardline position after all. Nevertheless, the diplomat laid down the opportunity to be proven wrong. Now it was up to Oliver—one man doing the job of three with a caseload screaming for several times that number—to make a convincing impression.

Oliver's province took in a million square miles of territory. As the waterfront grapevine spread word of his presence, messages began coming in day and night from shipping agents and masters for him to come to Bangkok, Singapore, Hong Kong, and so on. One trip saw him in the Philippines getting the *Enid Victory* back into the supply stream. The 445-foot ship, on her way to Vietnam with a load of ordnance, had an engine room explosion that disabled her and resulted in the death of the second assistant engineer. Oliver went to Subic Bay, where she had been towed, to investigate the casualty. He walked into a mess.

The only engineering officers around were the chief engineer, who was on his first trip in that capacity since getting his chief's license, and an elderly third assistant. The other third assistant had deserted the day before. The master had taken the first assistant engineer to Manila to sign him off for misconduct and to find the deserter and crew replacements. While the master was away a shipyard repair foreman informed Oliver that the ship was fixed. The captain, having anticipated this, and knowing that before the U.S. Navy declared a vessel operational she had to pass a sea trial, had left orders with the chief mate to take the ship out for the test, but only if a U.S. Navy pilot was present to guide her into open waters. Befitting this daffy drama of human foibles, Port Control sent word that no pilot was available. It did not matter anyway, because the chief engineer refused to get under way with a shorthanded engine room crew. To add to the plot a radio message was received from South Vietnam urging Oliver to speed up the ship's departure because her load of aircraft bombs was urgently needed for an operation in progress.

Oliver, who held a current master's license for any tonnage, asked if there was any objection to him taking out the *Enid Victory*. He had commanded Liberty ships and had sailed in Victory ships. They had many similarities. No one objected. Why should they? If anything bad happened Oliver would take the blame.

To sail with a full engine room crew Oliver persuaded engineers from ships in the anchorage to take the trip. The sea trial came off without problem, with the engineering plant working fine. But Oliver's job was not done yet. He left for Manila, where he found the master in a highly nervous state brought on by the death of one crewman, disobedience by another, and the desertion of a third, along with the strain of command. The master, having also lost confidence in his novice chief engineer, was looking to replace him. Realizing this would further delay the ship, Oliver reassured the captain that his chief engineer was competent, just cautious, and he arranged for the master to see the shipping agent doctor, who prescribed medication to calm the man down before he returned to Subic Bay. Next, Oliver drifted in and out of merchant seaman bars and hangouts, leaving word that he had something for the missing third assistant engineer. Greed and curiosity lured out the deserter, who found Oliver that night. Oliver gave the man what he had for him, a charge sheet for failure to join his ship, an offense that would result in suspension of his sailing papers. The man was furious, and although no blows were struck a barrage of unpleasantries were exchanged. The *Enid Victory* continued on to Vietnam and Oliver moved on to the next case.

Animal studies by zoologists often find their subjects' behavior rational and predictable, even when under duress. In contrast, psychologists and sociologists find the conduct of human beings, with their higher intellect, not only irrational and unpredictable, but harmful. Doctors and police officers regularly see examples of this. The same can be said of Coast Guard members assigned to merchant marine detail duty. In Southeast Asia they came upon tragic, strange, humorous, and violent behavior. The most serious was the first assistant engineer driven by such overpowering despair that he ended his life by plunging a screwdriver into his chest.

Odd behavior may grow from an obsession to be somewhere else. In the case of one seaman, ignored in previous hospital sick call visits to get himself shipped back to the United States, he appeared at the embassy, where he demonstrated before a consul the fact that he was physically unfit for sea by squeezing a milky substance from his left breast. Another mariner provoked repatriation first by urinating over the side of the ship onto a Philippine Customs launch. The master quickly offered profuse apologies, including a new shirt to the dampened customs officer. Then, as the ship left the dock, the bothersome seaman dashed below and turned off the main steam valve, causing a power loss that endangered the vessel's safety in the heavily trafficked harbor.

Provocations, even if justified, could result in unhappy consequences. Liquor had loosened the tongue of one seaman who, in weaving his intoxicated way to his quarters, berated the shipmates he passed. During the night someone slipped into his room to repay the scoldings. When the seaman awoke the next morning, gone was his prosthetic leg, as well as his spare, both evidently dropped overboard.

Another incident hospitalized a man, leaving his survival uncertain for a time. After the chief mate had written up a crewman in the ship's log for an infraction, someone entered his quarters while he slept and poured five gallons of primer paint over his head, filling his eyes, nose, ears, and mouth as he gasped for air.

Humor is often bred from the absurd, and Coast Guardsmen could not help but chuckle at some behavior, such as the complaint that a merchant seaman was running a brothel ashore—and overcharging his shipmates. In 1967, a seaman buried at sea in 1966 off the Vietnam coast drifted ashore. This sent the shipping advisor scrambling to the waterfront to find a ship to perform a reburial at sea and trusting that this time enough weights would keep the sailor from coming back from "liberty."

Then there was the trusting mariner who bought three grenades from an American soldier, who assured him they were impotent. Some while later, the mariner let his son, a seaman from another vessel, toy with one of the harmless grenades. The "dud" demolished the stateroom, blowing a two foot by four foot hole in the overhead, a two foot by three foot hole in a bulkhead, and knocking down the sink—but apparently all without any personal injury.

Merchant marine life has its savage moments, maybe more so in a war setting where societal constraints are lessened. A ship's delegate was attacked with a screwdriver by a seaman, who presumably did not like his work assignment. The blunt tool rented six inches of upper arm and its shaft protruded four inches from the other side. Foul play was suspected on another vessel when, shortly after a man confessed to the master that he was using narcotics and implicated 14 other crewmen, the informant was reported missing at sea.

There was no doubt in Danang of shipboard murder when a crewman stabbed another to death. It happened at a period when the matter of jurisdiction over merchant sailors was still in debate, but, in a surprise action, the military invoked the Uniform Code of Military Justice and convened a general court-martial that convicted the seaman and sent him to a federal prison.

All jobs have their nuisances: a postal carrier delivering mail house-to-house evades the jaws of nasty-tempered dogs; a gardener beautifying a landscape battles persistent unsightly weeds; and a shipping advisor traveling repeatedly in Vietnam idles for hours awaiting air transportation. Oliver knew the routine; he had replayed the scene often. He would present his priority orders from MSTS or the embassy at the air terminal desk, where he would receive a mechanical nod from the person on duty and be told to put his name on the standby list and have a seat. In the waiting room, afloat with a sea of uniforms that always seemed at high tide, his orders were no more pressing than anyone else's.

One particular trip up-country began as usual, with Oliver inscribing his name on the passenger sheet in the U.S. Air Force terminal at Tan Son Nhut Air Base and taking a seat. After a while he rose from the hard bench and hiked to the U.S. Army terminal, thinking he might catch a ride on an observer plane. But there the script was the same—sign and wait. On his way back to the main terminal he noticed a third component in the airfield complex. Scores of light airplanes, many of them Cessnas, sat on the ground around a stubby building. They belonged to Air America, a nominal commercial airline serving intelligence and clandestine operatives.

The scene is well-imagined from the perspective of the dispatcher languishing in the nearly empty waiting room. The outside door swings open, and through the sunlight that momentarily explodes inside the dim interior strides a rugged, tanned officer wearing army greens. The man radiates professionalism and the dispatcher has no doubt that he is proficient in using the .45-caliber semi-automatic pistol in the shoulder holster strapped across his chest. When the officer speaks it is in the manner of addressing an equal, which makes the dispatcher take a liking to this stranger who says he is in the Coast Guard. This is news; he had not heard that the Coast Guard was in Vietnam. He sees the Coast Guard cap service insignia and identification card, but he also knows that things are not always what they seem at Air America. The officer then produces a diplomatic passport and mentions something about being the shipping advisor for a U.S. Navy admiral in Japan. The dispatcher's mind processes the input: *...Army fatigues...Coast Guard insignia...works for a Navy admiral...has embassy clout.... What the hell is a shipping advisor?.... Boy, what the Central Intelligence Agency won't do to come up with cover!* After Oliver concludes his introduction the dispatcher blurts, "Yeah, where do you want to go?"

The airport waiting days had ended. From then on when Oliver walked into the Air America building smiles greeted him and someone would heartily call out, "Where to this time, Commander?" It was like having a private airline. Many flights took place in a two-seater, with just Oliver, the pilot, and lots of closeup scenery for company.

The walls of Oliver's office were decorated with weapons recovered from hostile mariners. They included straight razor, pipe wrench, stevedore hook, meat hook, serving fork, and various knives: pocket, switchblade, sheath, butcher, paring, and butter. Lethal fists were a popular weapon, and a marine investigator needed to be a persuasive talker to complete a tour without becoming a casualty by his own side. When Oliver boarded the *Cape San Martin* and removed the chief engineer for misconduct, it so upset the mariner that he boasted that he had been a heavyweight boxing champion in the Navy and promised that when they reached the dock he would punch Oliver into oblivion. On the way, the shipping advisor delivered his own verbal counterpunches, and by the time they reached the landing Oliver had won a technical knockout. The engineer had forgotten his pugilistic threats and invited Oliver uptown for an amicable cup of coffee.

When paging through generations of Coast Guard exploits the foremost quality found is fortitude. It is as if upon entering the Coast Guard an individual passes through an invisible passageway where "courage pods" are sown into the mind. These nuggets lie dormant until adversity vibrations crack their shells, releasing their power. This unusual organization, dedicated to fighting for its country and to saving lives, breeds an extraordinary will to overcome fear and hindrance. At the numerous small Coast Guard stations along the nation's shores, courage is as regular as daybreak. This has always been true. Back in the age when muscles instead of engines powered surfboats,

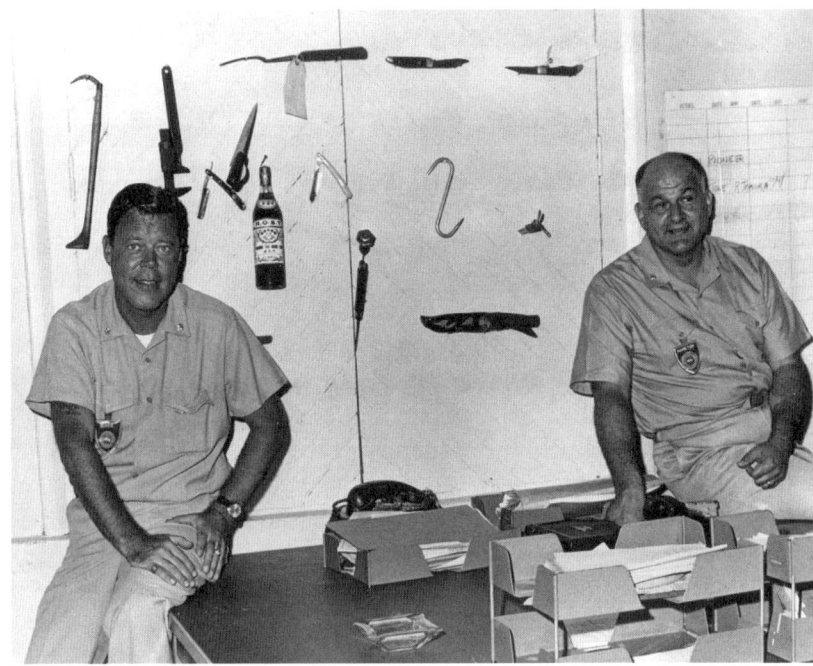

Dealing with merchant mariners had its dangers. The wall behind Coast Guard shipping advisor Commander E. Frank Oliver (left) with his assistant, Lieutenant Commander Joseph L. Hamilton, displays crude weapons taken from hostile seamen. (Courtesy of E. Frank Oliver)

men from these stations shoved the heavy craft into the stormy water, scrambled aboard, and pulled on oars to force their way through the breakers trying to throw them into the sea. Once through the surf they careened up and down the waves, taking a mauling from gale-force winds. Exhausted, hands bleeding, they would reach a foundering ship with the task hardly begun, for now they had to rescue the crew and make it back. Oliver manifested this same traditional mettle in the *Loma Victory* affair. Just his willingness to act against an armed, deranged merchant marine captain on an ammunition ship dissolved all opposition to establishing a merchant marine detail in Vietnam.

Lieutenant Gerald T. Willis, the Coast Guard officer commanding ELD #2 in Cam Ranh Bay, had agreed to call Oliver by radio whenever he was needed to keep a volatile situation from getting out of control because the U.S. Army would not intervene. Willis called Oliver as soon as he learned that the master on a ship backloading ammunition was roaming her decks with a gun, threatening to shoot into the holds and kill the chief mate. Once advised of the emergency nature of Oliver's trip, the Air Force promptly flew him to Cam Ranh Bay.

For months, tentacles of dark horrors had groped for the master's mind. Now, with thousands of tons of explosives on board and more coming, the imagined terrors got a grip and sent him rushing topside yelling for the loading to stop and ordering the cargo removed. The chief mate's attempt to reason with the captain drove him into a rage. He ran to his cabin for a gun and commenced hunting the decks for his second in command, who wisely locked himself in his stateroom.

Willis collected Oliver at the airport in a jeep and hurried back to the sentry-lined wharf. An army colonel, glad to see the shipping advisor, reported that cargo operations on the four ammunition ships had been suspended and all stevedores and military personnel withdrawn. While Oliver listened he stared down the deserted pier, where powerful lamp towers transformed it into a long lighted tunnel cut into the black sky. Scattered crates and forklifts showed signs of a hasty evacuation. Off to the left side at the far end hunkered the *Loma Victory,* a bomb needing to be defused. The officer was still talking. "We'll be here. If you need any help, let us know." Oliver reacted with a soundless chuckle. On the trip over he had no idea how this situation would unfold, but he had assumed that the Army would be a lot closer to him than a thousand feet. His audience waited. It was showtime. The gun under his left shoulder gave him some reassurance. Absently, he nodded in assent to the colonel, gave himself a mental prod, and stepped into the limelight.

The thick silence around him made him feel as if he were walking underwater. Even the rhythmic clop of his boots on the concrete seemed muted. Although he saw no one, he sensed that he was being watched from the ships towering on each side. Finally, the interminable walk ended and he was making the tall climb up the gangway. The hush had followed him to the top, where he paused to look around. No one was about. He made his way toward the captain's cabin on an upper deck. Inside the empty passageway his approach took on more caution. Recalling that the master once sailed for Matson Navigation Company, he called out, "Hey Cap, I'm Captain Oliver. I used to sail for Matson. We probably have some mutual shipmates." He listened and heard an indistinct reply. Turning the corner he saw an open doorway halfway down the passageway. He raised his voice again, "I came aboard to talk to you." In a few moments he stood in the doorway facing a medium-built, nondescript man in his late forties, casually dressed, sitting behind a desk. Next to his right hand on the blotter lay a .38-caliber revolver. The glazed countenance staring back warned Oliver that this man was on vacation from the world of reason. The master growled, "What do you want?"

Oliver edged ahead. "The Army told me they stopped loading ammunition and they asked me to come down to talk with you to see what you had in mind." There was no reply. He sat down on a chair on the other side of the desk and figured he would keep on talking until he saw the right moment to act.

"Cap, I think we may have been shipmates at one time," he continued in idle distracting chatter. Now and then the master uttered a terse sentence, but for the most part the conversation was one-sided. Throughout, the man's hand never moved away from the gun.

Before long, Oliver realized that the man was leaning back in his chair, creating a weight imbalance. Without pausing in his speech Oliver lunged forward and drove his right palm into the master's right shoulder, knocking him to the floor. Oliver snatched up the gun, turned it on the sprawled captain, and hollered for the chief mate, whose room was on the same level. When he appeared Oliver pulled out his handcuffs and told him to manacle the skipper. He then sent him for the soldiers. Oliver searched the premises, including the safe, which took lengthy prodding to get the captain to open. His search turned up a plentiful supply of pills, most of which were amphetamines, central nervous system stimulants. The master had been liberally borrowing from ship funds. Several thousands of dollars of his IOUs were in the safe. The chief mate admitted that for six months the captain had been on a diet of pills, alcohol, and marijuana, rendering him virtually useless to command, and that he (the chief mate) had been running the ship. Because the skipper was well-liked by the crew, no one would turn him in. Oliver designated the chief mate temporary master and returned to Saigon with his prisoner.

Before the Coast Guard's direct involvement, the merchant marine problem was comparable to a high school without a principal. Unruly students (mariners) went unpunished because the teachers (masters) lacked authoritative backup (principal), leaving the parents (shipping interests) clamoring for action. With the presence of the Coast Guard, known for its leadership in maritime affairs, the merchant seaman issue began receiving earnest attention and gradually came under control. Steps were taken, such as the embassy decreeing that American civilians accompanying the armed forces came under the Uniform Code of Military Justice, which meant that merchant mariners could be tried by court-martial.

Provost marshals in the respective ports had the latitude to go aboard an American merchant ship to stop trouble, but overwhelmed as they were in military matters, they opted to leave that job to the shipping companies and the Coast Guard. Oliver did his best to become on good terms with the provost marshals and urged them to heed a master when he called for help. But getting this cooperation was like a marathon dance: you could not rest. The dance ended in November 1968, at Cam Ranh Bay, during a meeting with the judge advocate of the 1st Logistical Command, provost marshal, support unit commanders, MSTS, and Coast Guard, where an accord was reached that military police would, with a ship captain's approval, go aboard to put down violence that endangered people, property, or the port.

There was another change that helped reduce the mariner problems. Oliver had observed that seamen who missed the sailing of their ship, or who downright deserted, loitered in Saigon enjoying the city's pleasures. Some of them, of course, caused trouble. What was happening was that a few less-than-honest shipping agents acting in collusion with hotel managers put these men up in hotels, where they were allowed to order anything they wanted from room service with the bills going to the ship. The hotel managers profited, the shipping agents profited, and the seamen enjoyed a free ride. Some seamen had to "wait" two months before catching another ship. So Oliver and a consulate officer talked this over with the Vietnamese police and the Director of Immigration, suggesting that the Vietnamese do what their Japanese and Filipino counterparts do regarding mariners who have failed to join their ship or deserted; bill them for their room and board, and particulars, such as arrest warrant and escort to aircraft. Immigration agreed to treat these individuals as illegal immigrants, but would only act against those causing trouble. Thus ended the Saigon vacations.

Oliver's impressive accomplishments changed minds at the embassy. He was asked to move his office into the embassy, even though he still remained with MSTS. Then, in mid-1967, the embassy asked the State Department to establish a Coast Guard merchant marine detail in Saigon.

A little past the halfway point of his tour Oliver's request for assistance was fulfilled, with the arrival of a lieutenant commander and a chief petty officer. When

Oliver's tour concluded, he and his staff had boarded more than 500 vessels and performed 263 investigations. The merchant marine detail that succeeded them continued this commendable record.

The Coast Guard merchant marine detail played an important part in keeping the flow of military supplies moving steadily into South Vietnam. Yes, there were troublesome mariners, but overall they represented only about two percent of the merchant marine, a figure comparable to military personnel running afoul of the Uniform Code of Military Justice. Oliver, having a great respect for those in the merchant marine detail, paid them this compliment with deep feeling: "They do a damn good job that nobody takes note of."

CHAPTER 9

COMBAT SEARCH AND RESCUE

AT 4,000 FEET COAST GUARD LIEUTENANT COMMANDER Lonnie L. Mixon dropped the nose of the HH-3E, aiming the helicopter for an 80-foot-wide slot halfway up a mountainside where *Carrot Top,* a nine-man reconnaissance team, awaited rescue.

More than seven hours earlier two Americans and seven South Vietnamese had jumped from a U.S. Marine Corps helicopter into Laos, not far from the South Vietnamese border on a line west of Danang. They were expected. A greeting committee shot down the aircraft as it exited the plateau and cornered the ground party. Throughout the morning and early afternoon aircraft rained down protective fire around the landing zone (LZ), with uncertain results because of the cloud blanket a thousand feet over the terrain. When *Carrot Top* radioed that hostile fire was sporadic Mixon went in for the pickup.

The clearing ran up against a 2,000-foot cliff face, the top of which poked through the cloud cover. Because of the rocky sides there was only one way in and out of this canyon table for his helicopter. Mixon came to an abrupt hover ten feet over the center of the sallow, elephant grass–covered LZ. Near the rock wall ahead and to the left several men waited alongside the bright orange fabric on the ground that they carried for pinpointing their retrieval location. Sitting on the right side of the cockpit, the same side as the rescue doorway, Mixon pivoted the aircraft, which measured three quarters the diameter of the circular clearing, to face his exit. With the rotor blade wash blowing the tall grass nearly flat, Mixon saw people stand up in front when halfway through his 180-degree turn. He thought they belonged with *Carrot Top,* but as he passed from his side vision he saw them raise their weapons. A crewman in back yelled, "Gunfire!" The copilot grabbed his rifle and shot back. Mixon finished the turn and threw the helicopter off the mountain. Gasoline gushed from the severed main fuel line, temporarily blinding the two crewmen in the cabin. The rotor blade windstorm coming in through the open cockpit windows whipped up the volatile fuel, coating everybody and everything. For a time Mixon refrained from working any switch or using the radio, fearing that a static electricity spark would obliterate them. They closed the windows. When they shut down the fuel boost pumps the leaking stopped. In the 45-minute flight back to Danang with several inches of gasoline sloshing around their ankles they had to forego lighting up much-needed, nerve-calming cigarettes.

After touching down they ran as fast as they could from the wounded bird, staining the runway with its flammable blood. Yet the day's work for Mixon and his crew was not over. The U.S. Air Force, not wishing to be accused of favoritism, gave them another HH-3E and sent them back to the scene. While they had been away another helicopter attempting the recovery careened from the LZ in flames, crash landing a few hundred yards away. *Carrot Top* was told to get to the crash site for pickup with the two survivors. Later that day, the six men left in the *Carrot Top* team, including the American advisors and the two airmen, were rescued.

This was life's pace for a year for the Coast Guard aviators who volunteered for the Air Force–Coast Guard pilot exchange program. The idea of a pilot exchange between these rescue services, one of which operated primarily over land and the other over water, was a natural. When the National Search and Rescue School, a joint Air Force–Coast Guard venture, was founded in 1966, speculation over how such an agreement might work began in earnest. Such a program, surely, would acquaint each service with the other's tactics, techniques, and equipment, and the resulting refined performance would benefit those in need of rescue. Although this is what the agreement would say, other immediate motives drove the men pushing for the arrangement. On the Coast Guard side there was unhappiness that aviation had no role in Vietnam. Of the service's many missions, the military one was already in place, with others (port security, aids to navigation, and commercial vessel safety) forthcoming. But where was Coast Guard's best known mission—search and rescue?

For the Air Force, the full-fledged combat search and rescue role in Southeast Asia had sneaked up like a cold virus because of the combination of a helter-skelter war and its lack of foresight. First came a throat tickle, then a stuffy nose. These and other encroaching symptoms were doctored, but the cures failed; and before the true illness was recognized and treated the patient was bedridden with chills and fever. As the insurgency in South Vietnam—provoked by North Vietnam in 1959—grew, so American combat escalated in both countries. When family feuding in Laos broke out into a civil war in 1960 and North Vietnam backed the Communist faction, the United States entered into it. Wherever in Laos and Cambodia that North Vietnam ran supplies into South Vietnam the United States attacked them. In 1970 Prince Norodom Sihanouk was deposed in Cambodia. The United States went after the North Vietnam–backed Communist forces there. Throughout it all, American ground troops remained largely in South Vietnam fighting "The Vietnam War," while American fliers scouting and attacking the whole frenzied landscape fought "The Southeast Asia War."

Early on, when planes went down, saving the aviators became a spontaneous effort using whatever was available. As air activity increased the need for coordination and rescue forces increased. The Air Force began marching toward this responsibility in December when it sent three officers and two enlisted men to Saigon to establish a search and rescue post in the Air Operations Center at Tan Son Nhut Air Base. They did what they could without any formal rescue aircraft in the country, and in April 1962 became Detachment Three, Pacific Air Rescue Center. The component of this unit that directed rescue efforts took the title of Joint Search and Rescue Center (JSARC) following a mutual rescue coordination agreement between the United States and South Vietnam. Still, the effort was formless.

A study done in 1963 by Major Alan W. Saunders, commander of the air rescue center, was prompted by firsthand knowledge that airmen who could have been saved were being captured or killed by the enemy, or, in some instances, dying because their rescuers lacked recovery skills. Campaigning for rescue improvements, Saunders's report documented that Army, Marine Corps, and South Vietnamese aircraft were not always available for rescue and were subject to recall at any time by their command. Foremost, the crews had no formal rescue training.

The Air Force had no doctrine for combat rescue; when a war came along it would just extend its peacetime procedures as needed. This was like using a Band-Aid for a shrapnel wound. The only helicopter in the Air Rescue Service was the short-range HH-43B Huskie, reliable for saving air crews from crashes at or near bases, but hardly something to send into the fury of heavy machine guns, especially without any predetermined methodology. In May 1964, the Joint Chiefs of Staff ordered that search and rescue forces be sent into Southeast Asia and the necessary tactics devised. The Air Force deployed what ill-suited aircraft it had: the HH-43B; the dependable but sluggish amphibious HU-16B Albatross; and the SC-54 Rescuemaster, a cargo plane modified for mission control work. On 1 July 1965, Detachment Three, Pacific Air Rescue Center became the 38th Air Rescue Squadron. That is, until further reorganization took place on 8 January 1966, when the U.S. Air Force's Air Rescue Service became the Aerospace Rescue and Recovery Service, and the 3rd Aerospace Rescue and Recovery Group (ARRGp) came into being to take charge of all rescue units and searches in the Vietnam theater. By the time the Air Force and the Coast Guard began talking pilot exchange, combat search and rescue had matured from using borrowed or makeshift equipment under improvised tactics to an operation with sound equipment and effective strategies. Still, the Air Force was short one important ingredient—experienced rescue pilots. To fill out their helicopter crews the Air Force yanked pilots out of transports, bombers, and fighters.

An agreement between the Air Force and Coast Guard was signed in March 1967 calling for a five-pilot swap for two-year assignments. From the Coast Guard the Air Force would get three helicopter pilots for the 37th Aerospace Rescue and Recovery Squadron (ARRSq) in Danang, and two fixed-wing C-130 pilots for the 31st ARRSq at Clark Air Force Base in the Philippines flying support for the war.

The Coast Guard found itself with plenty of volunteers. Eighty pilots, almost all those eligible by rank and flight hours, put in for the assignment. Chosen for fixed wing duty were lieutenants James "Casey" Quinn and Thomas F. Frischmann. The helicopter pilots were Lieutenant Commander Lonnie L. Mixon, Lieutenant Jack C. Rittichier, and Lieutenant Lance A. Eagan. Eager they were. Hotshots they were not. They were family men in their late twenties to middle thirties. Quinn, the oldest in the group, had five children. Not content to remain on the periphery in the Philippines, he convinced the Air Force to reassign him to the 39th ARRSq at Tuy Hoa, in South Vietnam. One thing these men, and those who came after, were convinced of, was that no other pilots in the world were better prepared and qualified to fly rescue than Coast Guard pilots. For them, saving lives was the reason they were born.

Rittichier was familiar with the Air Force, having flown B-47 bombers in its Strategic Air Command before yielding to the lure of Coast Guard aviation. He and Mixon were at Detroit Air Station before going to Vietnam. There, Mixon saw Rittichier's courage and passion for the Coast Guard. On 29 November 1966, Rittichier was Mixon's copilot when they lifted off in their HH-52A helicopter to fly 150 miles over Lake Huron in a snowstorm to save eight men on a foundering ship. Gale force winds buffeted the small helicopter, shaking the crew like dice in a gambler's cup. Terrible visibility forced them to fly low to get any kind of vision. They covered the final 80 miles speeding just 200 feet above the water to use the peek-a-boo shoreline for navigation reference. Moments after hoisting the last seaman off the bow the seething lake snapped the German freighter in half and swallowed her.

Rittichier had the collateral duty at the air station of public affairs officer. He took telling the public about the Coast Guard very seriously. Upon getting his orders he initiated an effort with the public affairs office at Coast Guard Headquarters to send them articles and information on the adventures of the exchange pilots. Because of this love for his Service, Eagan affectionately called him, "Mr. Coast Guard." So deep went the trio's Coast Guard pride that they made a pact not to tell anyone in the squadron that Rittichier had been in the Air Force, for this was to be a Coast Guard endeavor all the way and they were going to be the best at whatever they did while with the Air Force. However, their "gung ho" outlook would tinge their tour with a heavy personal sadness.

Rittichier was a relentless lifesaver; it was as if he took the rescue of every downed aviator as a direct challenge. Eighteen days after reporting to the 37th ARRSq he earned a Distinguished Flying Cross (DFC) for going into enemy fire to snatch up four Army fliers after their helicopter gunships had been shot down. Thirteen days later he flew through enemy anti-aircraft emplacements to land at a bomb-cratered landing zone littered with unexploded bombs and mines to prepare two downed helicopters for pickup. Eight days after that his prowess would earn him another DFC, this time for maneuvering under the yellow cast of flares among 100-foot-tall trees on a steep slope at night to save nine men in two trips—five of them seriously wounded. He had 13 saves in his two months with the squadron when, on 9 June 1968, he was going for number 14.

Mixon had left at daybreak to recover two downed Army fliers. Because of the jungle's density, their location was difficult to pin down, so he was running a little behind in getting back for relief. When he landed, Rittichier was waiting to go out in Mixon's helicopter. An A-4 had gone down well to the west of Hue and its Marine Corps pilot had radioed that his leg, and probably an arm, had been broken when he hit the ground. This meant that he was unable to evade. Air strikes were in progress to keep a strong enemy force away from him.

The pilot, who lay busted up beneath his parachute a few yards from a road in a North Vietnamese Army bivouac area, had gone from fighter pilot to enemy bait for the soldiers dug in out of sight, awaiting the helicopters. The first HH-3E to attempt the pickup made three approaches. Each time killing fire drove it away. Finally, the Jolly Green Giant had to depart to refuel, leaving Rittichier with the only rescue helicopter on scene. The odds of pulling this one off looked bad, but Rittichier did not think about whether he could or could not succeed—only that he had to. Down there was a hurt man who would be murdered if abandoned. He called for the gunships to cover him as he was going in. He flung his aircraft through concentrated fire into a hover over the pilot until the shooting became too intense and he had to pull away. The strike planes poured on more suppression fire. Rittichier came around into another hover over the downed pilot, his aircraft shuddering from the hits it was taking. Over the radio a pilot yelled to Rittichier, "Your left side is on fire, Jolly Green. Get outta there!" He pulled off to the east, but with rotor blades visibly slowing down, the helicopter could not rise. It hit the ground 1,300 yards from the Marine pilot, where a fireball consumed it within 30 seconds.

The sudden cremation of their comrades maddened the Americans. Again and again gunships and fighters ripped into the enemy, but they were well-entrenched. Three more helicopters tried reaching the pilot, only to be chased off torn and gouged when the air became diagrammed with tracers.

Eventually radio contact was lost with the pilot and when he no longer moved the mission was called off. It had been an improbable task to pull off a rescue amid a regiment-sized enemy camp. Still, when your business is rescue you have to try. The cost of the effort came to four crewmen killed, one helicopter destroyed, and three damaged. Rittichier's HH-3E was the tenth one lost in combat out of the 32 procured by the Air Force. Flyovers the next day found no sign of the Marine or his parachute. Standard helicopter procedure was for high bird, the second helicopter, to look after low bird, the one making the pick up. If low bird went down, high bird swooped in to rescue low bird's crew. When Rittichier attempted the recovery he had no high bird. In this instance it did not matter—the outcome would have been the same—but by going in without a backup Rittichier showed his commitment to lifesaving.

The Coast Guard's volunteer list evaporated with Rittichier's death. When the time came to assign the replacements for the first group, another solicitation notice had to be issued. To qualify, a pilot had to be a lieutenant or lieutenant commander with 550 flight hours, 300 of them in a helicopter. Only three men came forward, but that was enough, and saved some personnel officer from picking non-volunteers and living through many sleepless nights until knowing they came home alive. They each had the minimum flight hours called for, but only one had the qualifying rank. Of the others, one was a lieutenant (j.g.) selected for promotion and the other an ensign who would move up a rank before heading overseas. But the Air Force was not going to be picky and waived the rank qualifier. If these men wanted to fly combat search and rescue that was sufficient. The three, Lieutenant Richard V. Butchka, Lieutenant (j.g.) James M. Loomis, and Ensign Robert T. Ritchie, were all in their middle twenties. The consensus at Butchka's unit, San Diego Air Station, was that he was crazy to volunteer. The air station had been his first assignment out of flight school and his operations officer, astonished that he was going into combat with little more than 500 flight hours, did not expect Butchka to come back breathing.

Ritchie, a bachelor, at Houston Air Station, wanted to put in for Vietnam duty, but after seeing the requirements thought it would be a waste of time. His more pragmatic commanding officer encouraged him to apply, telling him that anything you want you ask for. For the most part, the source of military pilots comes from officers who request flight training. Ritchie, however, entered aviation by footpath rather than paved street. When he was a seaman at a Coast Guard lifeboat station in Massachusetts the Coast Guard had an Aviation Cadet Program that gave young enlisted members the opportunity to become pilots. Soon after applying he was off to flight school at Pensacola Naval Air Station in the special enlisted grade of Aviation Cadet. He graduated, was commissioned, and was assigned to Houston. Now he, Butchka, and Loomis were going to join the few in Coast Guard aviation ever to fly rescue under combat conditions. But first came a half year of hard training at five Air Force installations ranging from Florida to the Philippines.

Tutelage began with a global survival school at Fairchild Air Force Base (AFB), near Spokane, Washington. Here they learned how to forage for food and to evade capture in enemy territory, and they went through the mental and physical abuse that comes with being a prisoner of war. Next they went to Sheppard AFB outside of Wichita Falls, Texas, to learn to fly the Sikorsky HH-3E Jolly Green Giant, so dubbed because of its size and green and brown camouflage scheme. Its two 1,250-horsepower turbine engines drove it at speeds of more than 160 miles per hour, and it cruised at 100 miles per hour at 10,000 feet, well out of range of anti-aircraft guns. Upon looking for a suitable combat rescue helicopter, the Air Force decided on the H-3 after trying out the cargo version, but it needed enhancements before it became practical for battle. To increase its range, a 650-gallon fuel tank was installed, giving it nearly 30 percent more fuel than the standard tank. It was adapted for two jettisonable external tanks, each with 200-gallon capacity—the type used by the F-100 Super Sabre jet fighter. Its new 500-mile combat range was further increased with an air-to-air refueling system. To protect people and key components, a thousand pounds of half-inch titanium armor plating were distributed around the aircraft and a shatterproof canopy put in. For retrieving survivors, a 600-pound capacity, 240-foot cable hoist with a jungle penetrator was added.[1] When Kaman Aircraft Corporation, the maker of the HH-43B, was modifying that helicopter for Vietnam service, its engineers designed the penetrator to plunge through heavy foliage to a survivor on the ground. The 26-pound, pointed metal weight had three spring-loaded paddles at one end that when pulled down became seats. At the other end, spring-loaded arms, once released, offered protection when raised up through the branches. And finally, for self-defense, the helicopter had mounts for two M60 machine guns.

The Coast Guard version of the H-3 began gradually entering service in 1969, so this was a new aircraft for the earlier exchange pilots who came from the HH-52A. However, because it too was a Sikorsky aircraft they found many of the integral systems similar and formed a strong attachment for the higher-performance HH-3E. Rittichier expressed it this way: "As far as we were concerned it was love at first sight.[2]

The training continued at Eglin AFB, near Fort Walton Beach, Florida, for advanced combat crew flight training. Here they learned high hover recovery over forests; low-level, high-speed, quick-stop approaches to a point on the ground; and air-to-air refueling with the HC-130P. Hitting the refueling basket in a drogue streaming from a wing of the big four-engine airplane is one measure of a pilot's skill. The target tends five degrees left of the helicopter's centerline and to jab its fuel probe into the basket a pilot has to leave the drafting position into the buffeting air turbulence of the tanker's engines. Because the long probe, which extends beyond the rotor blades, dips when the helicopter accelerates, the pilot has to start above the basket and essentially dive at it. But, if the helicopter is moving too fast and the pilot slows down the probe will rise. Furthermore, the probe has to impact the drogue with at least 160 foot-pounds of force for a seal to occur. The whirling rotor makes a helicopter a virtual static electricity–making machine, and during refueling training Eagan learned what occurs when the seal is not tight. A ten-inch static spark ignited the fuel leaking around the valve, sending flames reaching for his aircraft. In response, Eagan kicked over the rudder to slide out of the way of the aerial torch and continued the refueling flying along sideways.

Training moved on to Francis E. Warren AFB in Cheyenne, Wyoming, for high-altitude flying exercises to prepare pilots for rescue in the mountainous areas of Southeast Asia. Their last instruction stop was at Clark AFB in the Philippines for jungle survival school, or as students and instructors called it, the College of Jungle Knowledge. Throughout their training the Coast Guard aviators did exceptionally well and were told so by their Air Force instructors, many of whom had come from flying combat search and rescue in the ongoing war. Rittichier stated that his group's proficiency was a product of their motivation to save lives, rather than individual brilliance.[3] He no doubt downplayed the flying skills to avoid sounding boastful, but the war medals amassed by all of the Coast Guard exchange aviators proved not only their incentive, but most certainly their flying prowess as well.

Given the task to pull off rescues in South and North Vietnam, Laos, Cambodia, and Thailand, the Air Force had to figure out where to best locate units to reach trouble spots in the least amount of time. Based upon experience, rescue analysts had determined that if a helicopter reached a downed airman within 15 minutes rescue probability was high, but if it took more than 30 minutes recovery chances dropped rapidly. With this in mind, rescue units were placed in South Vietnam and Thailand, with the 3rd ARRGp at Tan Son Nhut Air Base in overall command of planning, organizing, coordinating, and controlling rescue operations. The long-range helicopters were placed in the north end of South Vietnam and Thailand: the 37th ARRSq at Danang; the 40th ARRSq at Udorn, Thailand; and Detachment One, 40th ARRSq at Nakhon Phanom, Thailand, the latter two near the Laotian border. The short-range HH-43B/F helicopters came under the 38th ARRSq at Tan Son Nhut Air Base, with 14 scattered base detachments for local rescue work. On the coast, between Qui Nhon and Nha Trang in central South Vietnam, the 39th ARRSq was based at Tuy Hoa Air Base with its airborne mission control/tanker C-130s. To further cut down on response time into North Vietnam and Laos, helicopters flew orbits off the North Vietnamese coast and over Laos. They also deployed nearer the DMZ and in Laos on ground alert.

Even though the HH-3E performed well, rescue planners still desired an aircraft with greater speed and power. To cover the 150 nautical miles from their northernmost ground alert strip in Laos to Hanoi in a half hour would take a 300-knot helicopter. But designing a rescue specialty helicopter for the Southeast Asian battleground would be costly, and the war might be over before it ever became operational. The alternative was to find another off-the-shelf machine. Chosen was the U.S. Marine Corps heavy lift Sikorsky CH-53A. After modification for rescue it became the HH-53B, or Super Jolly Green Giant. Impressed by its size—nearly 12.5 feet longer than the HH-3E—aircrews called it the BUFF for "Big Ugly Fat Fellow." Though not much faster than the HH-3E, with a speed of around 190 knots, the HH-53B far surpassed it in lift power and defensive armament, which was illustrated by an HH-53B picking up a 12,000-pound A-1E and carrying it 56 miles from the central Laotian panhandle to Nakhon Phanom.[4] This added strength, delivering 40 percent more hover capability, made recoveries over mountains less frightening. Rotor blades need to grab onto air molecules to keep a helicopter airborne. At 10,000 feet air is two-thirds less dense than it is at sea level; therefore, at high altitudes, or in hot, humid weather, a pilot must sharpen the pitch of the blades to grip enough air, but this creates drag and slows down the revolutions per minute unless more power is applied. One of the checkoff items of escorting aircraft was to fly low over the survivor, taking air temperature and altitude readings to pass along to the helicopters. The copilot looks through the charts in the back of the flightbook to find the maximum weight they can be to hover without falling out of the sky. To lower weight pilots dumped fuel, which often left helicopters without enough to make it home. This was why air-to-air refueling was a lifesaver for the lifesavers.

Three 7.62-mm miniguns with a firing rate of 4,000 rounds per minute gave the HH-53B substantial firepower. Instead of four in a crew, it could carry six. The first HH-53Bs arrived in September 1967 and were assigned to the 40th ARRSq. Although still not the ideal rescue helicopter because its bulk kept it from maneuvering in tight areas and its getaway speed kept it within various gun ranges anywhere from a half minute to two and a half minutes before clearing the area, it stood as the finest rescue helicopter in the world at the time.

The basic rescue team had helicopters for recovery and airplanes for protection. For much of the war the bodyguarding fell to the A-1 Skyraider. A powerful reciprocating-engine aircraft that first flew in 1951, in this kind of war it was ideal for interdiction and close air support. The 15 hardpoints underneath accommodated an assortment of bombs, rockets, napalm, and other weaponry, while the wings held four 20-mm cannons. The A-1 had exceptional endurance—a theoretical 12 hours with maximum fuel—and could fly at attack levels lower than those at which anti-aircraft guns could be depressed. Rescue escort duty went to the best pilots. There were two A-1 squadrons. The A-1s from the 602 Special Operations Squadron at Nakhon Phanom had the call sign *Sandy* and those of the 6 Special Operations Squadron at Pleiku, South Vietnam were termed *Spad*.

A troublesome recovery effort usually included the HC-130, the HH-3E/HH53B, and the A-1, with whatever FAC and strike aircraft were necessary. Serving as mission controller, the HC-130 orchestrated the rescue by assigning radio frequencies to aircraft, briefing new arrivals on scene, and assigning tasks. It also refueled the helicopters. Tactics called for four A-1s and two Jolly Greens on scene. The A-1s, divided into two flights, *Sandy Low* and *Sandy High,* customarily carried for rescue work rockets, CBU, and 7.62-mm miniguns. If other types of ordnance were needed they could be called in. The helicopters and *Sandy High* were put into orbit, while *Sandy Low* assessed the situation. One of the *Sandy Low* pilots became the on-scene commander, with the job of locating the survivor, determining his condition, and getting the lowdown on the landscape and enemy presence. When conditions seemed best he sent a helicopter in for the pickup. This helicopter, designated "low bird," swooped in escorted by *Sandy High*. The other helicopter, "high bird," stayed ready to rescue the low bird crew if they ended up on the ground.

Few rescues were accomplished without opposition. After knocking out an American plane, the enemy immediately searched for its survivors in order to ambush the rescuers. When an airman bailed out, his survival radio automatically sent off an audible signal on the emergency frequency. To lose a radio meant certain death. Without one there was no way to get help. As a consequence, many aviators carried two radios. When an aviator arrived in Vietnam he supplied answers to personal questions, such as the names of his family, pets, or favorite sports teams. This information, accessible to JSARC, was used to confirm that the person on the radio was the survivor and not an impersonator setting a trap. Even so, in this excited state the mind can lock up the memory cells. This happened to one Marine flier, who could not remember the name of his wife, or anything else on his personal list, but he convinced the rescuers that he was a good guy by telling them that they had picked him up once before and he gave them the date.

Helicopters carried rescue specialists (RS), unique enlisted individuals trained to be "supermen." They could parachute and scuba dive. They were skilled in first aid, hand-to-hand combat, small arms, and in surviving alone in the desert, arctic, or jungle. It was they who left the helicopter to cut loose a pilot dangling upside down from his parachute caught in a tree or assist an injured flier. They were so dedicated to lifesaving they would plead with their pilots to put them on the ground to save someone's life even though it might mean losing their own. Sometimes neither survived because the rescue specialist and survivor were shot to death while being hoisted.

Primary home base for the Coast Guard helicopter pilots became the 37th ARRSq with its 14 HH-3Es. The squadron was authorized 21 each of pilots, copilots, rescue specialists, and flight engineers for flight crews, and had an overall squadron roster of around 250 men. At any one time, however, only 70 to 80 percent of that figure were actually attached. Most of the shortages were in copilots, flight engineers, and maintenance personnel.

An entry in the unit's historical report of April to June 1969 lamented that the squadron never had enough replacement pilots arriving fully qualified in the HH-3E, and only 25 percent of them were trained for aircraft commander. With respect to a particular aircraft, an aviator starts out as a copilot and through routine flying works up to first pilot, which means he may fly solo, but is not normally qualified to carry passengers. But with experience comes confidence, and if that is topped with good judgement a first pilot progresses to aircraft commander, or rescue crew commander. The Air Force had two more levels. Instructor pilot came next. At this tier one never had to fly as copilot. After that came flight examiner, and each squadron had one. This person headed the training program and gave the tests for moving up to the next level. That same historical report happily mentioned the arrival of Butchka, Loomis, and Ritchie—all aircraft commanders. And, although in the Coast Guard the threesome were junior in terms of helicopter hours, they were senior in helicopter hours to just about everyone in the 37th ARRSq and shortly thereafter were made instructor pilots, with Butchka elevated to flight examiner. Often, a junior Coast Guard officer found himself flying with a major or lieutenant colonel for a copilot, but the rank disparity never interfered with the mission. All the Coast Guard helicopter exchange aviators in Southeast Asia felt at ease with their assignment, and the Air Force treated them like their own.

The 37th ARRSq began receiving the HH-53B in April 1969 as the replacement for the HH-3E; thereby, those Coast Guard pilots that came after the second exchange group trained in the HH-53B.

A daily commitment for the squadron had one or two HH-3Es orbiting the Gulf of Tonkin; two HH-3Es on strip alert at Danang; and two likewise deployed to Quang Tri nearer the DMZ. At this sand-covered U.S. Marine Corps compound the pilots had their own tent. It had a floor, cots, and VHF-FM radio, and next to it was an outhouse. The pilots could walk over to the Marine mess for a hot meal or stay around the tent eating C-rations. Another HH-3E was kept ready for training or rescue backup in Danang. The 37th ARRSq also rotated air crews to serve brief stints with Detachment One, 40th ARRSq at Nakhon Phanom. It had two helicopters on ground alert at the base and two others either sitting on the ground at *Lima Site 98,* which was Long Tieng in northern Laos, or flying orbit over the area during air strikes. The friendly outposts in Laos, termed *Lima Sites,* were usually manned by Royal Laotian forces, with short dirt airfields run by Air America and Continental Air Services, civilian companies operating under United States government contract.

Two wicked impediments opposed a pilot's compassionate desire to recover survivors: formidable landscape and murderous anti-aircraft weapons. When a flier ejected he was apt to bounce into a mountain or plummet through dense growth to the jungle floor. The karst topography of northern Laos, while a spectacular geological phenomenon, became an enemy to a helicopter pilot trying to work in close to snag an aviator, who was lucky to have escaped being impaled or shattered on the jagged limestone. Jungle rescue was blind work. Through the triple canopy—three heights of tree growth—the rescuers often could not see the survivor, nor the survivor see them. A downed flier could vector a helicopter to him by sending up a smoke or flare signal.

To bring down rescue aircraft, the enemy employed concentrations of anti-aircraft guns. Red dots on the maps carried by helicopter pilots showed where these guns were known to be, and some locations on these maps were solid red. Under 3,000 feet the 14.5-mm and 12.7-mm heavy machine guns were effective. The 23-mm, 37-mm, and 57-mm guns enjoyed themselves at higher altitudes. The twin 37-mm M1939 gun—a minor variation of the Bofors 40-mm designed in Sweden and used all over the world—was probably the most prevalent weapon the rescuers came up against, as it was used to defend a variety of troop and supply concentrations. The mobile weapon sat on a four-wheeled trailer and could be easily positioned around a downed flier. It was a "point and shoot" weapon—with a simple sight to adjust for the target's direction and speed—that took five-round clips and had a firing rate of 80 rounds per minute.[5]

Three weeks after killing Rittichier, the North Vietnamese Army nearly wiped out the remaining Coast Guard helicopter exchange pilots during the *Scotch-3* affair.

In the beginning, the Thunderchief pilot thought he could keep airborne long enough to reach the sea, where he would parachute into the water for a safe and quick pickup. But his F-105 was dying too fast and he had to leave, now! Another pilot in the vicinity watched Lieutenant Colonel Jack Modica disappear into the North Vietnamese jungle and noted the location.

Knocked unconscious when he hit the ground, Modica came to almost two hours later, giving the North Vietnamese plenty of time to get to his position. And, even worse luck, something had happened to his back. He could barely move. Through his survival radio he filled in the FAC overhead on his situation and was told help was at hand.

The two surviving rescue helicopter pilots of the three the Coast Guard initially sent to South Vietnam—Lieutenant Commander Lonnie L. Mixon (left) and Lieutenant Lance A. Eagan—talk over air operations. (Courtesy of U.S. Coast Guard)

Any remnant of a safe and quick recovery left in Modica's mind evaporated in the vicious ambush that drove away the first Jolly Green Giant coming for him. When that helicopter had to leave because of low fuel, Mixon was next to try. The air strikes preceding him had little effect on the enemy gunners. They nailed him with accurate fire that ruptured a hydraulic line, damaged the fuel tank, and knocked out the electrical system. He pulled off to allow the strike planes do their business. Before darkness fully engulfed the area the rescuers felt they could press for one more try. Mixon told the group that his helicopter was still flyable, and that he would go make the attempt rather than get another damaged. This time Mixon became the center of a spectacular tracer light show that drove his helicopter away even more deeply wounded. Modica, having hidden himself as best he could, spent an apprehensive night listening to soldiers rustling through the jungle looking for him.

The next morning Eagan sat on strip alert at Quang Tri listening by radio to a recovery effort that was not going well. An A-1 had been downed, killing the pilot, and a badly shot-up HH-3E was returning to Danang with an undetonated rocket lodged in its belly. Before long, the attempt was halted and the rescuers regrouped to restudy the matter. Eagan learned from the other crews that the North Vietnamese were close to the survivor, because groundfire had come from around and directly below their helicopters. They agreed that sending an RS into that plight was foolhardy. Eagan concurred, even though his RS, 20-year-old Airman First Class Joel Talley, said he would go.

They resumed the operation in the afternoon, with Eagan to make the next try. He told his crew that when they lowered the penetrator Modica had to get on it on his own. Again, Talley volunteered to go down, but Eagan, not wanting to leave a crewman behind should he have to abort, firmly said no.

Eagan descended through the anti-aircraft fire in twisting evasive maneuvers. The concussion from airbursts staggered the helicopter like a boxer taking an opponent's blows, but like a good fighter it recovered quickly to stay in the fight. Then he was through it, into the quiet box canyon peering for *Scotch-3* through the triple canopy. The injured flier tried directing the rescuers by radio, with little success. Eagan told him to release smoke, but it was so dissipated by the ample branchwork that it was of no help. The flight engineer then caught a glimpse of Modica and guided Eagan to where he had seen him. Still no one shot at them. When Modica confirmed that he could not move, Talley again asked to go down. This time Eagan let him have his way.

After being lowered 125 feet, Talley got his bearings and started out through the tangle of vines and undergrowth. Eagan radioed Modica to call out or make some sort of signal. Talley spotted the pen flare and found Modica more than 50 yards from the helicopter, a distance he knew he could not haul the man. Eagan edged the aircraft nearer, the rotor blades lopping off tree branches as he went, until he could get no closer than ten yards to the towering, dominant tree that Modica lay against. Talley, who had been on the ground 16 minutes, would have to carry the pilot to the penetrator. At the dangling hoist he strapped in the pilot and himself, then pushed down his radio transmitter switch.

Breaking into his concentration to keep a steady hover against a buffeting wind, Eagan heard Talley say, "Take us up!" At that instant he caught sight of movement in front of him. A North Vietnamese soldier hidden in a tree had been listening on a radio for this moment to spring a well-disciplined trap with his opening shot. Locked in a stare at death, Eagan's senses switched to an altered state of heightened perception. He saw in slow motion the bullet coming at him, puncturing the windshield and sending powdered glass particles floating toward his visor. As soon as death had passed him—by inches—his senses reverted to normal.

But Eagan could not move off until Talley and Modica cleared the treetops. It was a helpless time, like standing before a firing squad where one's sole salvation depended on lousy marksmanship. He held his position some 15 seconds, more than enough time for him and his crew to be moved onto the killed-in-action list, then he heard a shout from the back that they were clear. Without hesitation Eagan pulled away, with Talley and Modica swaying below the aircraft. He flew back over the DMZ, putting down at Dong Ha, where, while a field hospital checked out Modica, Eagan and his crew checked out their Jolly. Armor plating and luck saved them. The intensity of the fire showed in their battle damage. They had taken 40 direct hits. The tail section had a gaping hole, four of the five rotor blades had been hit, and the self-sealing fuel tank had nine punctures. One bullet would have gone into the copilot had it not been deflected by the armor plating under his seat. In spite of the damage, Eagan, with his emotions still inflamed at combat heights, had expected to fly the aircraft back to base. After all, he had brought it this far. So he was somewhat surprised when it was deemed unflyable. The Jolly Green Giant did fly to Danang—but slung under a crane helicopter.

At the Officer's Club in Danang rested a large statue of a Jolly Green Giant where, after each rescue, with happy ceremony, there were rounds of drinks, poured over heads as well as swallowed, and the "save" number on the statue was changed. Next to the statue, the Army had a big hook with numbers. Every time the Army had to carry back one of the squadron's helicopters, that figure changed too, with appropriate toasting and partying.

Talley's courage did not get overlooked. On this, his first time under enemy fire and his first rescue with the 37th ARRSq, he was awarded the Air Force Cross.

Casey Quinn, the Coast Guard's only C-130 pilot flying combat search and rescue, amassed plenty of adventure during his 247 combat and 19 support missions. Eleven HC-130Ps were assigned to the 39th ARRSq. On a daily basis, two flew a morning mission, one near the DMZ and the other in northern Laos. They were replaced by two others in the afternoon, with each orbit having strip alert backup. A crew consisted of six men: pilot, copilot/navigator, radio operator, loadmaster, and two engineers. These flights lasted six to nine hours, sometimes longer. Trying to keep order during the rescue frenzy and trying to keep the Jollies fueled were their chief concerns. Even if he was not directly involved in a case, Quinn found his flights exciting because something was nearly always happening, such as the time Ritchie was over Laos looking for *Nail-53*, a downed OV-10 pilot.

Low overcast and thick canopy had slowed efforts to pinpoint the survivor, who was thought to be somewhere on the steep west slope. As Ritchie flew over the valley *Nail-53* heard the helicopter but could not see it. Once Ritchie felt he had the pilot fairly well located he lowered the penetrator. It was routine procedure for a survivor on the penetrator to signal he was ready to be pulled up by shaking the cable. Apparently, *Nail-53* dropped his radio during his excitement in searching for the hoist, because the helicopter lost voice contact with him. After a reasonable time the penetrator was raised and Ritchie moved to another spot, sending it down again. The fishing continued, but *Nail-53* was not biting. During this time the low fuel warning lights came on and Ritchie radioed the C-130 that he needed fuel. After stalling a few more minutes without a nibble he told the flight engineer to take up the penetrator because they had to get out of there. The flight engineer responded that it felt like someone was around the penetrator. Shortly thereafter came the pull-up signal. When low fuel lights come on a pilot has 15 to 20 minutes of gas left. Five minutes had already gone by since the initial warning. It took another agonizing half minute to reel in 210 feet of cable and get the survivor inside. Ritchie alerted the C-130 that his situation was critical—if he could not hit the drogue on the first try he would be in need of rescue. Under a full power surge he climbed out of the compact valley. As he cleared the ridgeline his heart was clutched by sudden fright. Something dark and massive came up under them. It was the Hercules with drogues streaming. Casey Quinn would never let a pilot run out of fuel if he could help it, and most certainly not a fellow Coast Guardsman. Ritchie ran his probe into the basket and they rose off the hilltops as one.

On that day, Quinn, who could fly the thickset cargo plane like a nimble fighter, had saved Ritchie's crew, but on another his skill saved his own crew. An F-105 had been shot down along the border of North Vietnam and Laos, just north of Mu Gia Pass. The two crewmen had ejected and touched down on North Vietnamese soil. Quinn, who was in an orbit on the Laotian side from the downed aviators, merely two to three jet minutes from the airfield at Vinh, North Vietnam, had six HH-53s and four A-1s with him when ordered to top off the helicopters with fuel in preparation for the pickup. Flying in trail, the helicopters waited their turn. One had just finished fueling when there was a horrific explosion. The Super Jolly Green Giant, hit by an air-to-air missile, disintegrated. They had been jumped by North Vietnamese MIG-21s coming up from low altitude. It was everyone for himself, but the MIGs were after the big, juicy HC-130. Quinn sent his plane diving and jinking toward earth to avoid a radar lock for their missiles. His wildly flopping drogues were ripped off among the trees. The plane took other damage, but Quinn had escaped.

The allure of an Air Force career is the chance to fly supersonic jet fighters or other challenging fixed wing aircraft. One just did not join up to fly the unglamorous eggbeater. That was for civilians—or the Army. Those who did find themselves in helicopters had been converted from fixed-wing duty or were individuals who in the Air Force's opinion were not quite good enough for anything else. Because the helicopter was perceived as a lesser aircraft, most of the pilots and the copilots in the rescue squadrons in Southeast Asia were there not by choice, but by order. Doubtless, some of them came to enjoy flying helicopters and began referring to them in a more masculine term, like "chopper," instead of the disparaging "whirlibird." Accordingly, when these aviators became acquainted with Coast Guard pilots, who not only seemed to live to fly helicopters, but who volunteered to fly combat search and rescue, they thought them wacky. One morning in particular only reinforced that perception.

At 0430, Butchka dragged himself into the shower room in preparation for the day ahead. He and Ritchie had been scheduled for strip alert, so when Loomis came in he asked him what he was doing up. Loomis explained that Ritchie had had an accident and had cut his chin pretty badly. The medics stitched him up and did not think that he would be flying. Before long, in came Ritchie, looking like the loser in a barroom brawl. He saw Loomis and asked him why he was up. Ritchie told Loomis to go back to sleep, that he was flying as scheduled. Butchka and Loomis retorted that Ritchie was not going up in his condition. About then the air base came under one of the biggest Viet Cong mortar and rocket attacks to date, sending the rest of the squadron scurrying into action or cover. But through it all, three naked Coast Guard pilots were arguing over who was and who was not flying.

Ritchie would not place his crew in jeopardy; if he said he could fly, he could. It was the same with rules; he would not bend them if it put his crew at risk. But, as rules for anything go, they are inanimate and do not flex when the condition for which they were written is not present. This happened when Ritchie landed at Nakhon Phanom with a half dozen bullet holes in the skin of the aircraft. None were critical, but this type of damage required that the helicopter be grounded for repair. Knowing they had to go out again, the flight engineer covered the holes with tape and sprayed black paint over the tape. When he and Ritchie performed a walk-around inspection the crewman remarked, "I can't find any holes, can you?"

Flight engineers were resourceful as well. One time Ritchie had to set his helicopter down on the beach because it was losing hydraulic fluid from the transmission. The culprit was a blown O-ring. Having the good fortune to be carrying Marines when this happened, they set up a perimeter guard until hydraulic fluid could be flown to them. But the fluid was useless without a new O-ring. The problem was temporarily solved when the flight engineer tore the hem off his T-shirt, shaped it into an O, and stuffed it in place. The jury-rig stemmed the leak long enough to make base.

Following the death of Lieutenant Jack C. Rittichier, from the first group, the Coast Guard's pilot volunteers list evaporated. But the Coast Guard was spared having to order non-volunteers to replace the initial deployment when these three men requested the duty: Lieutenant James M. Loomis (left), Lieutenant (j.g.) Robert T. Ritchie (center), and Lieutenant Richard V. Butchka (right). (Courtesy of U.S. Coast Guard)

People enjoy commemorating milestones that mark achievement or longevity. A married couple is proud of their 50th wedding anniversary, and a person's 100th birthday deserves notice. The rescue forces measured their milestones in lives saved. The six Coast Guard helicopter pilots of the first two exchange groups comprised only two and a half percent of the rescue pilots in Southeast Asia during that two-year period. Yet, as few as they were, they still accounted for a couple of record-setting plateaus. A few days before Christmas 1968, Eagan performed a risky hover, with his rotor blades whirring four feet from the face of a 900-foot cliff and almost his entire hoist cable played out in making the 3rd ARRGp's 1,500th save. While the commendation letters from Commander, 7th Air Force, COMUSMACV, and Commander, 3rd ARRGp praised all hands for this Air Force team achievement, those plaudits also reminded all that this milestone came courtesy of Lieutenant Lance A. Eagan of the United States Coast Guard.

The doldrums had taken up residence at the 37th ARRSq. On 15 June 1969, when the squadron had logged its 491st save, excitement began building toward getting number 500. The men could smell its nearness. But when summer ended that aroma was not much stronger. In fact, the last save, made on 8 October, was only number 497. Planes were still going down, but other squadrons seemed to be making most of the pickups. Then along came *Misty-11*.

Misty-11, an F-100 flying FAC, flamed out northeast of Saravane, Laos, forcing the two crewmen to eject. They touched down within a hundred yards of one another.

Misty-11A had a broken leg. *Misty-11B* was unhurt. Before sending in a helicopter the A-1s trolled low and slow, teasing the enemy to show themselves. Their repeated passes brought no response. Butchka, in the high bird slot orbiting at 3,000 feet, watched his roommate and liberty buddy, Captain Charles D. Langham, descend for the recovery while the Skyraiders dropped smoke along the road northwest of the survivors to shroud the rescue. Langham dropped into a hover, sending his RS down to assist *Misty-11A*. Within a minute the RS had the survivor on the penetrator. When the penetrator was 10 to 15 feet in the air Butchka saw the three sides of the blind canyon twinkling. The Skyraiders rushed in to suppress the fire, but the opening volley had shot the hoist assembly off its mounting, sending it crashing into the flight engineer's chest. He recovered, hit the switch to cut the cable, and yelled to Langham to pull off. Up above, Butchka spit out his wing tanks and went into a plunging descent of 2,500 feet per minute. Seeing Langham's aircraft smoking and throwing fluid, Butchka shouted for him to put it on the ground. Langham searched for a clear spot, flying at a hundred feet, without realizing his friend was right behind him. A mile and a half from the attack, Langham and crew jumped out of the helicopter down onto marshy undergrowth, their eyes searching upward for high bird. They did not have too far to look. Butchka's helicopter was in a 25-foot hover on the left side of Langham's, facing the same direction with its cable waiting off the nose of the wounded HH-3E. During the swift pickup Butchka's helicopter took a jolt in the right side by the load ramp that holed the skin with a gash eight inches long and two inches wide. Butchka was never sure whether it was caused by enemy fire or something else, but it was the general belief in the squadron that Butchka had moved in on his roommate so fast that Langham's rotor had not stopped spinning and that it had caused the damage. With the men safely on board, Butchka requested permission to go after the RS and *Misty-11A*, but was told to return home.

A helicopter from another squadron made three attempts to pick up the RS and injured flyer but, driven off by hostile fire each time, it finally had to withdraw because of severe battle damage. The next try fell to Ritchie. All day the helicopters had been following standard procedure by heading into the wind for the recovery. Ritchie decided to get his aircraft as light as practical by dumping fuel and approaching from downwind where the enemy would not expect him. The canyon, still smokey from the previous approaches, received another contribution from the A-1s to cover Ritchie. He went in quick. His hover lasted only a minute and the RS and *Misty-11A* were inside. Shooting had been sporadic during hover, but increased as he pulled away. He dashed over to pick up *Misty-11B*. However, the enemy was now alerted and drove him off. He started another attempt, but that was canceled because the poor visibility brought on by the thick smoke made it too hazardous to try. On his third effort, while in a hover taxi to relocate *Misty-11B,* enemy fire disabled his hoist. The flight engineer had to pull up the partially lowered cable hand-over-hand. At that point Ritchie's workday ended. He refueled and returned to Danang. *Misty-11B* was picked up by a helicopter from Nakhon Phanom, but even then a Coast Guard pilot was around. Loomis was flying high bird at the time.

At last the squadron had touched the half grand mark in saves. Most certainly, Air Force purists will not tout it, and Air Force historians will overlook it, in part because number 500 was one of the squadron's own men—largely because it was accomplished by a member of another branch of the armed forces. So it is up to Coast Guard historians to recall *Misty-11,* when, on 24 October 1969, Lieutenant Richard V. Butchka, USCG, rang up saves number 498, 499, and 500; and Lieutenant (j.g.) Robert T. Ritchie, USCG, chimed in with numbers 501 and 502.

Take a mental moment to sit on a hill and watch a helicopter hover and hoist. The endeavor looks undramatic even if it is drawing enemy fire. Now move that perch to inside the aircraft, where you have to yell to be heard over the din of engine roar and radio chatter. The helicopter, unhappy at its forced immobility, complains by vibrating, and you know that pounding against the air frame is not the wind—it is enemy rounds hitting the titanium armor. Then imagine yourself getting up every day to go to work as a professional practice target. That was the lot of a helicopter rescue crew in the Vietnam War. If that is not unnerving enough, consider what will happen to you if you are shot down, especially in Laos, where the sense of humor is grim and the taking of prisoners infrequent, where they display their contempt with acts such as tying a downed pilot to a tree, nailing his Geneva Convention card to his head, and then, after disemboweling him, leaving him with his life oozing away while his comrades helplessly circle overhead.

Where did these men get the courage to go out almost daily for a year to allow people to try killing them without defending themselves? Mixon did not know, other than to observe that some men found their strength in religion, and some found it in drink. As for motivations, they varied. For certain individuals it was just one of many military jobs they had to carry out in their career. A lot of men were driven by peer pressure: They forced themselves on to avoid the stigma of being perceived as weak. But for the most part, they were compelled by something deep within their souls echoing that human life is irreplaceable, and if at all possible, they should preserve it. Following the *Scotch-3* rescue two of the lifesavers tried to explain what they felt. While their words lack eloquence, they indicate a profound elation. Talley remarked that helping someone gave him a tremendous feeling, and Eagan's copilot, Major Robert E. Booth, said, "It was a great feeling and an exhilarating experience to take part in a rescue. It gives a person a great deal of satisfaction to know he's helped save a life."

An invisible but regular passenger in the Jollies was fear. Every time he got airborne, Butchka could not talk on the radio for the first 10 to 15 minutes, because his mouth was dry and his tongue swollen. Men came on with the dry heaves just sitting on alert. But fear can be controlled; its purpose is to alert the body's survival defenses. Once the rescue started fear got shoved under the seat to make room for professionalism, because the ultimate game was on, a frightfully deadly one called "determination." One side was determined to take the prize, and the other was determined not to let it be taken.

It is not clear how often the spoilers won, but the rescuers came away with 3,883 prizes—that is the number of lives they saved in the war.[6] War is a patchwork quilt of paradoxes. One patch is that at the same time that life is a disposable commodity, it is also to be saved at any cost. The Air Force rescue force assembled in Southeast Asia provided the world with thousands of examples of the goodness and unselfishness of humanity. The Coast Guard aviators who served on that team regarded that duty as the most fulfilling of their career. Their heroic performance brought honor upon their Service, and Coast Guard history will ever reflect that honorable action.

CHAPTER 10

Always Ready, Always Humane

Even in a democracy like the United States, where some people are immensely altruistic, the term "humanitarian" is given little thought in the context of the military. This is unwarranted, for every year service members assist communities wrecked by natural calamities and routinely perform charitable works. Similarly, their personal sacrifices as warriors often stem from a selfless free will to fight injustice. For one of the five armed forces the perception is just the opposite. A vast public segment, unaware of the United States Coast Guard's long war record, regards it solely as a rescue service. In spite of its more than two centuries of wartime gallantry, Americans, with regularity, are amazed that the Coast Guard had Vietnam War service. The Coast Guard is a truly unique government organization. Knowing how it evolved helps in understanding why this image prevails.

Coast Guard history flickered to life in the summer of 1789 when the United States government, only a few months old and in critical need of operating capital, passed a tariff act. Under British rule, sneaking goods into the country became an approved practice among colonists protesting what they regarded as unjustly exorbitant duties. Later, the British were no longer around, but the smuggling continued unabated for several reasons: it had become a way of life for many; there was apathy toward a new central government with which the citizenry had not yet established a rapport; and plain old avarice. The merchants liked the higher profits, while the consumers enjoyed relatively lower costs. As for the smuggler, he engaged in a regionally accepted vocation with no opposition at sea, and thus made a comfortable living at minimal risk.

Frustrated over the inability of the government to collect revenues, Alexander Hamilton, secretary of the republic's impoverished treasury, outlined in the spring of 1790 his plan to Congress for a fleet of ten revenue cutters to enforce customs laws. On 4 August 1790, Congress approved the building of the vessels, creating what is the present Coast Guard. Typical of this service, which defies succinct classification, it began essentially nameless, referred to only as a "system of cutters." As a result it carried many names, until the late 1800s when the designation "Revenue Cutter Service" stuck. Hamilton's sea force thwarted smuggling and the country started paying its bills. Aside from engaging smugglers these spunky sloops and schooners were the sole defenders of the coast until 1798, when the U.S. Navy came into being. In 1798 and 1799 revenue cutters and Navy ships battled French vessels during the undeclared war with France, setting the precedent whereby these sister services would team up against foes in the future.

Laden with law enforcement and military requirements, the cutters sailed into the next century and into another role. The government, realizing the large amount of time the cutters spent under way, outfitted them with rescue equipment for aiding distressed mariners. This action was prompted not so much by benevolence, but by economics. The angry Atlantic Ocean storms that disabled merchant ships, sending their valued cargoes to the bottom, were sinking the nation's economy as well. At midcentury the government started building lifeboat stations along the coast from where rescue crews could reach foundered vessels. In the 1870s these shore facilities came to be the Life-Saving Service and, like the revenue cutters, it also came under the Treasury Department. In the Twentieth Century the cutters cruised into a natural reorganization that on 30 January 1915 merged the Revenue Cutter Service and the Life-Saving Service into what we now call the U.S. Coast Guard.

Rescue at sea is true-life adventure performed by real people in an unsubmissive environment, garnished with natural drama. It commands wide attention. Moreover, when these heroics are repeated over and over by one organization, the public mind becomes conditioned that one means the other—that is, rescue means Coast Guard and Coast Guard means rescue. Any other role is just something to occupy time between saves. Some also find it hard to accept that the same individuals who are masters in search and rescue could be proficient in law enforcement and military defense. Yet, each demands the same asset—unfathomable perseverance to overcome numbing mental and physical fatigue.

Rescuers often undergo great hardship to save life. This was never truer than in the saga that started in November 1897, when winter jumped eight whaling ships with 265 men, or more, on Alaska's north coast near Point Barrow, then locking them in early ice. Provisions had been planned into December, when they intended to return to San Francisco. Now, somehow they had to survive on them until July, the soonest any supply ship might find leads through the ice. Death's spectre moved among the whalers, in no hurry to claim them. It found watching slow, painful death from starvation entertaining.

Rescue was left up to the Revenue Cutter Service. Its plan was to have the cutter *Bear* get as near as she could and then put a relief party ashore to trek overland with provisions, gathering a reindeer herd along the way to feed the trapped men. The expedition, commanded by slightly built Lieutenant David H. Jarvis, left the cutter 16 December with dog teams. The group, which included a Russian guide and two other ship's officers, one of them a doctor, had before them 1,500 miles of snow, ice, and rugged terrain to conquer. For three and one half months the party endured exhaustion, brutal winds, and temperatures that plummeted to 70 degrees below zero.

It would take a complete book to properly detail the sufferings and setbacks of the Jarvis expedition. Much of the equipment they had brought along was unsuitable for the harsh land. Their sleds were heavy and rigid and demanded 14 dogs to pull them.

The lighter sleds used by the Eskimos, strapped with seal and walrus hide to give elasticity from the pounding of rough travel, used only nine dogs. Their goatskin sleeping bags with canvas and rubber covers failed to keep out the cold, as did their dogskin and woolen clothing. For warmth, the natives used deerskin materials. Jarvis readily adjusted to conditions by learning from the natives and replaced these ill-suited items.

Three miles from where they landed was the village of Tanunak, where a Russian half-breed trader got them started for St. Michael. That initial leg exemplifies what the party endured throughout the trek. On the first day a blinding snowstorm befell them, confusing the guides on which direction to take. A wrong step and they would plummet off the 2,000-foot mountains into the sea. So steep were the slopes that the sleds could overrun the dogs. To avoid this, they unhitched the animals, wrapped chains around the runners to retard speed, climbed aboard, and rode the sleds downhill. Going up grades they often had to push the sleds or climb into harness themselves to help the dogs get over them. On the Yukon River, men, dogs, and sleds fell a foot through glaze ice to the solid ice below.

When Jarvis reached St. Michael after following a twisting course, he had traveled 375 miles, but as the crow flies he was little more than 200 miles closer to his objective. Before reaching St. Michael, Jarvis had split his party, sending the other officer to gather a provision train while he and the doctor sought reindeer. It must be noted that domesticated reindeer were in Alaska because of the Revenue Cutter Service—more exactly, due to the humanity of Captain Michael A. Healy. Healy, who spent much of his career policing the Alaska Territory in command of the cutters *Corwin* and *Bear,* had observed starvation encroaching on the natives as the unrestrained white man killed off sea creatures such as seals and walruses, the natives' food mainstays. In 1890, he met a Presbyterian missionary who had been appointed a federal agent for education among the natives and who was also concerned with the problem. Healy told him that he had seen Siberian natives living off reindeer. In agreement that it could work in Alaska they ran the *Bear* over to Siberia and brought back a dozen reindeer paid for by missionary funds. Once the government was convinced that the idea would work, federal money made future purchases and during the decade 1,100 deer rode the *Bear* from Siberia to Alaska.

On 19 January, Jarvis and the doctor reached Indian Charlie's place to acquire his 138 reindeer with a promise of replacements. Jarvis also hired the man to help drive them to Point Barrow. Leaving the doctor with the herd, Jarvis took Indian Charlie with him to find more reindeer. An American missionary, managing a reindeer herd to distribute its increase among the natives, agreed to supply 292 animals. Jarvis found others, to raise his total to 448. During the trackless drive to Point Barrow they were assailed by strong winds, snowstorms, and temperatures infrequently higher than 20 degrees below zero.

The Jarvis expedition neared the first whale ship, *Belvedere,* on 26 March. A small supply building sat on shore, with her scant provisions watched over by an armed guard. For a mile, a rope stretched across the sea ice to the ship, for use by the crew to grope their way ashore during low visibility or if calamity struck the ship without warning. They found 30 men aboard and the master seriously ill. Jarvis wrote in his log, "They couldn't believe we were real."

Three days later the reaction was the same when they arrived at Point Barrow, their destination. Jarvis, in assessing the conditions, saw that his assignment was far from over. Discipline had broken down among the sailors, who felt no longer bound to their ships, since their shipping contracts had expired. Some turned into common hoodlums, intimidating weaker sailors and abusing and looting the natives. In an abandoned building 22 feet wide by 55 feet long—the approximate dimensions of a double-wide mobile home—lived 78 men, most of them from those ships crushed by the ice. The structure contained one small window for light, and the walls were encrusted with ice. Filth and vermin clung to the men, along with a greasy soot that issued from the seal-oil lamps they burned for warmth. Some sailors were too weak to move from their bunks. Had his expedition not gotten through, Jarvis realized that when the *Bear* arrived barbarism and death might have been all that remained around Point Barrow.

In his capacity as a federal law officer in the Territory, Jarvis took charge. He sent sailors back to their ships to continue as if they were still signed on. He ordered all white men to stay out of the native villages. He solved the overcrowding by obtaining other buildings for housing and made hygienic inspections of all living quarters and ships. He enforced exercise with activities such as hunting and playing baseball on ice. He commenced a methodical slaughter of reindeer to distribute meat rations. Of the 448 deer Jarvis started with, he arrived with 382, losing the others to wolves, dogs, and exhaustion. Only one man died after the relief party arrived and that was of a heart attack.

On 28 July, the *Bear* crept to within a few miles from shore. Among those who crossed the ice with Jarvis to the vessel were 97 sailors whose ships had been lost. They were taken aboard, and shortly thereafter, when the ice relaxed for the summer, the *Bear* and the freed whaling ships departed Alaska, completing one of history's most unbelievable victories by man over adversity.

Another remarkable feat unfolded on the night of 17 February 1952 as the tanker *Pendleton* pitched and rolled toward Boston. Her master, encountering a troublesome blend of rough seas and poor visibility, decided to delay entering port until conditions improved, but they only worsened into a classic New England nor'easter. Just before 0600 the 500-foot ship took a violent lurch. She screamed, alerting the crew of her terrible agony. When the wailing stopped the fore and aft halves of *Pendleton* drifted apart. Forty miles away, in one of those inexplicable coincidences, a similar tanker, the *Fort Mercer,* also broke in two.

Chatham, Massachusetts sits on the southeast elbow of Cape Cod. On this day, the town was sprawled against the heel of land with its fingers clawed into the earth to keep the blizzard winds from throwing it into the ocean. At the Coast Guard station Boatswain's Mate First Class Bernie C. Webber made a futile attempt to shake off the frigid cold. He thought about the seas the 70-mile-an-hour winds were raising and concluded that going out on a rescue in it would be a sure trip to the grave. So, when the order came to dispatch a boat to the *Fort Mercer* a sadness fell over the station. Many believed they would never see their mates alive again.

Later, radar picked up the stern half of *Pendleton* five miles offshore. The officer-in-charge, Chief Warrant Officer Daniel W. Cluff, a stalwart Southerner, fearing that if the hulk drifted into the Chatham bar she would capsize and drown anyone aboard, turned to Bernie and drawled, "Webber, pick yourself a crew. Y'all got to take the 36500 over the bar and assist that thar ship. Ya heah?"[1] The men Bernie wanted were not around, but three young Coast Guardsmen, without hesitation, volunteered to go with him. Among them was the unit's junior engineman, and one of the two seamen was not even assigned there. He was waiting for better weather to catch a ride to his lightship out on station.

They chugged away from the dock at 1755 in menacing darkness. The wet snow and piercing cold had already penetrated through their clothing in the open cockpit. At her maximum speed of eight knots the 36-foot motor lifeboat neared the roiling bar, the first danger to clear. The men sang to bolster their courage until a mean wave kicked the boat clear of the water. She crashed down on her side. Moments after Bernie regained control another wave slammed home, breaking the windshield. Seawater rushed through the opening, knocking Bernie down and tearing the compass off its mount. There was no surcease from these batterings, which shoved the lifeboat into extreme angles, causing the engine to lose prime and quit. Each time this happened the engineman crawled into the tiny compartment to restart it. Bernie now knew what blindness must be like—his visibility was zero and he had no radar. His only navigation device was the magnetic compass. Although he had a vague idea where the ship was he did not know where he was.

Guided by a supernatural insight, Bernie dueled seas higher than the length of his craft, bringing them an hour later beneath the towering stern half of *Pendleton*. The Coast Guardsmen were overwhelmed with disappointment when no one seemed to be aboard. Then a head peered above the taffrail, and another, and another, then another. A Jacob's ladder came flying over the rail. As soon as it uncoiled against the starboard side its rungs began filling with frantic figures. Bernie's nautical instincts took over as he judged the swells to maneuver up to the undulating ladder. With each starboard roll of the ship the ladder swayed away from the hull, dipping the seaman at the bottom into the salty water. When the hull rolled back to port the ladder slapped the men against the steel. In disbelief Bernie watched an endless line of men spill off the tanker down the ladder. How many his small craft could hold he did not know, but he was not leaving anyone. Those who leaped for the lifeboat and missed were quickly grabbed from the sea by the outstretched arms of Bernie's crew.

This went on for an hour, until only one man remained, a huge individual of more than 300 pounds, and big in heart as well. It was his encouragement that had held the crew together when the disaster struck. When he jumped he missed the bouncing lifeboat but somehow managed to clutch his ship's propeller. As Bernie neared the man a wave threw his boat against the tanker. Before he could line up for another approach the derelict took a severe roll, and the large man was never seen again. Bernie could not dwell on his despair over losing the last sailor. He had 32 others to get back. Ideally, he wanted to make it to the Chatham bar, but, unsure of his location, he hoped at least to run aground close enough to shore to give each one a chance to reach land as best he could. With the seas pushing them, the ride inland was not as violent as the trip out. Again providence rode along, and the lifeboat entered Chatham as if riding a rail. Inside the station they happily learned that the other rescue crew had made it back safely, although they had not found any survivors on the bow half of the *Pendleton,* to which they were diverted. Bernie's superiors and news reporters craved details of the remarkable rescue, but they would have to wait. For him and his crew, warmth and sleep came first.

Coast Guard history bulges with records of the service's humanity as shown by Jarvis and Webber, where individuals leave behind their comfort to confront death, to help strangers. The Coast Guardsmen in Vietnam brought with them the same respect for human life. It is worth mentioning that lifesaving hero Bernie Webber served in South Vietnam with Squadron One's initial group.

Although Coast Guardsmen's roles in Vietnam were not humanitarian-centered, except for those flying combat search and rescue, they still found humane opportunities. The routine of boarding fishing junks furnished one such outlet. Fishermen disliked these interruptions, which deprived them of critical time in making the successful catches needed to feed family and bring income. Wives and children often accompanied the leather-skinned fishermen to assist with the fishing. When the Coast Guardsmen found all in order they showed their caring in small ways. Sometimes they handed out items donated from organizations in the United States: toiletries, sewing kits, clothing, and such. More often the gifts came from whatever they had handy, such as medical supplies or fruit. Upon pulling away from a junk, few Coast Guardsmen were not moved when looking back and seeing a three-year-old boy in yellow T-shirt and red shorts clutching to his chest a big apple in each miniature hand. On his face, bemusement, as his fledgling mind tried to comprehend this kindness in his war-torn world, where the opposite behavior prevailed.

The composite Coast Guard attitude toward the South Vietnamese people was that of guardian as well as ally in arms. How it regarded civilian property is an illustration. Because boardings took place around-the-clock and in varying sea states, collisions and damage occurred. When that happened, COGARDACTV made restitution to the owner.

To be sure, Coast Guardsmen were resolute in their military duty, but search and rescue aroused their juices. It was something as well-known to them as a family member or their take-home pay, which, like either of those, they could talk about for endless hours. It was the task for which they trained, practiced, and performed more than any other. So when a distress came up, large or small, it was treated like an SOS that the *Titanic* was sinking.

The *Joy Taylor* was no esteemed cruise ship, but the cargo vessel taking on water en route to Saigon from Singapore needed help quick. Fortunately, the cutter *Morgenthau*'s alert morning radio watchstanders heard her SOS on 29 December 1970. Told by *Joy Taylor* that she could not stay afloat long enough to make port, the cutter shut down her diesel engines and awakened the powerful turbines for greater speed. Four and a half hours later *Morgenthau* found the *Joy Taylor* with a severe list, 275 miles south-southwest of Saigon, struggling to reach Condore Island at six water-laden knots. Flooding at a rate of 200 gallons an hour, the master estimated he had already taken on 30 tons of water. The shifting of her ponderous oil drum cargo in the heavy seas threatened her stability. After the cutter arrived the ship began leaning even further, and stacks of drums on deck broke loose and tumbled overboard. With her decks awash she could no longer maneuver, and her time remaining on the surface ebbed away. When the master ordered his crew to abandon ship the lifeboats on the high side were unlaunchable and those on the low side unusable, so the 23 men had to leap into

Inspecting fishing junks for enemy personnel and contraband took up a lot of patrol time. Most junks carried only fishermen and their families simply making a living. To assuage the inconvenience of interrupting their fishing, Coast Guardsmen passed out medical supplies or fruit. Here a South Vietnamese boy clutches apples given him. (Photograph by author)

the sea, where the cutter's lifeboats waited to pick them up. A little later all hands watched the *Joy Taylor* roll over and drown.

Another classic sea rescue occurred nearer the coast, where, on 16 December 1967, the Philippine tug *Alyee,* towing four barges from Saigon to Cam Ranh Bay, came to trouble when whipping seas submerged the last barge. If the captain stopped to get rid of the drag, the tug and other barges would be pulled under, yet he could barely make headway. Three cutters responded to the call for help—*Half Moon, Point Cypress,* and USCGC *Point Kennedy* (WPB 82320).

For the job of cutting loose the barge, *Half Moon* sent Boatswain's Mate First Class Russell Kipkowski, Damage Controlman First Class Arley N. Hudson, and Damage Controlman Third Class Ronald J. Hessel, in the 25-foot lifeboat. They were thoroughly soaked by the 14-foot waves when the time came for Hudson and Hessel to make the dangerous leap over to the third barge, a jump they successfully made, toting a portable cutting torch. Fighting against winds trying to blow them off the slippery steel deck, they burned through the wrist-thick cable. Safely back on the *Half Moon,* Kipkowski expressed his relief by joking, "It was so rough out there that even the fish that came to the surface looked seasick." Maybe even more relieved was Felipe De Ceña, the tug's master, who closed his message of thanks with, "May the Lord bless you all."[2]

To supply the Marines at Dong Ha near the DMZ, the Navy set up Naval Support Activity Detachment, Cua Viet LST Ramp, inside the river entrance. At the ramp ships offloaded ammunition and fuel. From there they were put into smaller craft for the last seven miles of transit upriver. What had once been a secluded locale of broad empty sandy beach had become a military eyesore of wooden huts, gray machinery, and piles of crates. On 10 March 1968, the landscape got messier when five days short of a year since the first arrival of LSTs at the new facility an enemy artillery barrage hit the ammunition stacks, igniting an inferno.

It took a supreme effort by everyone to save the base from total destruction. Again, the Coast Guard came to help. The *Point Arden,* nearby on patrol, dropped off a rescue and assistance team, then joined a harbor tug and a landing craft hosing the fire at the LST ramp. While there, a huge detonation 75 yards away blew in her bridge windows and damaged her electrical, electronic, and machinery systems. South of the ramp her shore party fought flames fed by gasoline gushing from a five-inch rubber line. They succeeded in shutting off the flow and extinguishing the fire—a feat that probably saved the main ammunition dump.[3] *Point Arden* next took on the role of floating emergency room when she brought on a doctor to attend the casualties being shuttled aboard. During this time another major explosion shook the cutter, taking out her primary ship-to-shore communications. The firefighting lasted four arduous hours. Three Coast Guardsmen were wounded by flying shrapnel, but in the end the critical supply link to the Marines was saved.

Over the course of time sailors become inured to the calamities of life at sea, dealing with each event in its turn. Even the alarm of taking on water is accepted with relative calm. But one cry dissolves all composure—"Fire!" The fear of burning alive becomes greater at sea, because you are beyond anyone's help except your own. In at least two instances in Vietnam, the Coast Guard was, fortunately, on the scene when fire broke out.

On 3 August 1970, the *Yakutat* sat tight, held taut by anchor flukes hooked into the sea's bottom. Crewmen lugged shells and powder cases from the magazines into the upper handling room in preparation for the night's gunfire mission. Three thousand yards astern of her, anchored in 30 feet of water, the USS *Jennings County* (LST-846) advised that she had put out a fire in her auxiliary engine spaces and needed no assistance, but communications would be irregular as the fire had knocked out all power. A little more than an hour later she called for a dewatering pump. The cutter sent it, and, as a precaution, a rescue and assistance team packing assorted firefighting equipment. From the LST a Coast Guardsman informed the *Yakutat* by portable radio that the fire had restarted and was out of control. Furthermore, the fire pump was dead and all portable fire extinguishers used up. Moments later the *Jennings County* cried for immediate help.

The cutter sent over a second assistance crew and with disciplined haste restowed 80 rounds of ammunition and snugged anchors against the hawseholes. Upon nearing the LST the *Yakutat* men were shocked to see black smoke rising from every opening and flames licking bulkheads with the enthusiasm of a kid licking a popsicle. Withstanding blistering heat, the deck force moored the starboard side to the *Jennings County.*

In short order firefighting parties with ten hoses and men armed with portable fire extinguishers charged onto the other ship, in a scene reminiscent of buccaneer days.

Fires below deck, most especially in engine compartments, are the most grueling. In an environment of already overheated air from running machinery, fire intensifies the temperature. The closed space fills quickly with blinding, acrid smoke from burning oils and greases. Without an oxygen breathing apparatus (OBA) a crewman is incapacitated before doing any good. The searing metal gratings and decks cannot be touched without protective apparel. The firefighter encased in rubberized clothing, with face covered by an OBA mask, rapidly perspires from the exertions of hauling a water-stiffened canvas hose. The inside moisture with no outlet adds a clammy discomfort to the firefighter, who is fighting panic as well as fire. This is what the Coast Guardsmen and sailors endured until just before 0100, two and a quarter hours after the reflash, when the fire came under control.

The cutter stayed alongside *Jennings County* for the next 55 hours until a tug arrived to tow her to port. During that interval *Yakutat* dewatered her, fed both weary crews, and provided the inert ship with communications and emergency power. If it were not for the *Yakutat,* the LST would have perished. The soonest that any other help could have arrived was late the next morning.

Just after the *Point League* passed a 75-foot white-hulled South Vietnamese motor cargo junk, on 29 December 1966, flames erupted from her. The cutter came about to find four men clustered in the bow, a man swimming alongside, and three others 100 yards away clinging to floating oil drums. After picking up the swimmer the WPB skipper turned his cutter into the deep swells to slow down her lively pitch and roll. Each Vietnamese sailor jumping into the sea grabbed a Coast Guard ring buoy and by it was pulled to the cutter, where a Coast Guardsman waited in the water to help him up the side. After picking up the three at the drums the Coast Guard crew turned their attention to the fire. There their water hoses were aided by an unexpected fire suppressant source. Bubbling from the bursting bottled cargo on deck, beer foam was coating the fire. Once the topside blaze was out they entered the burning engine compartment where the problem had begun. They towed the saved vessel to Vung Tau.

In August 1966 the *Point Hudson* took part in a particularly extraordinary rescue after two fishermen in a junk wildly waved to get her attention. The men related that there had been three of them until one had taken ill and left in a U.S. Navy PCF for medical attention. They returned to their village and explained to their friend's father what had taken place. The father disbelieved their story, accusing them of murdering his son and throwing the body into the sea. Afraid for their lives, they fled to find their friend to prove their innocence. That had been three days ago. When they saw the cutter they thought of appealing to the Coast Guard for help. The Coast Guardsmen checked with the U.S. Navy and learned that the third man was in a hospital in Vung Tau. This information was relayed to the village chief, who passed the good news to the parents, thereby averting a bizarre tragedy.

Coast Guardsmen brought their compassion ashore as well. Upon learning that the inhabitants of the scattered islands in the Gulf of Thailand drank contaminated water, they gave the matter collective thought and came up with a plan that sent a contingent of them off to Hon Thom, an island not far south of Division Eleven, to try out their idea. They dug a trench perpendicular to an underground water flow. Leaving the end near the water open, they enclosed the rest in concrete. At the opposite end they erected a storage tank, connecting it to the concrete trench with a three-inch-diameter pipe. Small stones were placed in the bottom of the tank for filtration, resulting in a steady, non-contaminated water supply. News of this success reached another island, where water came from what could be collected from rainfall or brought in from other places. The inhabitants asked the Coast Guard to teach them how to build a well. Working side by side with the villagers the Coast Guard had a functioning water supply going in six days.

Wherever the men of the Coast Guard saw poverty, they saw human beings in need and tried somehow to make life for them a little better, if just for the moment. It was the ragged, smiling, playful children that touched their hearts the most. Consequently, homemade playground sets began to appear in rural communities, such as the one constructed onboard *Chase* by their damage control force and placed in the Vietnamese Navy compound at Coastal Group 16. The 50 children living there were delighted with their gift, which had a slide, seesaw, jungle gym, and four swings. At an old church building seven miles from Vung Tau, Lieutenant James F. Hunt of Division Thirteen was moved to act by the ordeal of a Catholic nun and 82 orphans. Four months earlier she had been running an orphanage of 200 children in Kien Hoa Province until the Viet Cong moved in and set up anti-aircraft batteries around the building to fire at American aircraft. The aircraft fired back. After a time the Viet Cong drove off the nun and the remaining children—those who had survived the bombings and who were not 13 and older. The latter were kept with the guerrillas. The sister started the trek with 100 children and 20 pounds of rice to feed them. In three days they covered nearly 60 miles over rugged country before reaching safety, but 18 children had died or were lost along the way. Seeing these orphans in garments that would more aptly be called shredding, Hunt began writing Coast Guard wives' clubs, church organizations, and individuals in the United States asking for donations. A plentiful response brought in clothing, diapers, new and used soap (Coast Guard wives had gone into hotels and motels asking for their partially used soap bars), and even money. The goods were delivered to the orphanage by Division Thirteen men, and some of them became regular visitors during their infrequent time off just to talk to and play with the children.

The most recurring benevolence came in the form of medical care rendered by an effort called Medical Civil Action Program (MEDCAP). The Squadron Three cutters, with their doctors and hospital corpsmen, were best equipped to treat a range of ailments. Village "house calls" soon became a normal inclusion on patrol and a statistic in a ship's deployment summary. *Morgenthau*'s concluding figures listed 25 MEDCAPs treating more than 2,500 patients. This people-to-people endeavor was taken seriously. The USCGC *Taney* (WHEC-37) left her doctor in Qui Nhon when the ship left for Sasebo, Japan for shipyard maintenance. While she was gone he organized 16 MEDCAPs treating more than 3,200 villagers, plus another 300 patients in hospitals. Sometimes these good deeds brought other benefits. After two medical visits by *Half Moon*'s crew to a fishing village, where they gave leprosy and tuberculosis cases palliative treatment, started a basic hygiene program, supplied salves for fungal infections, and furnished vitamins for the children, the U.S. Navy patrols in that area subsequently reported the fishermen less reticent about passing along information regarding Viet Cong activities.

One of the most organized of the hospital corpsmen performing MEDCAPs was Chief Hospital Corpsman Joseph White, who prepackaged his pharmaceuticals with labels written in Vietnamese and code numbers so he knew what was in each one. Therefore, if he wanted to dispense aspirin to be taken in twos every four hours he reached for the container bearing his number for that dosage. His patients did not always consume his medications, because of a religious taboo, but they retained them in prominent view as a status symbol. Periodically, his prepacked drugs fell into enemy hands, and when later found some great distance away they yielded useful information about Viet Cong troop movements. Suspicion or diffidence usually greeted the first visit to a village. After explaining their presence, the Coast Guardsmen would set up a table in the open and wait for curiosity to prevail. Eventually someone came forward, a cut would be cleaned and bandaged, then another would take the chance, and before much longer it was just like any visit to a medical clinic—long lines and long waits.

On the southwest side of the Viet Cong–held Ca Mau Peninsula, a few miles inland from where the Ong Doc River spills into the Gulf of Thailand, Song Ong Doc fidgeted between attacks. This pro-government village of 3,000 people pushed up against the north bank of the river was like a young goat surrounded by grown alligators—a temptation too great to ignore. Many of its residents had been brought out of Viet Cong–controlled hamlets to live in this mythically secure community. To sift out any lingering Viet Cong sympathies, people were housed in sections according to the length of time they had been away from guerrilla contact. Protecting Song Ong Doc was no easy task for a half dozen American advisors and 120 regional force soldiers. The latter, having their families living with them, had added incentive to protect the town. The Viet Cong prowled freely to the north, east, and south across the river. This hazard brought *Market Time* units into a long relationship with Song Ong Doc. In the beginning Coast Guard and Navy inshore patrol craft used their limited firepower to turn back incursions.

Then along came Squadron Three. The first big cutter assigned to the gulf sector, Area 9B, was the *Bering Strait*. Her officers met with Major Wayne B. Laverty, the senior U.S. Army advisor at Song Ong Doc, who explained his layout: on the north and east a few hundred yards of marshiness, then a dirt bank with outpost bunkers, 70 yards beyond that a barbed-wire belt, followed by a quarter mile clearing of forest. On the south the narrow river kept the enemy at bay. With the Viet Cong in control of the land, entry into Song Ong Doc was limited to boat or helicopter. Laverty was heartened when advised of the destructive force that the ship's deck gun could deliver at long ranges. The news that a floating artillery battery would be looking out for them was most welcome. When the *Bering Strait* crew saw the advisors' spartan existence and lack of essential military equipment, they constructed them a barbecue grill and a stand for their heavy machine gun. It was then that Laverty began to comprehend how self-supporting a ship was, where wood and metal scrap could be fashioned into something useful. The major, who cared a great deal for the South Vietnamese people, began inviting the Coast Guardsmen ashore for orientation, while at the same time nudging their innate goodness toward village needs.

What they saw was a remote dirt clearing in a sparsely populated jungle peninsula where men struggled to raise families with the interference of impromptu mortar and small arms fire. Its lone overworked generator quavered in pushing electricity into frail, crowded dwellings. The only representation of modern times was military hardware. What they smelled was raw sewage, dead fish, and pungent spices. Even under these desperate conditions the people radiated an uncommon cheerfulness. This "don't feel sorry for me" philosophy played a part in bonding the Coast Guard and Song Ong

Doc together. The Vietnamese liked the sincere attention, and the crews enjoyed the stopovers as a diversion from patrolling rigors. But moreover, the war that had seemed so abstract from sea now had a face—and a meaning.

The *Androscoggin* crew took on the role of close relatives, a shipload of uncles and cousins who, when in the neighborhood, dropped by for a visit. This was fairly frequently, for the ship spent all or part of four of her five Vietnam patrols in Area 9B. Her first time off—Song Ong Doc—began as it went for all cutters. The advisors and district chief were invited aboard for a meal, where everyone became acquainted and discussed the current military situation. The conversation moved on to how the crew might be of service to the village. This was 21 December 1967, so naturally a children's Christmas party topped the list.

At 0915, on the day before Christmas, the commanding officer, three officers, and eight enlisted men loaded down with 500 boxes of candy and 45 gallons of ice cream piled into two PCFs for their first look at Song Ong Doc. Forty-five minutes later community and military leaders, village elders, all the school's teachers, and selected children greeted them at the landing with speeches and letters. An attractive lei of paper flowers was placed around the commanding officer's neck, and the next senior officer also received a lei, but one half as large. The difference was not lost on the commanding officer, who wrote of the matter, "These people have one of the most sensitive perceptions of the nuances of protocol I have ever seen."[4]

As a swarm they moved up the stony unpaved lane, passing beneath a large banner propped up by slender wood poles. The sign, in neatly printed capital letters, read, "Welcome the captain and the crew of the 'Coast Guard 68' to Song Ong Doc."

Looking around, the Coast Guardsmen saw an architectural museum collection. Had they been taking this walk in the previous century nothing would have appeared out of time: primitive huts of stalks and leaves, simple square lodgings of boards and discarded wood, and single-story French colonial buildings with white masonry walls and louvered shutters covering glassless windows, such as the school the entourage was about to pour into. A long veranda dressed the 20-foot-wide schoolhouse. From inside the building that ran back 100 feet came the muted buzz of hundreds of children talking. The gushing welcome that began at the river continued with more speeches until it came time for the children to act. One by one they stepped up to the head table, some in slow shyness, some with the quick step of bravado. Each delivered a handwritten Christmas greeting to the captain, who thanked them in Vietnamese. Next the ice cream and candy were passed out. Outdoor game competition followed. Watching kids with their legs stuffed in burlap bags hop to the finish line brought merriment to the onlookers. The Coast Guardsmen took part in handing out prizes to the winners.

Their day continued with a tour of the advisory team compound and then a grand lunch arranged by the district chief. Although the cuttermen had taken their places at the two long tables with some trepidation when they failed to recognize some of the food, they did not leave hungry. The opening course consisted of pieces of raw fish, which they picked up with chopsticks and dipped into boiling spiced water, then dabbed the now cooked fish into a bean sauce and ate it with wild mint leaves. A feast of fried shrimp, fried fish (with heads), and baked chicken, all of which they topped with nuoc mam, the fermented fish sauce, followed. But they were not done; the main course had not yet been served. When it arrived it proved to be rice with chicken and a fiery pepper sauce. Fortunately, plenty of Vietnamese beer was on hand to cool the palate. If there were any more courses simmering in the kitchen, the Americans were spared further assault on their stomachs with the timely arrival of a chaplain, who was delivered by armed helicopter to hold church services.

The festivities did not slow down after services, for it was time for the village sampan race, a popular and serious event. The seagoing men appreciated the verve of the winner, who got all he could from his craft, which sank crossing the finish line. *Androscoggin*'s crew entered into competition of their own, taking on the locals in volleyball. These Vietnamese were good. The Coast Guardsmen won one of the three games, but they sensed that maybe Oriental manners played a part in that single victory. At 1830, all hands were back aboard the cutter, weary but content.

For the remainder of the patrol the *Androscoggin* shared her time between improving village life and fighting its enemies. Shore details painted the schoolhouse and the medical staff held sick call. It was well for one fishermen with a gangrenous finger that the ship's doctor was available to amputate it, saving his arm and ultimately his life. The gun crew kept busy pounding Viet Cong positions around Song Ong Doc. Two Viet Cong companies were discovered northeast of the village on 3 January 1968. Under the guidance of a spotter plane the cutter devastated the target with 100 percent coverage. The effort resulted in several secondary explosions and a compliment from the FAC, who remarked that in his six months in Vietnam he had not seen a prettier shoot.

Six months later, not long before she was scheduled to depart Vietnam, *Androscoggin*'s crewmen were back inside the schoolhouse as guests for graduation ceremonies where they witnessed the custom of rewarding the graduates with school supplies, an incentive for students to keep up their studies over the summer. Everything proceeded in dignified order until the Coast Guard began passing out their presents—400 dolls and 400 yo-yos.

This was what it was like between the Coast Guard and Song Ong Doc, a microcosm of an idealized tie between the governments of the United States and the Republic of Vietnam. Each cutter contributed to Song Ong Doc in a tangible way, most leaving behind some visible remembrance. The playground equipment in the schoolyard boasted that it was presented by the *Barataria*. The *Androscoggin* had a brass bell made in Hong Kong and presented it to the school engraved that it came from the ship's crew. The men on the *Dallas* built the village a new dispensary. The mental imprints left upon the villagers' minds were, without argument, worthy ones. In this obscure freckle on the planet, Americans and Vietnamese exhibited how easily diverse cultures could get along.

Desk duty in Saigon could not suppress the humanitarian soul of the headquarters' staff. It too found ways to reach out with kindness. A usual city sight were groups of roaming boys scrounging for survival, most orphaned, some from families too impoverished to provide for them. Filthy, diseased, and wearing tatters, these urchins were one of those annoyances that city dwellers endured by ignoring it. But Loforte could not. Bothered by this dead-end existence, he stuffed the staff microbus with first-aid supplies and, each evening after work in the parking lot outside his quarters, he opened an urchin clinic, patching cuts and treating sores. Before long, every week or so the kids were whisked off to a Vietnamese dispensary for showers, a fill-up on vitamin pills, and proper medication, especially for scabies, a highly contagious skin infection

The Coast Guard's headquarters staff in Saigon took special interest in the city's street kids. After the boys' shower, Captain William N. Banks helps one of them into clothing provided by the staff. (Courtesy of U.S. Coast Guard)

caused by a mite that troubled all the kids with its maddening itch. Guardianship of the "dead-end kids" continued to expand. After dispensary visits they were dressed in clothing from stateside donations. Haircuts were arranged. A laundress was found to wash towels and clothes. They were taken on picnics and to sights such as the Saigon Zoo. The Coast Guardsmen attempted to make their lives less dreadful, even though it exacted great patience when the kids they left clean and freshly clothed often returned from their punishing street life grimy and in rags.

When the men on the USCGC *Point Young* (WPB 82303) reached into their wallets to send a generous donation to a U.S. Navy chaplain in Saigon for use in his charitable work among the Vietnamese, that small thoughtfulness blossomed into the Coast Guard's most noble humanitarian undertaking in Vietnam. The chaplain, impressed by this spontaneous magnanimity, went to Loforte to discuss with him where the money might be best used. The chaplain suggested that Loforte visit an elementary school for girls as one possibility. Little girls soften up even the most hardened of men, but nothing wrings more tenderness from a man than a charming blind girl, and Loforte, who was far from being hard-hearted, found himself among 20 of them.

On his way back from the school his mind swirled with thoughts of helping that went beyond the *Point Young* donation. Much was needed: living conditions were primitive and basic school materials were in short supply. True, the government allotted the school eight dollars a month for each girl up to age 16, and sporadic donations came in from diverse sources, but it did not even come near to providing food and clothing. As for medical and dental care, it was nonexistent. Still, as critical as these physical items were, they could be addressed with money.

Something more compelling was possessing Loforte: a recognition in these castoff, sightless human beings, the desperation for what money cannot purchase—companionship and affection. Back in the office an idea came to him. He spread word to the Coast Guardsmen in Vietnam about the Saigon Blind School for Girls, explaining that all the girls were totally blind, most since infancy. They came from families without means to support them and from orphanages. Normally 18 to 20 girls, ranging in ages from 6 to 14, lived there during the school year. The girls that went on to high school in the city, but who had no home, were allowed to continue to live there. He pitched them the notion of "adopting" the school and received overwhelming response in favor of it. Volunteer donations of 50 cents a man each month were suggested, and the basic plan was to provide whatever seemed most needed with the funds available.

An early addition to the school was a large electric range to replace the tired old kerosene one. The absence of electric refrigeration limited the food that could be kept on hand, until the Coast Guard bought a modern refrigerator. These appliances were purchased in Thailand and Japan and brought over by most expedient means, such as the automatic washing machine, which made the trip in the hold of an ammunition ship. Coast Guardsmen passing through the city stopped in on the girls and just about every Sunday afternoon members from the Saigon staff visited. Upon their arrival they would be surrounded by girlish giggling and chatter. With inquiring fingers the girls would trace across the faces, arms, and chests of the men, seeking out distinguishing features to identify them by. The girls found the visits ideal for practicing English. Sometimes they were taken to a swimming pool. Even though they could not swim, they still enjoyed splashing in the water. Clothing and other necessities donated from Coast Guard Wives Clubs poured in. One batch of the materials hitched a ride in the aircraft taking the Coast Guard commandant on an inspection tour of his Southeast Asian forces. Every year, the Coast Guard put on a Merry Christmas party and the girls entertained with a play and song.

The health of the girls was always on the minds of the men. With the high cost of medical and dental checkups beyond their—and the school's—financial reach, they kept alert for the means to obtain the care. For example, they befriended a small group of American nurses affiliated with USAID who helped arrange for inoculations and examinations. Once they persuaded a Navy doctor to go out to the school and give each girl a physical examination. A military dentist visiting Saigon from Nha Bhe ended up spending his Saturday afternoons giving dental care at the school. When, after three weeks, he had to return to Nha Be without treating all the girls, the relentless Coast Guard benefactors transported them to his clinic until all the teeth involved were extracted, filled, or cleaned. Eventually they found a Vietnamese woman who had received her dentistry training in the United States, and persuaded her to give regular dental treatment at a much lower cost than her normal rates. In her goodness, she continued treating the girls without immediate payment, knowing that when the monthly donations caught up with the bill she would be paid.

When the Coast Guard was notified that 13-year-old Tram Thi Hue might see if given a corneal transplant, it jumped into action to make it happen. A transplant needs to be done within a short time frame to be useful. With the replacement cornea coming into Saigon from out of the country, precise flight connections were needed to get it and the girl to the Navy hospital ship offshore where the operation was to occur. To facilitate this, interservice aircraft hops were prearranged. Every time Tram Thi Hue, accompanied by Lieutenant Richard E. Ahrens of COGARDACTV, touched down, another aircraft was waiting to fly them to the next point. At Danang, they were met by Lieutenant Rittichier, who flew them to the hospital ship in an Air Force Jolly Green Giant. In a few days the corneal transplant was shuttled to sea the same way. Although the operation did not succeed, everyone felt better for trying, and it demonstrated how committed the Coast Guard was to those girls.

A major goal of the blind girls project was to send a top student to school in the United States. The institution they had in mind was the prestigious Perkins School for the Blind in Watertown, Massachusetts, just west of Boston. The school prepared blind children to enter society as independent and contributing citizens. Besides academics, the curriculum included grooming habits, manners, and other social and recreational skills. The school had links with Vietnam, for it was where the sighted Vietnamese woman in charge of the Saigon school had studied to teach the sightless. It also was where staff officer Lieutenant Commander Richard A. Bauman's aunt had gone to learn braille after her vision had diminished to a fifth of what was normal. Fourteen-year-old Nguyen Thi Chien, who had been a student at the blind school for seven years and had just completed her first year of high school with academic honors, was chosen. Communications were opened with Perkins seeking a scholarship for Chien. In July 1967, after a series of correspondence with the school's administrators, word came that she would be given a full-residence, $5,000-a-year scholarship, if the Coast Guard would pay her transportation, her incidental expenses at school, and provide a sponsor while she was in the country.

Obtaining admission to the school turned out to be a pleasant endeavor, much like eating ice cream, compared to obtaining permission for Chien to leave the country, an iffy struggle much like chewing overcooked liver. One Coast Guard officer observed that the French handed down two legacies to the Vietnamese: the baking of French bread akin to the best made in Paris, and a bureaucracy second to none. Banks, who picked up where Loforte left off, expressed his frustration with this 17–23 July 1967 unit diary entry:

> ...the procedure here for obtaining an exit visa belongs to another world. After 17 visits to various agencies, the end is still not in sight and we are by no means certain we are on the right road.

The process began with a visit to the U.S. Consul to ask advice while delivering Chien's acceptance letter from Perkins. Told that they faced a big hurdle in obtaining a Vietnamese passport and exit visa, the Coast Guardsmen nonetheless pushed the throttle full ahead and steamed into unknown waters. The first thing to do was to get her certified as healthy. So they ran her through the medical and dental gauntlet. It did not matter that she was blind, she was still draft-eligible, meaning she had to get clearance from the defense authorities.

At the Ministry of Education they came up against a miasma of disinterest toward letting the girl go. They beat down this resistance with written approval from scores of

A proud accomplishment for the Coast Guard came when 14-year-old blind
Nguyen Thi Chien was put aboard an airplane to fly to the United States
to continue her education at the Perkins School for the Blind.
(Courtesy of U.S. Coast Guard)

titled officials and through the informal influence of individuals with connections at the ministry. Now, with their paper-bulging portfolio they merrily strolled into the police station to apply for the passport, expecting to leave with it that day. Sorry. After a dozen return visits, it seemed everyone in the department, even the janitor, scrutinized the papers. Finally they were informed that they still needed a letter from the Ministry of Security. No problem. In a couple of days they returned to the police station with the requested letter, where they were given another broadside. The endorsement stipulated that the police investigate Chien's parents before she could leave the country. Well, no one had seen Chien's parents, who had lived up near the DMZ in enemy-held territory for eight years. It appeared that a technicality had torpedoed their dream. The Vietnamese did not go in for waivers in the routine course of business, and Chien's blindness did not seem to reduce her as a potential security risk. The Coast Guardsmen trudged back to the Ministry of Security, pestering for another audience with the Adjutant General. Although their Western affrontery angered the bureaucrats, their request was passed along. A further face-to-face meeting was not necessary: shortly thereafter, a paper came back with the seal and signature of the ranking official over the words, "Chien, The Blind Girl, Exception." The police issued the documents allowing her departure, but this was not the end of the matter. A week later, it was noticed that her exit visa was only good for 15 days. This meant that it would expire seven days before her flight. An extension was granted, but only after several days of uncertainty and worry when they had to leave the passport overnight with the police.

At last, the hoped-for day arrived. A big gathering of Coast Guardsmen, teachers, classmates, and friends said goodbye to Chien on 26 August 1967 as she stepped into the commercial airliner. Only eight passengers were aboard, and she deservedly received special attention from the crew. Loforte, by then retired and living in Hawaii, met her at the airport in Honolulu, where the airplane had a four-hour layover. To keep Chien company he brought along a group of Vietnamese students.

A week and a half before Chien took off from Saigon, Priscilla C. Banks, the wife of the Coast Guard Activities, Vietnam, commander, received a letter from her husband that announced, "Congratulations! You have been made the Resident Sponsor for Chien during her planned three year course of instruction at Perkins." The letter gave the time and day that Chien would be landing in Portland, Maine, which was near their summer cottage, where she would spend a week until staff officer Bauman's parents came up from Boston to take her to start school 5 September. The letter included a check to buy clothing for the girl. Chien's airplane circled the airport for 45 minutes until the fog lifted enough for it to land. Some spectators may have wondered why the Vietnamese girl was wearing sunglasses in this mist, but not the welcoming party, which included men from the South Portland Coast Guard Base, of which several were Vietnam veterans. Chien, who would take the name Maria, walked into their embrace and began her American experience.

Many Coast Guardsmen reached out to the Vietnamese. There was Lieutenant (j.g.) Milton C. Richards Jr., a quiet spoken Virginian who saw how desperately poor these people were and wanted to do something for them. He expressed his wish to help the villagers of Cat Lo to his good friend, a South Vietnamese Navy warrant officer, and they came up with the idea of giving English language classes. Therefore, when Richards was not on duty at Division Thirteen or filling in for an officer on patrol, he teamed with his Navy friend teaching English to the Vietnamese.

In September 1968, Petty Officer Carlton C. Richards's tour in Vietnam was over, but not behind him. Beguiled by a five-year-old girl in a Saigon orphanage, he wrote his wife about little Nguyen Thi Nam and they agreed to adopt the child. However, he was unable to complete the tedious, lengthy proceedings during his tour. A fellow Coast Guardsman still in Vietnam picked up where his buddy left off and dealt with lawyers, embassy officials, and government authorities to bring about a happy ending in July 1969, when the little girl landed in the United States and into the arms of new parents.

The Coast Guard's motto of *Semper Paratus*—"Always Ready"—is uncertain in origin. It may well have been a phrase spouted in a ripe moment that caught on, to be uttered whenever unexpected orders appeared sending men into detestable tasks. Captain Francis Saltus Van Boskerck, who received his commission in the Revenue Cutter Service on 20 May 1891, recalled it being the service's watchword for as long as he could remember. It gained official recognition in 1910, when it appeared on the Coast Guard ensign. Van Boskerck heightened recognition of the motto by writing the music and the lyrics to *Semper Paratus,* which went on to become the service's marching song and anthem. While *Always Ready* flawlessly defines the United States Coast Guard, a subtitle could well be added—*Always Humane.*

CHAPTER 11

GQ!

"C'MON, THEY GOT THE CHIEF!" These words from the petty officer bursting into the cabin jerked the *Point Orient*'s executive officer awake and sent him charging up to the bridge. There he learned that the commanding officer and the chief engineman had taken off in the Boston Whaler smallboat for three sampans at the river mouth of a restricted zone. When it neared the sampans the Vietnamese threw themselves down and heavy fire from three shore positions intersected at the small boat. The *Point Orient* quickly closed with her machine guns blazing, allowing the Whaler to get clear of the morning ambush, but the chief was dead.

That's how it went on the inshore patrol, where death and pain lacked the courtesy of announcing their visits. At night, when the senses expect trouble, such rudeness was tolerable, but during daylight, when tranquil blue water was caressing lazy sandy beach under a cloudless sky, the intrusion of ripped flesh seemed irreverent.

Of all units in *Market Time,* the inshore vessels faced the greatest peril. Unlike the aircraft and offshore ships, largely safeguarded by distance, every day they navigated among the furtive adversary. Without a doubt each WPB and PCF hull merited a Purple Heart medal. For their crews there was no such thing as being safe, just fortunate. Unlucky, early in 1966, was the PCF that taught the tragic lesson that booby traps were not just a soldier's care when she came upon a Viet Cong flag flapping from a bamboo pole attached to a wooden raft. The men showed good sense by tossing grenades around the object, believing that they would detonate any hidden explosive. Nonetheless, as a sailor cut away the souvenir a blast occurred, killing four of the six men and sinking the boat. Someone on shore happily watching the sailors take the bait had electrically set off a mine.

Armed with multiple .50-caliber machine guns, the inshore craft could mince most targets, but their remarkable mortar transformed them into slight but formidable gunboats. While it took hundreds of machine gun rounds to reduce a target, it only took one mortar shell an instant to splatter that same objective.

Three types of the 81-mm-diameter, two-foot-long mortar shell were carried: high-explosive, illumination, and white phosphorus—the latter for creating smoke or setting fires. The fuzes used were point-detonating, time, and proximity. The tripod-mounted Mark 2, Model 0 naval weapon could be swiveled from one side of the vessel to the other and raised up and down just as a machine gun. Unlike a conventional dropfire land mortar, which is basically a tube closed at one end with a nail in the bottom to ignite the round, this version could be trigger-fired as well, giving it the capability of shooting from nearly horizontal, a tactical plus in close combat, especially against another vessel. Indispensable for coastal operations and regarded highly safe, it did bring unexpected grief. The first time was in October 1966. During NGFS a high-explosive shell in the mortar barrel of PCF-9 blew up, killing three sailors and seriously injuring two others. Then, in March 1967, during a practice shoot, the mortar on PCF-39 exploded, taking one life and maiming three men. It was to happen once more, this time in August 1969 to the *Point Arden* during a harassment and interdiction shoot. Dead were the executive officer and the engineman first class.

It was commonly believed within the WPB and PCF divisions that firing the mortar with two rounds in the barrel would blow up the gun. This was founded on the assumption that when the fuze of the bottom round crushed against the one on top of it all fuze safety features to prevent an in-bore detonation were overridden. So convinced that double loads were the cause of these mishaps, mortar crews had little fear for their own safety. They just tried to avoid a double-round firing. On the *Point Dume,* when the "resume fire" order was given following a short pause, a round was dropped into the tube. But before being triggered, one of the gun crew asked if anyone remembered the previous round being fired. No one was sure. To check it the barrel was tapped against its depression stops and out jiggled two shells.

Of course there were investigations. Tests were made. Theories were advanced. A problem with proving or disproving the double-load conviction was that the survivors could not attest with certainty whether or not this was done. One theory offered by ordnance experts was that a burning ember in the barrel set off the propellent bags in the high-order (rapid rise in pressure) explosion needed to set off the main charge. This cookoff supposition appeared to be disproved in a locally conducted test, and in combat against a North Vietnamese trawler when the *Point Orient,* while trigger-firing rounds every eight seconds, had three of them go off by themselves because of embers and heat inside the barrel. A Royal Australian Navy explosives specialist who ran experiments with fuzes was adamant that a double load would not cause the gun to blow up.

This was somewhat substantiated on one cutter when a round dropped into the barrel went off upon hitting the point of one already there without causing any trouble. The most likely culprit in the exploding barrel disasters was deteriorated powder in the booster charge. Tests conducted on the same lot of rounds that were used in the PCF-39 mishap showed some breakdown in the powder of the 1955-manufactured ammunition. This would increase the powder's sensitivity to shock, bringing about a premature explosion.

Obviously, the enemy was totally unsympathetic in this matter, as they were doing their best to take out these inshore pests with recoilless rifles or any weapon on hand with a chance of striking home. One Viet Cong sniper's bullet, at the extreme range of

1,900 yards, creased the finger of the chief boatswain's mate on the USCGC *Point Garnet* (WPB 82310), and then buried itself in one of his legs. Another long-distance rifle shot wounded the commanding and executive officers on the USCGC *Point Ellis* (WPB 82330). The bullet struck aluminum window molding on the starboard side of the bridge, causing the copper jacket and lead to separate. The copper piece traveled across the bridge, hitting the commanding officer in the forearm, while the slug went through the executive officer's arm and entered his shoulder, where it deflected off the flak jacket armor into his body, stopping in his spine, and bringing paralysis to his legs. Doctors successfully operated on this serious wound, and the officer was soon back patrolling.

The "frontiers of the United States extend to every hostile shore," wrote Captain LeRoy Taylor, USN, in 1960.[1] As head of the Foreign Weapons Production Branch in the Office of the Chief of Naval Operations, he was mindful that armed conflicts involving coastal nations obliged American vessels to work a tight shoreline and criticized his service's failure in developing this capability. He wanted the Navy to build boats 80 to 100 feet in length, drawing six to seven feet of water. Ironically, what he described was already under construction, but for a naval relative—the United States Coast Guard.

The Coast Guard's deteriorating wood hull 83-footer fleet needed replacement (60 vessels of this class participated in the Normandy Invasion of World War II). Sought was a cutter that could operate under all weather conditions close to shore or out at sea, yet be economical to build and maintain. Her primary missions would be search and rescue and law enforcement, but, should war come along, she would be expected to confront and defeat an enemy. The result was an 82-foot steel-hulled craft with an aluminum superstructure that could stay at sea unreplenished for a week and cruise a thousand miles. Designed by Coast Guard naval engineers, with valuable input from the men who operated such craft, the cutters were built at the Coast Guard's Curtis Bay shipyard outside of Baltimore, Maryland. They would become outstanding seafarers in peace and in war.

Because 60 percent of the expense of running a cutter went for crew pay and allowances, the naval architects kept features simple and central to keep crew size low. This was evident on the bridge, with its 360-degree view of the deck. Up there, the operator, from the adjustable helmsman chair before a truck-type steering wheel equipped with power steering, could start the engines, manipulate the throttles, peer into the radar, talk on the radio, observe the fathometer, read navigation indicators, and reach above to rotate the searchlight. A panel on the bridge with red and green lights monitored the condition of the engineering plant, precluding the need to have someone in the engine room all the time. So well-conceived was the design that just four people could run the 82-footer. But because of the practical need of resting watchstanders, a modest complement of eight was settled upon, with berthing for 13 to accommodate passengers and wartime manning.

Among the cutter's notable features were transom exhausts, eliminating the bulky conventional smokestack and seven sealed-beamed lights (three on each side, and one aft) recessed into the hull and useful at night for picking up survivors and close-in maneuvering. Two diesel engines transferred 600 horsepower to each of the twin screws. If a propeller became damaged it could be easily replaced while the boat sat in the water. The addition of a three-knot creep speed was ideal for conserving fuel on lengthy patrols. Designed to run at 18 knots, she ostensibly lost one knot under the tonnage added for Vietnam duty—although in a speed trial dash back to Danang from patrol, the *Point Dume* logged 19 knots.

The domestic duty 82-footer spent 25 percent of her time at sea. The wartime WPB pushed that figure to 70 percent. In three years of stateside duty, one cutter totaled 2,905 underway hours, while in Vietnam that same vessel logged 3,880 hours at sea in just nine months.

The 82-footer was lively. So much so, that when moored, the wake from a passing skiff had the crew lifting their plates from the table to keep the food from rolling off. In her short life before going to Vietnam, the craft was repeatedly praised for her foul weather endurance. A typical report came from one entering the North Carolina coast at Cape Fear River amid 35-knot winds and 15- to 20-foot seas. The vessel broached and lay on her side for 20 seconds before snapping upright. The phlegmatic officer-in-charge wrote in the log, "Everything OK. These boats are well built and could probably weather almost anything."[2] Up to January 1964, the 82-footers went identified only by hull number. Then, esteem was added to their personality when they were given the names of land points. It was cutter 82329 that had the 90-degree lay down off North Carolina. She became the *Point Welcome*.

Changing the peacetime 82-footer into a war craft was as simple as changing a mild chili con carne recipe into one spicy hot by adding a few ingredients. The zesty additions were large-bore weapons, plenty of ammunition, a variety of radio frequencies, and three crewmen. Normally run by a chief and first class petty officer, for overseas duty two commissioned officers took over respectively as captain and executive officer. To care for the ordnance a gunner's mate became the third added member. The average age of the crews on the 26 Vietnam WPBs was, appropriately, 26. This gave the boats an ideal warrior blend of youthful passion and ripening good sense.

Skippers for the 82-footer were solicited from regular officers, essentially graduates of the Coast Guard Academy presently commanding 95-foot patrol boats. Executive officer slots went to qualified reserve officers, those men commissioned through other programs, such as Officer Candidate School. A number of them rose to WPB command during their combat tour. Officer and enlisted billets were filled by volunteers. If openings exceeded volunteers the best qualified were chosen. The Coast Guard was earnest in sending its best to Vietnam. To underscore this policy Headquarters included the following admonition in its solicitation directive:

> The arduous duty requirements can bring out the worst aspects of character in socially disoriented individuals, the alcoholic, the authority flaunters and the rebellious. The WPB's spend over 70% of their time at sea. During inport periods there is little or no shore leave. Explosive Loading Detachments work 12 to 20 hours a day. Every Coastguardsman in Vietnam is on a 7-day work schedule, with 12 hours a day the rule rather than the exception. The emotionally immature individual and personnel who are disciplinary problems are placed in almost continuous position of unrelenting stress for a year. The physically deficient are taxed to their extreme. It is therefore imperative that transferring authorities carefully screen all personnel prior to transfer to insure

that individuals with histories of hardships, physical disabilities, or repeated disciplinary offenses are not transferred to Vietnam. The unusually arduous nature of duty in Vietnam is a reality which requires the highest caliber of individual to successfully accomplish the Coast Guard's mission.

While a WPB crewman felt proud in belonging to Squadron One and held similar feelings for his Division, he boasted most about his cutter. Where family members are bonded by blood, these men living in close quarters, sharing sea duty hardships, and meeting combat dangers together formed a kinship perhaps closer than found in family. While on liberty they took any slur or criticism against their cutter as a personal attack. They defended any shipmate's wayward behavior without hesitation as one brother to another. Even though each boat performed the same job, that inherent human instinct, competitiveness, thrived between vessels. Each man believed his boat did her tasks better than any other. This feeling penetrated so deeply that when another cutter brought off an outstanding act his outward guise, while congratulatory, belied the suppressed envy tearing him up inside.

Patrol lengths varied by necessity, but in general, they ran six days out and two days in port during the dry season and four days out and two days in during monsoon season. The short in-ports were time enough to resupply, do maintenance unable to be done at sea, take care of personal business, and "recreate" at one of the service clubs. In the main, crews preferred being under way. In spite of the dangers, life at sea was far less regimented than ashore. In port the dress code was proper: serviceable hat, chambray shirt, dungarees, and regulation footwear. Under way, propriety bowed to practicality in deference to the high heat and humidity. Once out of sight of the base, the entire crew donned T-shirt, pants cut off above the knees, and rubber sandals or boat shoes. However, at "General Quarters!" dress reverted to the conventional if time allowed. Battle station additions included steel helmet and flak jacket. The boats carried apparel that protected abdomen and groin, but the men shunned these armored diapers because their bulkiness retarded mobility.

Boardings had become so routine that crewmen infrequently wore flak jackets when a junk was alongside, but did so more often when going on a craft where they might drift away from the cutter's immediate protection. Sometimes a crew member chose to be overly cautious. On one occasion this brought a good laugh when an executive officer made his first boarding. Outfitted for the worst to happen, the big, athletic ensign stood poised at the gunwale in helmet, flak jacket, jungle boots, and bearing a cocked .45-caliber pistol. The slightly built Vietnamese fishermen in the junk staring up at this hulking fighting man might have been impressed, but only up to the point where the American started his leap—and certainly not when he crashed through the wooden deck and put a hole in the keel, as well as when his gun discharged.

There were pragmatic Coast Guardsmen who wanted to see for themselves if their flak jackets were to be trusted. Several men from Division Thirteen gathered at the rifle range to test the fiberglass and ceramic sandwich sheet armor. From one hundred yards .223-, .30-, and .45-caliber rounds could not penetrate the vest. A hand grenade exploded on it could not get through the armor. But, as they expected, .30-caliber armor-piercing ammunition went through it as though it were a knitted sweater.

The eleven-man WPB crews found their 17 x 82 foot, three-story home quite appealing, if a little snug. They most appreciated the air-conditioned interior and sympathized with those on land who had to endure the debilitating tropical heat without it. Interior access came by way of a watertight door on the starboard side aft of the deckhouse. An outside ladder on the port side of the deckhouse led up to the bridge. Directly forward of the access doorway, across a narrow athwartship passageway not much wider than a coffee table, was the door to the cabin. Tucked in a niche on the right between the doors sat a scuttlebutt. Inside the cabin immediately to starboard rested two metal lockers. One held small arms, and the other was crammed full of 18 cannisters of Willy-Peter, or white phosphorous mortar rounds. Continuing down the starboard was a side drop desk, followed by two box-frame bunk beds, ending with lockers for personal effects. Across the cabin were more lockers and two more bunk beds. Occupying the center of the room between bunks was a drop-leaf table. A head took up the back left corner. The cabin was office and quarters for the commanding officer, executive officer, and chief boatswain's mate, with the fourth bunk taken by the Vietnamese liaison rider or chief engineman. (The arrangement varied from boat to boat.)

Back in the narrow passageway, aft of the deckhouse, close to the port bulkhead, a door opened onto a ladder descending into the engine room. Opposite this door a ladder went up to the bridge hatch for use in the foulest weather. Stacked alongside it stood the generating sources of the cutter's electronics. In the middle of the passageway facing forward was a third door. Pulling it open revealed another sharply inclined ladder going below. Fully loaded M16 rifles were mounted on the left of the slim entrance for quick accessibility. At the bottom of the ladder was the 16-foot-long, 7-foot-high messing and recreation compartment. Immediately to the left was the stainless steel galley, a U-shaped layout suitable in dimensions for one person preparing meals. To the right was the cook's dry stores closet, its shelves of cans and boxes visible through the wire crosshatched door. On the other side of the dry stores forward bulkhead began the dark green settee, which continued at a right angle up the starboard side. Arranged before the settee were two metal tables with just enough separation between them to get to the cushioned bench.

Circular seats hinged to the aisle side of the tables could be swung out for additional seating. A sticky, green, rubberized mat covered the tables to keep dishware from sliding. Above the starboard portion of the settee ran a shelf. Generally a catchall for this and that, it was where the large reel-to-reel audiotape player was installed. With understandable regularity it replayed a disc jockey show from a St. Louis, Missouri, radio station dedicated to the men of the United States Coast Guard in Vietnam. A shelf in the front bulkhead at the end of the second table held a television, useful for picking up American armed forces programming when in port. Sharing the galley side of the compartment was a compact berthing area with a drape-covered opening. The three stacked pipe-frame bunks inside were used by first class petty officers and above, and by guests.

The watertight door at the front of the mess deck led into the main crew's quarters, a cozy ten feet long. Each side had three pipe bunks with canvas stretched within the frame laced around the tubular metal and topped with a thin mattress. When not in use they could be folded up, or "triced," against the bulkhead. Not only was this the roughest riding part of the boat for sleepers, it was the noisiest when the mortar right above it was going off during illumination or harassment activity. Beyond the crew's quarters came the crew's head, with hardly enough space to accommodate the sink, shower, and commode.

Topside, the main deck layout could be categorized into approximately four 20-foot sections: forecastle, deckhouse, quarterdeck, and fantail. Starting from the bow, centered five feet from the stem and past a pair of fore and aft mooring bitts, lay a small hatch just wide enough for an average size man to fit through. Access down into the hold was by vertical ladder. The shelves mostly held cans of protective coatings, giving the space the appropriate name of paint locker.

Next in line came the mortar–machine gun battery mounted on a raised circular grating. Behind this forecastle centerpiece squatted two large cubes welded to the deck up against the facing of the deckhouse. These were the ready service ammunition lockers. Hinged at the top, the doors when undogged and laid back over the boxes exposed neat rows of mortar cannisters: high-explosive in the starboard one and illumination in the port one. Inboard of the port locker sat the fuze setter with its circular cutout where the tip of a round was inserted so a lug on the fuze mated with a keyway to set the number of seconds on a mechanical time fuze. Lodged between the boxes was a hatchway leading into the crew's quarters. Primarily an escape outlet, at times it was opened when the air conditioning failed in order to get air moving below to make sleeping possible.

The shoulder-high forward third of the deckhouse gripped an anchor and liferaft on its flat surface. From here the superstructure rose up like a butte to form the pilothouse. A narrow walkway along each side of the superstructure ended with two steps down to the quarterdeck behind it.

This patch of deck received the most wear. It was from here that the gangway was run out, and, at sea, the business of boarding took place. Dominating this space in its centerline cradle hunkered the Boston Whaler. A spiderweb of cables connected the boat to the boom protruding from the superstructure, the means by which it was lowered into the water. Next to the small boat's port side sat a bin containing flak jackets and lifejackets. A machine gun dressed the amidship rail on each side of the cutter. The fantail, beginning at the end of the small boat, followed with a centerline metal framework confining fifty 100-round cans of .50-caliber ammunition. Continuing down the middle came two hatches, the larger leading into the main hold, housing a large freezer and a sundry of nautical paraphernalia. The smaller hatch opened into the lazarette, another storage hold, and one where many of the WPBs kept spare machine gun barrels. A portable pump sat on each side of the deck, one for dewatering and one for firefighting. The stern corners of the fantail rounded off the layout with machine guns.

Some have characterized the inshore patrols as tedious simply because many did not include a fire fight. It must be remembered that *Market Time* was designed to take away the coast as an infiltration option, not amass a high enemy body count. Unless poorly conceived and executed, which *Market Time* was not, a good indicator of a blockade's success was less enemy presence. Sustaining this potency demanded constant vigilance, which in itself defeats tedium. In the five years that the WPBs patrolled, the enemy's ability or desire to challenge the naval blockade fluctuated with its

The inshore cutter's crew faced lonesomeness and foreboding similar to that of an infantry squad on patrol in hostile territory—battle could come with little or no warning. (Photograph by author)

wartime ups and downs. Consequently, crews operating during the lulls might consider their participation a disappointment because they went to war so primed to fight. Nonetheless, at the outset of every patrol each man felt some trepidation, for each foray represented the next perilous, and perhaps final, page of his life. These naval patrols shared the plight of army patrols—a few men on their own in hostile surroundings. In those preface hours of steaming to station, each man's private thoughts were steeping in the latest intelligence on enemy activity, rumors picked up ashore (which often turned out to be false or gross exaggerations), and what might happen this trip. Competing with these thoughts were musings of home. Although he did not think about this page ending his biography, there was always one nagging dread trying to emerge from a crewman's subconscious that he had to forcefully shove back. This was fear that somehow he would let down his shipmates, and thereby fail his country, his family, and himself.

The single most time-consuming aspect of patrol was culling contraband and foes from hundreds of junks, both large and small. The careful examination of a 70-foot cargo junk by USCGC *Point Partridge* (WPB 82305) turned up a false compartment hiding 3,500 pounds of contraband rice from communist China. In another instance, the *Point Arden* took notice of two fishing junks in a transaction where the occupants of one did not look pleased about handing money to the occupants of the other. The Coast Guardsmen took into custody the Viet Cong tax collectors and 31,000 piasters.

With thousands of fishing junks along the coast, boardings sometimes became chaotic when fishermen crowded alongside the cutter, each desiring to be inspected before others so as to be quickly on their way. (Photograph by author)

Realizing that most of the Vietnamese they encountered were hardworking people trying to make a living, the Coast Guard endeavored to be as congenial as possible during boardings. The goodwill could also dispose a fisherman to report on enemy activities, or move a Viet Cong guerrilla to change sides, as more than 12,000 did in the first eight months of 1966, responding to a program called Chieu Hoi, or Open Arms. The inshore boats displayed a metal sign written in Vietnamese explaining Chieu Hoi. For further encouragement pamphlets and safe conduct passes were handed out during boardings. South Vietnam promised Viet Cong and North Vietnamese "ralliers" a new life of freedom, and, if they wanted it, vocational training. When they switched sides they were sent to a returnee center, where they were given food, clothing, medical care, and, for a month or two, a daily money allowance. Turning in a weapon earned them a monetary reward.

Vietnamese sometimes found themselves taking an unplanned ride on a cutter if their name appeared on the Viet Cong suspect list, if they had no identification card, or if their card had expired or been altered. Detainees were passed on to a Coastal Force junk and taken in for evaluation. While some were found to be enemies, most were deserters, draft dodgers, or hapless civilians. In Coast Guard custody, detainees were confined to the fantail, with boredom for company. One day a young engineman thought about the workload he faced and then about the idleness confronting a quartet of detainees. He concluded he would be happier with less to do and they would be happier with anything to do; so, he dragged over the portable firefighting pump and passed out

When junks refused to leave areas designated as restricted, they were towed out of the zone. (Photograph by author)

wire brushes. The Vietnamese broke out in grins and showed industry in scraping off rust and paint.

Another time a lone detainee held overnight was secured against the small boat with an arm handcuffed to the cradle. Sometime during the midwatch the helmsman, having been spelled at the wheel, stepped out of the bridge to stretch, just in time to see the detainee pull his scrawny arm through the cuff. The man walked to the stern rail and urinated into the sea. His comfort restored, he slipped back into the cuff and went to sleep. Obviously, he was not a fanatical Viet Cong guerrilla or he might have grabbed an M16 from the passageway racks and used it to take out as many Coast Guardsmen as he could before they got him.

When a cutter ran short of something, she would seek out a passing vessel. The bigger Navy ships were a good source, especially for ice cream. On an extended patrol with no warship about, the USCGC *Point Grace* (WPB 82323) hailed a Japanese-crewed MSTS ship for water. After the cutter made fast alongside, a polite Japanese crewman handed down water—a whole glass of it.

One means of identifying vessels at night was by signaling a challenge code in flashing light. A friendly vessel would flash in return with predesignated code letters. Replies from U.S. Navy ships were prompt and professional. However, with merchant ships you could never be sure how they would respond, such as the gruff one given the *Point Hudson,* "What the hell do you want?" Into the cutter's log went the entry, "Obviously American." Another merchant ship simply replied, "Boo!"

The naval tradition of animal mascots aboard units continued in Vietnam. Although dogs were the most popular, there were some unusual critters found aboard. The crewmen on the *Point Comfort* (WPB 82317) traded a pack of American cigarettes

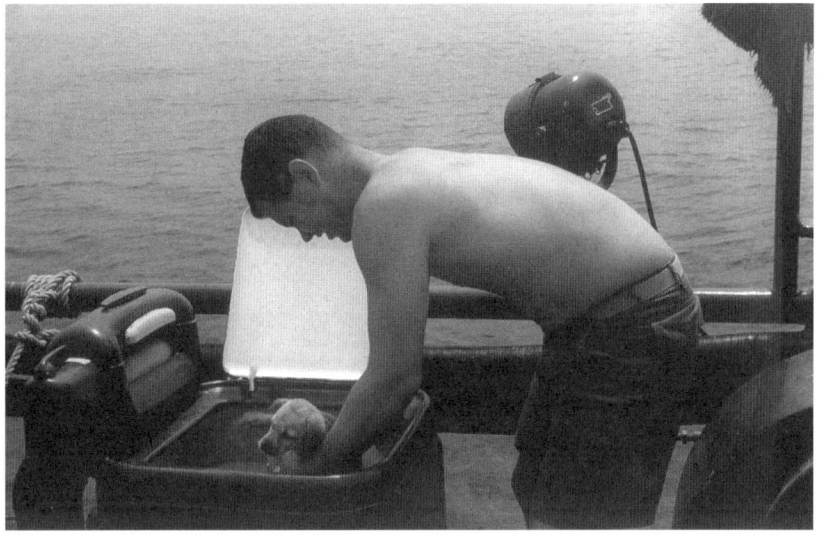

Mascots were common on the cutters. Here, Dumey, on *Point Dume,* gets a washing machine bath by Lieutenant Ronald E. Fritz, the skipper. (Photograph by author)

with a Vietnamese fisherman to get a duckling. But they did not show the same imagination in naming their new mascot "Charlie." After the *Point Hudson*'s crew showed care for an old man in a sampan by giving him a washcloth and soap for his skin ulcers and several small boxes of dry cereal, he showed his thanks by giving them a baby crocodile, with a string wisely tied around its snout. Deciding to keep it for a mascot, they leashed it inside the small boat. That night a hideous scream ripped a seam in the quiet of the river patrol. The crocodile had gotten free, and when a crewman stepped on deck for some fresh air the temptation of a meaty big toe was too great for young jaws to resist. The next day the amphibian was discharged from mascot duty and turned loose in the river.

As a clock continuously passes through the minutes of each hour, so did military regimen continue uninterrupted by war. Divisions held monthly personnel inspections, with the crews of boats in port required to take part in the formation. The occasion was also used to award decorations. Division commanders held the nominal title of commodore, and when a new officer took command he personally toured each boat, scrutinizing the appearance of cutter and crew for neatness. This is sometimes mistaken for competence. In the womanless world of the WPBs, pinups from girlie magazines adorned bulkheads, bulletin boards, and lockers. One new commodore did not object to these alluring morale builders, but he had a quaint policy that limited the number of pinups to three per man. If the object was to achieve restraint, it still left the eleven-man crew with 33 bosomy pulse-raisers.

On patrol the WPB worked for an operational commander, not the division. The division's primary task was making sure that these units could perform their assignments. All the boats underwent periodic operational readiness reviews, where staff

When a cutter was relieved on station, mail and information were passed over in a bag attached to a line. These transfers became hazardous maneuvers during the monsoon season, when seas were unruly. (Photograph by author)

members, usually accompanied by the commodore, made patrols evaluating the crews during drills and the mission. These trips also gave commodores excellent insight regarding the leadership capabilities of their boat skippers. Hence only the best men remained in command for any length of time.

South Vietnam had two seasons: dry and wet. In the dry season winds blew outward from land and in the rainy, or monsoon, season the winds swept in from the sea across the land. The rainy season came in two parts: the Southwest Monsoon running from May to October coming across the Gulf of Thailand, and the Northeast Monsoon blowing in above Nha Trang on the central coast from September into January. Monsoon disrupted inshore surveillance. The smallish PCFs were not foul weather tough. In May 1966, two PCFs sustained broken windshields and one had flooding in the six- to nine-foot seas, prompting the assessment that these craft had marginal capability in winds above 15 to 20 knots. Therefore, when the seas turned rowdy the PCFs stayed home, leaving surveillance gaps, which the WPBs did their best to cover by stretching their patrol sectors. The obvious solution was seasonal boat shifting. Navy PCFs followed blue skies and calm seas, condemning Coast Guard WPBs to the foul weather. This sometimes left a Coast Guard division in dry season with only three WPBs. As expected, the decision rankled WPBs' crews, but it also primed their self-esteem. While the U.S. Navy's vast size and superiority in ships tended to puff up a sailor's pride and led to haughtiness toward the diminutive Coast Guard, every Coast Guard member knew that one of his own was the equivalent of ten of them.

In October 1967, the commander of Naval Forces, Vietnam—well aware of the Coast Guard's value to his operation and the importance of joint service harmony—issued this message:

1. With the onset of the NE monsoon season floating units of Coast Guard Squadron One are once again being required to shift operating areas into more turbulent waters to take advantage of the WPBs' superior seakeeping qualities and the traditionally excellent seamanship of Coast Guard crews. Since their assignment to Market Time in 1965 the WPBs and their crews have borne the brunt of rough weather assignments remaining on the inshore patrol stations under all conditions of sea and weather.
2. The Coast Guard's contribution to Market Time is recognized and appreciated by Naval Forces Vietnam.
3. Well done.

The WPBs showed not only that they could stay afloat in bad weather, but that they could fight in it. On 27 December 1966 *Point Dume* delivered gunfire support to allied forces engaging enemy positions at Cap Mia. For four hours the WPB blocked the river mouth and adjacent shoreline, delivering mortar and machine gun fire into Viet Cong soldiers scrambling to escape the air strikes behind them. In the after action report the cutter's skipper wrote, "It should be noted that during the entire Operation a heavy sea of from 20–30 feet prevailed, making firing conditions extremely difficult. There were times for instance, that the after gun crews were ankle deep in water."

Few sounds flip an individual from full sleep into full wakefulness as does a General Quarters klaxon chasing a crew to battle stations. The incessant gonging has the effect of an intimidating boot camp instructor with his loud mouth in your ear shouting the dire things that will be done to you unless you "Move it!" Driven by this urgency you hurry to your billet concentrating on equipment to grab or hatches to secure in a mighty effort to suppress imagined fears. But, once at your battle station and the situation becomes clear—even if terrifying—alarm is overcome by determination.

On a craft the size of the WPB everyone takes part in combat. At the bow an engineman passes mortar shells to the cook, who drops them into the barrel for the chief boatswain's mate, whose finger on the trigger is ready to serve an explosive meal. Inside the bridge the commanding and executive officers direct the crew and navigate the craft, with small arms within reach if needed. Aft, a man is on each machine gun, with the remaining crewmen ready to replace spent cans of ammunition and join the battle with rifles.

When Captain LeRoy Taylor urged the Navy to build boats for coastal warfare he listed 17 ways they could be used. With the exception of mine laying, Coast Guard WPBs in Vietnam executed all those military roles. It is unlikely that Captain William E. Angel, USA, was aware of Taylor's in-house tussle with naval policy makers. A soldier concerned with land objectives does not lose sleep worrying about getting help from the big-ship Navy far out at sea. But, on 20 October 1965, while commanding a Special Forces detachment near Ha Tien, he witnessed one of Taylor's uses for inshore craft, "the support of the wet flank of any of our troop movements or of their positions being held."

That night a small Popular Forces outpost radioed Special Forces Detachment A-421 that they were under attack by at least a Viet Cong platoon. In turn the detachment radioed USCGC *Point Clear* (WPB 82315). Sensing victory, the Viet Cong pressed ahead for the *coup de grace*. The cutter closed fast, with machine guns raking the attackers while popping mortar illumination rounds overhead so that the defenders could see their targets. But it was not enough. With the outpost running out of ammunition and about to be overrun it called for mortar. Using hand grenade bursts at the scene for target reference, the *Point Clear* dropped high-explosive shells on the encroaching Viet Cong only 60 yards from the defenders, which sent the enemy fleeing in retreat. So impressed with the "wet flank" salvation, Angel wrote a letter thanking Squadron One, stating that his visit to the battle site at daylight "confirmed the fact that the Coast Guard was the prime factor in turning back the VC."

In the beginning, WPBs infrequently used their weaponry in behalf of land units. The *Market Time* directors preferred not to digress from hunting down infiltrators. But experience, backed up by studies early in 1968 by COMNAVFORV, changed this when indicators pointed out that aircraft patrols were the best way to detect infiltration from the sea and that using inshore and offshore vessels more for gunfire support would not degrade the blockade's effectiveness. The turnaround was dramatic. From 1965 to 1967 Squadron One only averaged 11 gunfire support missions a month. Beginning in July 1968 that average soared to 242 a month. A firing mission on 3 March 1968 by the *Point Caution* for the Army's 1st Air Cavalry Division further encouraged this use of WPBs. The cutter struck a suspected enemy encampment with 1,000 rounds of .50-caliber ammunition, and 45 rounds of 81-mm mortar (35 high explosive and 10 white phosphorus). Ground units later inserted into the vicinity counted 84 dead enemy troops.

Early in 1968 *Point Gammon* used her mortar to rid Coastal Group 14 of a nuisance when she was called upon to knock out Viet Cong loudspeakers on the outskirts of the base, filling the night air with Communist propaganda. The cutter was on the mark, as secondary explosions were observed and the night was still again. In the morning a patrol found the destroyed public address system and two Viet Cong casualties—one dead and one wounded.

Prominent on Taylor's list was putting ashore and pulling out reconnaissance or raiding teams. This was something that the WPBs became very active in doing along the entire South Vietnamese coast. As early as September 1965 two cutters transported a raiding party of 34 South Vietnamese irregulars and two U.S. Army Special Forces advisors to the northeast coast of Phu Quoc Island. Also that month at the other end of the country the Marine Corps commander of the First Force Reconnaissance Company, with the mission of covert intelligence-gathering in Viet Cong–controlled areas, approached Division Twelve about inserting and recovering his four- and five-man scout groups. On these ventures the pickup was made days later at a different location. Other similar missions were accomplished within a few tidy hours. A 20-man Vietnamese Navy SEAL team, with their two American advisors, was taken aboard *Point Grey* at Phan Tiet at 1600 hours and carried 35 miles to Point Legan, where the SEALs went ashore to ambush a Viet Cong supply platoon. Within 15 minutes after landing, the attack began. *Point Grey* contributed by sending up illumination over the scene and lobbing high-explosive shells just beyond the fighting to cut off enemy retreat. By 2130, all the raiders were back on the cutter, unharmed, after killing seven guerrillas and capturing 500 pounds of rice, 40 pounds of dried fish, and miscellaneous papers.

More perilous than putting people ashore was their extraction, because of the likelihood that the enemy knew of their presence. Shortly past 0100 on 22 January 1969, the *Point Banks* was ordered to evacuate nine South Vietnamese soldiers surrounded on three sides by two Viet Cong platoons. To keep the trapped men from being overrun, the cutter, two U.S. Navy boats, and a C-47 gunship opened fired on the Viet Cong. The commanding officer asked for two volunteers to take the Boston Whaler in for the rescue. Gunner's Mate Second Class Willis J. Goff and Engineman Second Class Larry D. Villarreal stepped forward without hesitation. In the small boat, Goff crouched behind the M60 machine gun as Villarreal guided it over the wind-churned seas and also dodged "friendly" fire. Their eyes searched for a sign of the besieged men, who were supposed to show their location with a light. The attempt to make a night landing through unfamiliar and uncharted waters became more complicated when not one, but three lights, each in a different location, came on. Villarreal pushed the sturdy craft over the fitful surf and right into a flurry of enemy fire. At that moment four of the trapped soldiers burst from the jungle, running across the sand for their lives. Goff triggered the machine gun to cover their flight. They splashed through the surf and hurled themselves into the Boston Whaler. Villarreal spun the helm and swerved for the *Point Banks*. On the return to the beach for the rest of the men, water inside the boat sloshed against their legs and several times the sea almost capsized them. Villarreal did a masterful job of keeping them afloat, the task made more trying every time the sea brought the engine to a sputtering stop and it had to be restarted. The Viet Cong concentrated their guns on their expected visitors, but somehow the Coast Guardsmen gained the beach unharmed, loaded up the five soldiers, and made their getaway. For their heroic deed the U.S. Navy awarded Goff and Villarreal Silver Stars.

Not all enemy intercepts had the adrenaline-charged excitement of coming upon a North Vietnamese trawler making a run for the river. Sometimes an anti-infiltration success became known well after the fact. Cutter crews appraised patrol areas as either "action likely," "action possible," or "action no-way." Station 1A1, which hugged the coast by the DMZ, fell into the first category. Station 1A2, seaward of 1A1, fell into the detested latter category. Here, out of sight of land, where traffic was infrequent, little boarding took place. Combat-tested crews were especially peeved when deployed there, surmising it a punishment for some unknown offense, because this station was infrequently filled. To the contrary, when a boat was sent there it was usually prompted by something in the intelligence reports.

In mid-July 1967, *Point Dume* found her keel soaking in 1A2 with a grumpy gang. The veteran crew, most with combat experience, were annoyed at this "exile." It was compounded by adjustment to a new commanding officer who, although he had been aboard a month, had still not won over the men. His penchant for holding drills, his high-endurance cutter style of regimentation, and his overwariness of bringing his vessel close to shore without good reason, contrasted sharply with the style of the beloved previous skipper, whose philosophy was more like, "You can shine your shoes when you get back home. We're here to kill Cong."

On the third day—a breezeless tropical scorcher with temperatures above 100 degrees—crew apathy shuffled about the boat until 1900 when the GQ! alarm freed each man of indifference, sending him to his station revitalized. The *Point Dume* charged seaward along the 17th parallel, closing on a target picked up on radar. Enthusiasm quickly waned when they saw a large, innocuous sailing junk awaiting their approach. The boarding turned up nothing suspicious. All five Vietnamese had identification cards proving they were from Danang, and they explained that they were fishing out of Hue, a normal activity for this time of year. The Vietnamese liaison chief petty officer evaluated them as innocent fishermen. The cutter crew agreed. The nearest Coastal Group also concurred with this assessment by radio, saying that the junk could be let go. Although the new skipper had no concrete evidence to detain them, he felt uneasy about releasing them. It bothered him that they were this far out at the boundary of the warring countries. Deciding to detain them, he put an armed crewman aboard and towed the sailboat until handing it off to a Coastal Group boat the next day. At that point the Coast Guardsmen dismissed the incident from thought. Closer questioning at the Coastal Force base did not revise its original conclusion, but Division Twelve's commander, in support of the WPB skipper's sixth sense, sent another WPB up the coast to bring the detainees to Danang for scrutiny by naval intelligence officers. Without doubt, the *Point Dume* captain felt great satisfaction a week later when he learned that this interrogation uncovered 75,000 piasters sewn into the clothing of the five Vietnamese. One of them admitted being a North Vietnamese naval officer with a mission to infiltrate at Nha Trang and travel to Saigon gathering information on the enemy. The other four were North Vietnamese Navy petty officers who were to return north after sneaking the officer ashore. It was no surprise that the WPB's liaison had been fooled. The intelligence people revealed that the identification papers were "the most complete and beautifully forged set of papers yet encountered."

Less than a year later, south of Danang, the *Point Orient* made a similar capture when they stopped a 45-foot sailing junk 85 miles south of Danang. The six occupants, claiming to be fishermen on their way from Danang to Nha Trang, however, did not have flawlessly forged papers. Their identification cards, dated four to six years earlier, looked conspicuously new. But real papers would not have helped them elude capture. Fishermen did not have such smooth hands and faces; they carried too much clothing with them; their sailing papers did not have an authorized departure seal from Danang; the junk lacked bait and fish; and a search uncovered a large amount of rice and salt, plus a quantity of medicine—all items needed by the enemy. Later interrogation revealed that they were North Vietnamese Army officers attempting to reach South Vietnam to carry out clandestine military operations.

When Taylor proposed the development of a patrol boat fleet he was really arguing for versatility. Originally deployed as one of the anti-infiltration elements, the Coast Guard 82-footer became an unintended working model of his concept as the operational commanders in Vietnam discovered the cutter's value in other ways. As a consequence they were borrowed from *Market Time* as necessary to take part in special offensives, which were often grand-scale amphibious landings. When troops swarmed into an enemy stronghold the cutters blocked the foes' retreat by sea. They also guarded the big naval ships from deadly surreptitious attack by small, high-speed craft. The list of these military operations is long, with such names as *Dragon Fire, Nevada, Ballistic Charge,* and *Deckhouse V.* In the latter, an invasion by American and South Vietnamese marines had been postponed twice because of rough water when someone decided to call for the Coast Guard. The *Point Kennedy* was borrowed and she led the landing craft convoy through the treacherous mouth of the Co Chien River, at night, up to the landing beaches. The Viet Cong showed its appreciation by sending a 57-mm recoilless rifle round through her starboard wing spray shield. To the Coast Guardsmen's relief the round failed to explode.

Operation Jackstay was prominent for the WPBs. In the spring of 1966, American and South Vietnamese soldiers invaded the Viet Cong sanctuary south of Saigon and the Coast Guard went into the labyrinth of rivers and canals to deprive the Viet Cong of supplies of food and fresh water. Here, Coast Guardsmen faced close quarters combat and their most deadly fighting in the war.

In May 1967, *Operation Beau Charger*, a massive amphibious landing, sent U.S Marines into the DMZ to sweep it clear of North Vietnamese artillery and troops. To the task group sailors aboard the landing ships, helicopter carriers, cruisers, and destroyers, the attachment of an 82-foot WPB and a 50-foot PCF to this fleet of giants for "security" must have encouraged much uncomplimentary humor. Aboard the *Point Dume* no one was laughing; she was in hostile waters above the DMZ off North Vietnam running a barrier from Cap Lay to Hon Gio, or Tiger Island, and facing much uncertainty. The 14-mile line was split into two 7-mile segments, with the mainland side named *Blondie* and the island half named *Dagwood*. The cutter and the PCF took turns covering them. Not long after arriving, the cutter was told to clear "Green Beach"—just below the river mouth—of Vietnamese craft. During this time North Vietnamese artillery opened fire on them. Though the nearest round hit 500 yards away, they were fully aware that they were a marked target.

The gunner's mate on *Point Dume* was making his third patrol. He had been aboard 18 days and in Vietnam for 22. Like everyone else he had been elated, and apprehensive, when learning that the next assignment would almost assuredly place them in the fighting. A slender, 24-year-old of medium height, he had volunteered for Vietnam out of patriotism and belief that this is where a military man belongs. There was also a question that chronically edged from his subconscious into his conscious mind that only war could answer. He had to know how he would conduct himself in combat. The crew's emotional high at the beginning of the trip had sagged to disappointment after three uneventful days. The gunner's mate had dropped into his bunk to get some sleep before going on the mid-watch (midnight to 0400) resigned that his question would not be answered on this outing. He was wrong.

Close to 2200 the GQ! alarm jerked him awake, sending him clawing for his steel-toed brogans. On deck he pulled on a flak jacket. The deck of the speeding cutter pitched sharply back and forth beneath his feet, causing him to lurch to his station, Mount 55, the starboard aft machine gun. He unlashed the canvas mount cover, clamped on the sound-powered phones, and topped his head with the bulky phone-talker helmet. He pulled out the elevation and train locking pins, then yanked the gun's retracting handle all the way back and let it go. The powerful spring slammed the action up against the breech, chambering a round with a satisfying clang. As he was hunched over, with hands gripping the vertical wood handles, thumbs poised above the upside down U-shaped trigger, his eyes sighted down the barrel while his ears listened for orders from the bridge.

They were intercepting a sampan moving down the North Vietnamese coast. He felt the concussion of their mortar firing and saw the illumination shell turn a portion of the night wicked yellow. All the activity was on the port side. He heard a jumble of voices on deck yelling toward the water. They were alongside the sampan. Its three occupants had tried to escape by jumping into the water, but the trio, clad in sodden black pajama outfits, were pulled aboard. Then the portside machine guns opened up on the sampan, shredding it into rubbish. Battle stations were secured and the gunner's mate went below to finish his nap.

It lasted until the GQ! alarm sent him back to his gun 20 minutes later. They were racing for the mainland again. This time four contacts showed up on radar, one a fast-moving steel hull. At about 1,500 yards from the North Vietnamese patrol boat, the skipper ordered an illumination round fired. The flare acted like a signal for the war to start. The gunner's mate kept his eyes locked on a white scar on the black sea; this was his target reference—the gunboat's wake. Under the pressure of his thumbs, the gun convulsed in his hands. His loader was yelling something to him, but in the din of gunfire and the captain's commands in the earphones it was impossible to make the words out. When his gun went silent he jerked the empty can from the tray and stepped aside for his loader to drop in a full one. The loader, raising his voice again, wanted to know why he was shooting into the water. The perplexed gunner's mate had no idea what the loader meant. Then, in a timely lull in the cutter's firing they heard a dim rat-tat-tat-tat and looked down in astonishment at geysers of water high-stepping toward the hull where they were standing. In a fluid instant he recharged the breech and returned fire. It was a naval version of an aerial dogfight. The two gunboats careened, charged, and retreated in maneuvering to apply killing bursts. If the wake patterns of the vessels could have been preserved they would have resembled the crayon scribbling of a small child. The gunner's mate thought that he might burn up the barrel's rifling when he was interrupted by the skipper's voice in the earcups telling them that the enemy had increased speed and was pulling away. Now it was the North Vietnamese artillery's turn. Realizing he had been lured into their range, the skipper broke off pursuit and dodged away in divergent course changes. Looking back, the gunner's mate saw a red artillery tracer floating its way toward the fantail. When it blinked out he thought for certain the round was still coming for them and experienced the total helplessness that comes in war when there is no place to hide. He felt exposed and disarmed. So he did what combatants usually do in such a moment—he took in a deep breath and stayed at his post. While the *Point Dume* was engaged, the PCF was also set up. She had tangled with a fast boat that pulled her close to Tiger Island, where that garrison's artillery practiced on her. It was a close call, but WPB and PCF both got away without casualties.

The next GQ! came during the mid-watch. It was no surprise this time to the gunner's mate, who was at the helm when the alarm went off. The watch had been keeping track of several radar blips loitering off Cap Lay when the task force commander ordered the cutter to assist a destroyer. Back again behind his machine gun, he wondered what they were in for this time. However, before reaching the destroyer new orders turned them around to investigate a reported contact, which turned out to be nothing. Battle stations were secured.

After finishing his watch, the gunner's mate was torn from sleep again. For the fourth time this night he dashed to his GQ! station, now to deal with junks loaded with supplies slinking for Tiger Island. The PCF had tried to board two of them. Ignoring warning shots to halt, one craft fled northward while the three men in the other jumped into the sea. Found in the abandoned 30-foot junk were crates of mortar ammunition, 100-pound sacks of rice, and small arms. Poised over his gun, straining his eyes to pick up movement on the water, the gunner's mate felt as though a bag pierced with pinholes had been put over his head; such was the darkness that it even subdued starlight.

He had not given the whereabouts of the PCF a thought until a "hellacious blast" whipped his attention to port in time to see their sea partner silhouetted in a blossom of light. Someone shouted over the phones, "The Swift's gone!" But there was no time to bother over the PCF's fate because they were suddenly among a strung-out line of junks.

An eerie silence enveloped the scene. Conversation over the sound-powered phones ceased, the cutter came to a stop, and everyone seemed to be holding their breath while the junks, propelled by oars, floated down the starboard side. From the edge of the gunner mate's vision something twinkling with red sparks arced toward the bow. It bounced off the flared steel hull and exploded. His pressure on the trigger increased, anticipating the order to commence fire. The junk that had lobbed the grenade was now moving by him so close that he had the machine gun hard against the depression stop to sight on it. Still no word came to fire. Unaware that the building tension was increasing his trigger pressure, the short burst of fire totally surprised him. In his muzzle flash the image of people standing in the junk burned into his mind. The skipper, wary that attacking this close might detonate the enemy's cargo and harm his men, yelled, "Cease fire!"

When the junks had passed them, artillery shells from Tiger Island began dropping around the cutter. The *Point Dume*'s engines roared to life, and her jump into a run almost knocked the gunner's mate off his feet. The skipper radioed the PCF, which had miraculously escaped the attack on her, to sink as many of the junks as possible. The cutter made broadside approaches so that three machine guns at once ripped into a junk. The silence had evaporated; all was now noise, now war. During the chaos, rounds from the Swift's twin machine gun turret dug at the water in front of the cutter. While concentrating his own fire on the enemy the gunner's mate heard the captain calmly telling the PCF that they were shooting at the WPB. When there was no letup—understandable because the machine gun turret sat on top of the pilothouse, making it difficult to hear a radio call—the captain repeated his message in a higher pitch. With the gun still banging away at them, the third call was in a voice as loud as the skipper could muster. This time the shooting ceased.

With most of the junks destroyed or damaged, it was time to get clear of the artillery again. This time a destroyer came on to assist by throwing suppression fire at the island. Under a demand for more power the cutter came about for the final sprint when the engines stalled midway into the turn. The crew waited helplessly while the engineers solved the problem. They hoped it would be soon, for it would not take artillery spotters long to hit a stationary target. The relief was great when the diesels came back to life.

The gunner's mate, after securing the ordnance, dropped into his bunk still wearing his flak jacket. From above he heard the metallic tinkling of spent .50-caliber brass rolling over the deck. Not all of them had been picked up in the dark and tossed overboard. The sound reminded him that come daylight he would have weapons to clean. Before sleep closed in he remembered that he still had 11 months and a week to do in Vietnam. He chuckled at the thought that he might never take off his flak jacket, not even to shower.

The young gunner's mate had learned the answer to his question of how he would perform under enemy fire by responding much the same as any military person that first time in combat, when training and discipline automatically take charge and bring him to react as though he had done it before.

And so it went for the men on the 82-footers: a series of random skirmishes while carrying out their duty of undermining the enemy's goal to rule South Vietnam. When a Coast Guardsman's 12-month tour ended he was replaced by another, so that 26 WPBs—286 men—continuously patrolled the length of the country. When plucked from the aggregate of thousands of aircraft, tanks, artillery, watercraft, and more than two million men and women who took part in the war, this figure is far from awe-inspiring. But this tiny force, which the Navy brought in to fill a void until it had its own boats and crews, had shown so much diversity and professionalism that it evoked a comment of one Navy chief of staff that he was angry at the Coast Guard for doing such a good job and showing up the Navy. This was not an isolated opinion. Commonly, when a critical mission came up it was given to the Coast Guard. Yes, this was partly because of the better capabilities of the WPB, and partly because inshore patrolling is a Coast Guard strength. But it was due in large part to the Coast Guard's knack for getting a job done. *Market Time* was a well-drawn operation, but it may be argued that without these valiant 26 cutters, its successes would not have been as great.

CHAPTER 12

VIETNAMIZATION—THE END OF THE LINE

POLITICAL CONSIDERATIONS PUT THE UNITED STATES in Vietnam and political considerations took the United States out.

Following France's exit from Indochina in 1954, President Dwight D. Eisenhower, a Republican, moved in to check communism's spread through building up South Vietnam's armed forces. Hanoi's leaders were undeterred. Communist documents captured in the mid-1960s disclosed that in January 1959 North Vietnam had decided to take over South Vietnam through armed insurrection. In May, the campaign formally began. By 1961 the Viet Cong—under North Vietnam's direction—had gained control of vast territory in the south. The United States now had a Democrat president. President John F. Kennedy, not wanting his party to be accused of faintheartedness by the Republicans, ordered thousands more military "advisors" to South Vietnam. To increase the mobility of its army, Kennedy sent over helicopters with American pilots. Nevertheless, by 1965, with the backing of political rhetoric and military supplies from Communist China and the Soviet Union, the North Vietnamese squeeze on South Vietnam had become critical.

Since the end of World War II the planet had become a deadly board game, with the Communist team of China and the Soviet Union against the Free World team of the United States and its Western allies virtually contesting for every country. Hence, keeping South Vietnam on the Free World side of the board became a matter of "them versus us." Aware that most Americans believed withdrawal now would throw away Southeast Asia to the Communists, the succeeding president, Lyndon B. Johnson, also a Democrat, rightly surmised that a pullout would arouse a controversy that would "shatter" his presidency with an endless national debate and wreck his domestic Great Society agenda. He made the pragmatic decision to send combat troops into the fight.

If at this point Johnson would have turned the war over to his military professionals and concentrated his time on his domestic programs, the Vietnam era, despite the instable South Vietnamese government, in all likelihood would have been short, conclusive, and with less loss of American lives. Instead it became a civilian-run war, with

Johnson, Secretary of Defense Robert S. McNamara, and others in the administration formulating military strategy and tactics. These self-styled "imitation generals" used a "limited war" approach, which they theorized would check Communist takeovers of Third World countries without starting a nuclear war with China or the Soviet Union. It did not occur to the administration's intellectual advisors that because nuclear war was so mutually destructive neither China nor the Soviet Union was about to invite nuclear eradication over a tug-of-war for a small Southeast Asian peninsula of impoverished agrarian nations.

Limited war calls for gradualism—that is, incrementally applying diplomatic, economic, and military leverage to dissuade an adversary. Johnson's civilian advisors feared that if the military conducted the war it would do what was necessary to win in short order by stepping over their restriction-laden strategies, and as a result, bring Chinese and Soviet troops to North Vietnam's aid. It was like trying to win a fight without hurting the other side's feelings. Johnson himself leaned over maps and aerial photographs, picking out the North Vietnamese targets to bomb. So it went: the civilians ran a piecemeal war in which, whenever the enemy prevailed, the military took the blame.

The American and allied forces did an outstanding job of keeping the enemy in disarray despite the restraints under which they had to operate. But with American casualties mounting in a conflict that appeared would last as long as the medieval Hundred Years' War, a segment of the American public became vocally critical of a war in which Americans were dying on foreign soil over ideology in support of an Asian government that willy-nilly changed heads of state, and did not seem as committed as the United States in opposing North Vietnam's takeover of their own country. While American public support began crumbling, there was no letup on North Vietnam's part. It continually threw in every resource it had to conquer the south, including using women and children to fight and haul supplies. North Vietnam did not comprehend that it was supposed to be fighting a limited war. It operated on the assumption that you fought to win at all costs. As such, the selective on-again, off-again bombing of their country did not translate into a show of American resolve. To the contrary, it showed weakness. So the North Vietnamese steeled themselves to endure hardships and setbacks until the Americans just went away, which they did when further military commitment had become a political liability.

The November 1968 the American presidential election brought back a Republican president. According to the Republican ideal, the involvement—which had begun under Eisenhower—would fittingly come to a close under Richard M. Nixon, who had been Eisenhower's vice-president. This would happen by turning the war completely over to the South Vietnamese government—which had not worked before. Few, if any, actually believed it would work this time. To assuage political and national consciences over what was, in truth, running away from an unpleasant mission, this retreatism was peddled as "Vietnamization." As the South Vietnamese learned to do the tasks the Americans had been carrying on, and how to use the large amount of military equipment being left behind, their U.S. counterparts would leave the country. The phaseout took time. On 29 March 1973, the last American combat troops left South Vietnam, resetting the war clock back to 1959.

In this war American forces carried out their orders very well. They never lost a major battle. Heroism was commonplace. They showed an extraordinary ability to improvise and overcome seemingly impossible obstacles. They believed in the fighting to keep people from subjugation. Accordingly, when Vietnamization came along there was no cheering. They had come to know and like the Vietnamese people. They abhorred the atrocities committed by the Viet Cong upon men, women, and children in the villages. Now they were leaving with their job unfinished. They felt disgust. It was a slap in the face for all that their comrades had achieved through their deaths and grievous wounds. Their sacrifices had been nothing more than part of political considerations.

And so the respective armed services began the process of turning their duties over to the South Vietnamese. For the Coast Guard, Vietnamization became tangible in the first week of February 1969, when two South Vietnamese Navy lieutenants reported aboard the *Point League* and the *Point Garnet* in Division Thirteen as prospective commanding officers. The men of Squadron One had been hearing rumors of this turnover business and hoped it was not to be, but when these officers replaced the American executive officers on these cutters the process had become hurtful reality. Coast Guardsmen felt an invasion of privacy, as though strangers off the street had moved into their house. Clearly, professional pride was pricked. None believed that the South Vietnamese could handle the cutters, maintain them, and use them to fight with the proficiency of United States Coast Guardsmen. This was true to the extent that the Coast Guard had nearly two centuries of tradition in its wake, while the South Vietnamese Navy, born 6 March 1952, was still an adolescent trying to make its mind up what to be. Nonetheless, orders dictated that a cutter entering Vietnamization had to be in the South Vietnamese Navy within four months.

Each Service had to devise a plan for ACTOV (Accelerated Turnover to the Vietnamese), the military title for Vietnamization. The crux of the program was that when a Vietnamese learned an American's job that American went home. The Coast Guard came up with a sound plan for indoctrinating the Vietnamese crews, but its acronym, SCATTOR (Small Craft Assets, Training and Turnover of Resources), indicated disfavor over the pullout. Coast Guard and Navy approaches differed only in that the Coast Guard brought on board the prospective skipper first, where the Navy left him for last. Concurrently, on shore, the Coast Guard phased Vietnamese sailors into the cutter repair force in a companion program called VECTOR, awkwardly standing for the "Vietnamese Engineering Capabilities, Training of Rating."

Lieutenant (j.g.) Christopher R. Gillespie typified the young Coast Guard officer; middle 20s, gung ho for his service, and a hard-to-suppress optimism. After six months on WPBs, and scheduled for a Division Twelve staff job, he asked to be SCATTOR project officer when it came to Danang, emphasizing that he believed he could make the plan work. He received the extra duty along with the operational order from COGARDACTV outlining how the training should go. From it, he developed a training manual that later the other divisions would use and that the Navy would adopt for PCF transitions. Each cutter beginning Vietnamization received a manual, along with checklists and a lesson plan for each item on the lists. Besides the general tasks every crew member had to perform, there were lists tailored to each rating—boatswain's mate, gunner's mate, and so forth. After a Vietnamese sailor learned his counterpart's duties the Coast Guardsman left the cutter for reassignment in the squadron or transfer back to the United States.

A major problem was that the Americans and the Vietnamese could not understand one another. Gillespie's solution was to provide English-Vietnamese and Vietnamese-English dictionaries along with small chalkboards, the latter useful in drawing diagrams and writing messages.

Notwithstanding positive outlooks such as Gillespie's and conscientious efforts by Coast Guard crew members, SCATTOR sailed in the heavy seas of diverse cultures further divided by differing perspectives. Americans trying to help South Vietnam could not understand what seemed to them ingratitude by the Vietnamese sailor for not taking training in earnest. But the Vietnamese, particularly among the enlisted, did not come from an environment (as did the Americans) where food, clothing, and shelter—life's basic necessities—were virtually assured. The Vietnamese sailor's main concern was not the war, but in caring for his family. On top of this, most did not want to be in the navy: they hated bad-weather patrolling and the family separations. At the other end of the naval spectrum were Vietnamese officers from aristocratic backgrounds, who, used to easy living, were not well-motivated to put up with the rigors of small patrol craft duty.

Absenteeism retarded the program. Officer and enlisted alike thought little of being absent without leave. It was common for the skipper of a cutter to seek out Gillespie after a patrol to tell him that so-and-so did not show up and the cutter left without him. Gillespie would find the wayward sailor, usually at his home, and take him to the South Vietnamese Naval Base for punishment, which amounted to something innocuous, such as raking leaves or cleaning up docks. Oh yes—he was also told not to miss the boat again. Similarly, as soon as mooring lines were made fast after patrol the Vietnamese went home, leaving the in-port maintenance to the Coast Guard.

When October came the Squadron One turnover timetable was laboring three months behind schedule, due largely to a shortage of Vietnamese sailors. Vietnamese crews on the *Point Ellis* and the *Point White* had to be combined because neither had a full complement to meet the turnover date. To address this bottleneck two Coast Guard officers were detached to South Vietnamese Naval Headquarters in Saigon. Their persuasiveness not only revived the manpower flow, but the men coming aboard now were better qualified than those they had been getting. It turned out that the South Vietnamese Navy had been holding back experienced sailors until assignments opened for the larger U.S. Navy vessels being turned over.

Still, Vietnamization was not moving fast enough for nervous politicians wanting to show war protesters evidence of American disengagement. In response the naval assets program became further accelerated. Indoctrination dipped from 18 weeks to 15, to 11. This compression brought overcrowding. Cutters had to go out with 11 Americans and 12 Vietnamese, a situation ripe for intramural turmoil. The culturally accepted practices of Vietnamese men holding hands and of sleeping together—neither of which had to do with sexual desire—repelled the Americans and lowered their tolerance, despite trying hard to be understanding. An empty bunk in such cramped quarters was too compelling for the Vietnamese to ignore, and likewise it was asking much of a Coast Guardsman to show restraint upon coming off an exhausting four-hour night watch to find his "rack" filled with two slumbering Vietnamese sailors. In short order the Vietnamese dreamers found themselves sprawled on the cold steel deck.

Although Vietnamese sailors did not care for American cooked food, they felt no disdain toward the fresh and canned food, which they carried home in quantity without permission. For the most part the Coast Guard showed compassion for this larcenous means of providing for one's family. But charity reached its limit for the cook aboard one WPB who entered his galley to find five Vietnamese sailors cheerfully boiling all 15 dozen of the cutter's egg supply. The enraged cook snatched up a cleaver and took after the fleeing amateur chefs, who now only wished to avoid becoming diced fish food.

Time constraints forced the training to continue through monsoon season, much to the distress of many Vietnamese crewmen, who became so seasick that they could not be cajoled to work under threat of death, which, given the circumstances, they might have welcomed.

In the end, each WPB overcame these travails to give birth to a full Vietnamese naval crew. The only midwifery remaining, done by the departing Coast Guard skipper, was observing the newborn's actions on a *Market Time* patrol. This was followed by a joint Coast Guard, Navy, and South Vietnamese Navy team running the crew through a standard operational readiness inspection. That left remaining the formality of the ceremony.

The first occurred on 16 May 1969, with the transfer of *Point League* and *Point Garnet* at the South Vietnamese Navy Base in Saigon. It was a flamboyant affair, with the audience seated on the pier under an open-sided tent facing the bow-to-bow moored cutters. The white dress military uniforms in the crowd stood out in sharp contrast against the dark gray vessels. Among the dignitaries were the commander of U.S. Naval Forces, Vietnam and the deputy commander of Royal Thai Forces, Vietnam. Deserving participants in the SCATTOR endeavor were presented with achievement awards and Captain Ralph W. Niesz, COMCOGARDACTV and Commodore Tran Van Chon, the South Vietnamese Navy's Chief of Naval Operations, spoke optimistically about the future. Then came the finale. The two naval leaders in turn bent over a small table and signed the documents transferring the cutters to South Vietnam. This done, all hands stood at attention. Hand salutes were rendered as a South Vietnamese Navy Band played the American national anthem during the lowering of the American flags, Coast Guard ensigns, and commissioning pennants. To the playing of the South Vietnamese national anthem the Republic of Vietnam yellow and red flags were hoisted in their place. The Coast Guard crews filed ashore and the South Vietnamese crew marched aboard. The *League* and the *Garnet* were now, respectively, the *Le Phuoc Duc* (PB 700) and the *Le Van Nga* (PB 701). The WPBs would take names of Navy petty officers killed in action. In this manner Squadron One dwindled away to join that dusty historical category of small-scale operations that made large contributions, but are known mostly by those who took part.

Less than a month later, on 5 June, Division Eleven ceased to exist and on 16 March 1970, Division Twelve was disestablished, leaving, after 14 July, the *Point Cypress* and the *Point Marone* of Squadron One. Pulled off *Market Time* for special operations in the Viet Cong–infested lower Mekong Delta, they finished out the squadron's annals with a flurry of combat. On 19 and 20 July they attacked the Than Phu Secret Zone, sending Kit Carson scouts (former Viet Cong) ashore on search and destroy probes, backing them up with gunfire from their decks and their deployed Boston

Whalers. The assault killed and captured Viet Cong troops, destroyed sampans and structures, and confiscated boxes of enemy documents. A week later, loaded with more soldiers and an Australian explosives ordnance detachment, the vessels cruised into the My Thanh River, destroying fortifications.

The concluding action came on the last patrol, appropriately on 4 August, the Coast Guard's 180th birthday. Continuing their purge of enemy forces, they crept ahead in a narrow canal off the Co Chien River with 25 Kit Carson Scouts aboard each vessel. Unable to detect enemy presence through the thick shoreline growth on this clear afternoon, the cutters came about. To turn around in the 120-foot-wide canal each WPB had to push her nose against the bank, then swing the stern to complete a T-shaped maneuver. When nothing happened during this vulnerable time the men felt more at ease. Then the *Point Marone,* leading the way 30 feet off the starboard bank, slid into the mental crosshairs of a patient enemy soldier manning a mine detonator. The explosion transmitted a concussion in the shallow water from bank to bank that had the destructive force of an earthquake. Windows shattered on the bridge. Flying glass shards ripped the Coast Guard skipper's face. A Vietnamese sailor on the starboard aft machine gun died when his talker phone chest plate was embedded into his body. Nearby, a Vietnamese sailor's arm disappeared at the elbow, severed by a jagged chunk of metal that continued on into his chest, killing him. A Kit Carson scout fell dead from a blow to his chest. The enemy fire that followed up the blast was answered and overwhelmed by at least six .50-caliber machine guns and some 50 rifles. The *Marone,* mud-splattered and listing to starboard, kept moving clear of the ambush. This was fortunate, for had she been disabled she would have trapped the *Cypress* behind her, leaving both of them imperiled.

Eleven days later, patched and painted, the *Marone* joined the *Cypress* for the last of the turnover ceremonies. On the same day, 15 August 1970, at 1100, 18 months after SCATTOR began, Division Thirteen and Squadron One ceased existence.

To be a significant naval force the South Vietnamese Navy needed more than river and coastal craft. It needed blue-water ships. In March 1969, a formidable contingent of American and South Vietnamese admirals ferried to a Squadron Three cutter anchored in the Saigon River for the express purpose of evaluating her facilities and capabilities for South Vietnamese use. Vietnamization was coming to Squadron Three.

Early in June 1969 on Midway Island, President Nixon met with South Vietnamese president Nguyen Van Thieu and offered him an armed forces package that would equip 170,000 more military personnel and upgrade army, air force, and navy hardware. This added package, which included two Navy destroyer escorts and two Coast Guard high-endurance cutters, would give South Vietnam the all-weather detection and intercept capability it lacked. The potent 5-inch guns of the cutters would also extend their naval gunfire range.

The two cutters chosen for turnover were a pair from the first Squadron Three deployment, the *Bering Strait* and the *Yakutat.* In February 1970, a South Vietnamese naval officer and some 15 enlisted sailors reported aboard each ship, respectively, in Honolulu, Hawaii and New Bedford, Massachusetts. These nucleus crews spoke fluent English, with all the enlisted men recent graduates from United States armed forces specialty training schools. The 6 February edition of the *Honolulu Advertiser* had this

Coast Guard Engineman First Class Raymond C. Mullins training his South Vietnamese Navy counterpart, Nguyen Van Phat, during the Vietnamization era as the United States eases itself out of the war. (Courtesy of U.S. Navy)

article headline, "CG wants to keep Viet trainees happy." The writeup told of *Bering Strait* Coast Guardsmen scouring grocery markets in search of nuoc mam, the ubiquitous fish sauce Vietnamese use in their food. The chief master-at-arms grumpily substantiated the headline in remarks to others that the ship treated the Vietnamese like visitors instead of trainees. No wonder, since rice cookers were scattered throughout the ship and the Vietnamese were taken on tours and given a lot of special liberty. This was supposedly done to help the men adjust to their foreign surroundings, with the understanding that once the ship got under way they would be worked hard.

After some independent patrolling, the two ships joined up in Hawaii and crossed the ocean to Subic Bay in May. Shortly thereafter, the mixed crews began *Market Time* patrols. By the end of June, roughly a third of the Vietnamese complement needed to man each ship was aboard. About a third of these had completely replaced Coast Guardsmen.

All the cultural problems experienced by Squadron One were repeated with Squadron Three, and then some. There was the Vietnamese seaman who declined to mess cook because menial galley labor was not appropriate for the son of a man who owned a big hotel in Saigon. Even though the other Vietnamese seamen saw nothing wrong in this, such preferential treatment is not customary in the American armed forces, and so the privileged sailor found his arms in greasy, soapy water scrubbing pots and pans. He reacted in typical fashion of one who is used to having his way and not getting it, by depriving something of himself from others. He had been the ship's interpreter. Now, all at once, he lost his ability to understand English.

As quickly as practical, commanding officers qualified the Vietnamese to carry out the external functions that dealt with Vietnamese civilians to deemphasize the American presence and elevate the people's confidence in their government's representatives. Boardings and civic actions, such as medical care, fell into this grouping. The philosophy showed merit. Le Quang Dung, trained as a Hospital Corpsman in the United States, worked alongside Coast Guard Chief Hospital Corpsman Joseph White on community sick call. In one village on his route a traveling South Vietnamese army medic could not gain the people's trust to treat them. But after seeing him associating with White and Le Quang Dung their esteem for him rose and they accepted his care.

Predictably, Coast Guard and Navy press releases made only favorable statements regarding Vietnamese crew assimilation. While generally true, these statements were superficial and misleading. One paragraph touted that in four months the *Yakutat* fired more than 64 tons of 5-inch projectiles, while during her entire 1967 deployment only a mere 19 tons were expended. Another paragraph said that the *Bering Strait* gunfire activity during the "training period" had also increased by comparison. From this the public audience could readily conclude, with great relief, that Vietnamization was surpassing expectations. But a peek behind the curtain reveals that the mission had changed since 1967 and these cutters were now required to put more time on the gun line. Press releases gave little detail to the crucial matter of performance—that is, how the Vietnamese crews were actually progressing. A revealing source for this could be found in a commanding officer's monthly operational summary. What Commander Paul D. Henneberry, commanding officer, *Bering Strait*, wrote shows the simultaneous pessimism and optimism aboard these cutters in transition:

> *The state of training and ability of the ship to respond to requirements is currently poor. While we can and have responded to all operations; our response is marginal. This is due to the loss of 40 experienced CG personnel and the arrival of 36 relatively inexperienced VNN sailors during September. The problem will be compounded in a few days when we lose 30 more CG and gain 30 new VNN personnel. The training program is less effective now because (1) the newer VNN arrivals are less fluent in English than the earlier groups, (2) the training program must be recycled to the most basic level each time a new group comes aboard, and (3) the newer Petty Officer arrivals are frequently senior to those we have on board and almost without exception will not listen to advice from the more junior yet more experienced VNN Petty Officers. The latter problem is a cultural one (save face) which we must accept and live with. It is expensive in terms of man hours because we*

> *must use our few senior Petty Officers to train senior VNN Petty Officers on a man for man basis.*
>
> *This past patrol has been particularly frustrating and hair raising due mostly to the noticeably slower response of the ship as a team in all areas of admin, and ops. The fact remains however that it did respond to the most active period of op (sic) to date—including several all night gunfire support missions. Operations, Deck and Engineering Departments are now headed, administered and operated by VN officers. All internal comms circuits are manned by VN. B-1 engineroom is manned, operated and maintained exclusively by VN. Despite the fact that this report does not reflect great optimism, I am none the less confident that our Vietnamese shipmates are learning and will by January be able to operate the ship. It is doubtful that GQ stations will be manned and ready in 3 minutes...a man overboard picked up in 5 minutes....I am reasonably sure ship will operate marginally and 3–6 months will bring remarkable improvements.*[1]

Captain Richard E. Hoover, who commanded Squadron Three, might have witnessed Henneberry's forecast of "remarkable improvements" six months after the *Bering Strait* was transferred to South Vietnam. Hoover had visited the ship just after she came in from patrol. He cheerfully wrote in the squadron diary,

> The ship and her crew presented a smart appearance. State of cleanliness and preservation was excellent. All machinery and equipment reported operating normally except for the evaporator (awaiting parts) and surface search radar, also awaiting parts.[2]

Although impressed with appearance, he did not reveal if the ship could yet fish up a man overboard within five minutes.

In a colorful ceremony at the South Vietnamese Navy shipyard in Saigon on 1 January 1971 that opened with prayer from a U.S. Navy chaplain and closed with blessings by a Buddhist monk, the *Bering Strait* and the *Yakutat* became, respectively, *Tran Quang Khai* (HQ-2) and *Tran Nhat Duat* (HQ-3). The number of cutters in Squadron Three had been reduced from five to four some six months earlier. This transaction dropped that number to two, and the Coast Guard commandant had already made it known that more ships were available for South Vietnam.

The beginning of the end of the Coast Guard presence in Vietnam started with the turnover of the Squadron One cutters to South Vietnam. Here, South Vietnamese sailors take possession of two cutters during the close of official ceremonies. (Courtesy of U.S. Navy)

The last two cutters serving in Squadron Three would not return to their Portland, Maine home port. Toward the end of their deployment they began training replacement South Vietnamese crews and on 21 December, after less than three months of indoctrination, the USCGC *Castle Rock* (WHEC-383) became the *Tran Binh Trong* (HQ-5) and the USCGC *Cook Inlet* (WHEC-384) became the *Tran Quoc Toan* (HQ-6). With no ships to direct, Squadron Three was officially disestablished on 30 January 1972.

In the following months three more Coast Guard cutters were given to the South Vietnamese Navy after suitable crew break-in. Like the others they were 311-foot former World War II seaplane tenders. On 15 July 1972, the USCGC *Absecon* (WHEC-374) became the *Tham Ngu Lao* (HQ-15), and on 21 June 1972, the USCGC *Chincoteague* (WHEC-375) became the *Ly Thoung Kiet* (HQ-16) and the USCGC *McCulloch* (WHEC-386) became the *Ngo Kuyen* (HQ-17).

After Squadron One dissolved in 1970 a hundred Coast Guardsmen still remained in Vietnam. Coast Guard Activities, Vietnam, became Senior Coast Guard Officer, Vietnam (SCGOV), with a smaller staff, and a sub-unit of SEASEC. Still functioning were the Port Security & Waterways Detail, Explosive Loading Detachments, Aids to Navigation Detail, LORAN Stations, and Merchant Marine Detail.

The U.S. Army Vietnamization plan called for the progressive turnover of all ports to South Vietnam. This added teaching to the regular duties of the men of the PSWD and the ELDs. They taught South Vietnamese soldiers who would be replacing the stevedores under U.S. contract how to unload ships. For their own replacements, they held courses for specially selected soldiers. One such course concluded on 17 November 1971 with the SCGOV presiding at the graduation in Cat Lai of a dozen new South Vietnamese dangerous cargomen. The happy occasion was followed by a lavish buffet prepared by the wives and girlfriends of the graduates. But ship captains did not share the Coast Guard's confidence and were not ready to accept these South Vietnamese overseers. The Coast Guard had to appeal to the Military Sealift Command Officer, Vietnam, to direct their acceptance. The MSCOV agreed, with the exception that any ammunition returning to the United States be loaded under Coast Guard scrutiny.

It was reasonable to believe that South Vietnam could carry on the roles the Coast Guard was turning over. But one area gave COMCOGARDACTV, and successor, SCGOV, the most difficulty to achieve successfully. This was maintaining an effective aids to navigation system. On 14 November 1968 COMCOGARDACTV advised Coast Guard Headquarters "...the Directorate of Navigation does not have the capability at present to assume the responsibility of maintaining the aids to navigation installed in support of U.S. missions by the USCG. It is doubtful if they ever will have the capability."[3] The letter concluded with the optimism that the South Vietnamese Navy might take it over. This hope was short-lived when it was vehemently opposed by the Directorate of Navigation. Correctly perceiving the sensitive political ramifications involved, the Coast Guard never brought up the subject again.

Even before Vietnamization it had always been the intent to hand over responsibility for the navigational aids network as soon as South Vietnam could handle it. The 1967 staff study forecasted that the Vietnamese would be in charge on 1 January 1969. But six months past that date, when Headquarters asked for a status update, nothing had changed. Not only was the Coast Guard still in charge, it was even caring for those Vietnamese buoys considered necessary to U.S. shipping.

Another letter to Headquarters, in June 1969, related that in a meeting with Directorate of Navigation and USAID representatives the pointed question of when the government could take over was asked. A Vietnamese official evaded the query by saying that he would have to consult higher authority, while the USAID officials showed indifference. The letter described the latter as "apathetic," calling them "short-timers" with no apparent desire to implement a new project.[4] In defense of the USAID they were in the midst of a staff upheaval; as a result, for a short time thereafter and until that problem sorted itself out, the agency authorized the Coast Guard direct liaison with the South Vietnamese.

Still, in the end, the Coast Guard accepted the reality that South Vietnam would never commit the people, equipment, or funds to run an expanded ATON program. Therefore, the devised turnover plan modified the current setup so that it fell within the country's capabilities, and would still meet the needs of military and commercial shipping. This was to be achieved by replacing most of the lighted and unlighted buoys with fixed lighted structures and fixed day beacons. Buoys required more attention and were expensive to keep up. They were constantly being dragged off station, sunk, or damaged, whereas fixed aids, many located ashore, were not as vulnerable. The Coast Guard would also replace obsolete and nonstandard equipment on South Vietnamese minor lights and lighted buoys, making them maintenance-compatible. Ample replacement aids and spare parts were to be part of the transfer package for each of the country's four designated phaseout areas. The Joint Chiefs of Staff accepted the Coast Guard plan on 10 February 1970 and South Vietnam agreed in principle. In December the parties signed a formal agreement.

But what sounded fine in meetings and looked fine on paper still had to be accomplished in reality. Hindrances were plentiful. The South Vietnamese buoy tender, *Cuu Long,* was still a floating, or more so a non-floating and chronic headache. In November 1970, she entered drydock to have her hull scraped and painted for the first time in six years. But a clean bottom could not make her run better when she had engines so obsolete that parts had to be made for them. On 25 February 1971, the prospective captain refused to get the vessel under way, citing equipment deficiencies. Apparently, he found a better job elsewhere too, because in June the *Cuu Long* had neither a master nor a chief mechanic. Low wages made finding any replacements scarce. Something kept coming up to keep her snuggling the dock, such as having all her steam lines replaced. There were other misfortunes. A boat carrying a contract survey team assigned to build some of the fixed aids hit a mine, killing seven of the nine surveyors. A month before that another survey boat designated for this project sank in a storm, taking the master along with her.

The realization that aids to navigation was of little importance to South Vietnam was expressed by Commander Peter D. Corson, the SCGOV, in this August 1971 unit diary entry:

> *The prognosis for satisfactory GVN acceptance of the ATON mission as we know it is poor. All the equipment in the world would make no difference. It is not a question of knowledge as the people with whom we deal are experts. They need scarcely any instruction on ATON maintenance procedure. The only reason ATON are needed here now is to support the U.S. mission and the VN people don't give a "Damn" about that. They have the expertise and the equipment but are missing the need, the will, and the inclination. These things we can't give them. We will continue to try however.*

And by example they did try. In May 1972 the ATON Coordinator and his lone remaining assistant spent three days fabricating and setting five buoys in the channel leading into Tan My harbor. To do this they collected 55-gallon drums and cable from Tan My LORAN Station, and from a local junkyard gathered up an old electric motor and cement blocks to use for sinkers. The buoys had been urgently requested by NAVFORV for South Vietnamese and U.S. Navy LSTs delivering supplies and evacuating war refugees at the time of North Vietnam's spring offensive into South Vietnam.

If the government seemed casual about navigational aids, citizens found them useful. One afternoon a work party from the Coast Guard buoy tender *Basswood* was ashore installing a dayboard near a small village. The usual crowd of spectators had gathered to watch. As the dayboard was being hoisted by a small block and tackle, an elderly man stepped forward, cut the line and calmly walked off with the dayboard.

The *Basswood* entered South Vietnamese waters 23 April 1972 for the last Coast Guard buoy tender deployment. One of her tasks was fabricating steel battery boxes and welding them onto fixed light structures, a procedure that greatly reduced vandalism. When she departed Vietnam 6 May 1972 she reported all aids left in the best possible condition.

That concluded the effort to give the country an effective marine aids to navigation network. Not all the modifications intended were accomplished, because delays and costly repairs used up time and funding. Still, an adequate system was left in place. The ATON Detail stayed on a while longer, providing technical advice, distributing supplies, and performing emergency repairs.

The end of the line came in 1973. The SCGOV, PSWD, ELDs, and ATON Detail shut down on 11 February. Earlier, in November, the U.S. Air Force moved its helicopter rescue force from Danang to Nakkon Phanom, Thailand, taking the Coast Guard aviators along. The last Merchant Marine Detail officer left the country 1 May 1973. The two LORAN Stations in South Vietnam continued operation, but, in keeping with the peace agreement that American military personnel leave the country, they were manned by civilians under contract, most of them Coast Guardsmen who had retired or had gotten out when their time was up.

The significant Vietnam adventure for the U.S. Coast Guard lasted eight years and garnered military and public praise. But the time lapse between wars works as a light-dimming switch. Bright glory fades away into forgotten blackness, leaving, as always between major wars, Coast Guard military history reclining in solitude until the next conflict, when the current generation rediscovers the Coast Guard as a fighting force.

As they have done throughout history, and as they did in Vietnam, when big trouble comes along, Coast Guard members will head off to fight without fanfare, heeding the cry, "Somebody, get the Coast Guard!"

Epilogue

It was business as usual in the Southeast Asia Section office in Bangkok until the American Embassy in Saigon telephoned the afternoon of 18 March 1975. A week earlier the section staff had visited Tan My LORAN Station, where everything appeared peaceful. Now a voice on the telephone was asking about the plan for evacuating it.

North Vietnam had begun its all-out onslaught to conquer South Vietnam. Its soldiers spilled over the landscape virtually unopposed. Some South Vietnamese units valiantly held their ground to the death, but most soldiers fled in panic. The day after the embassy call Tan My's crew was pulled out and the LORAN Station stopped transmitting forever.

Six weeks later, the teletype in the SEASEC Office clattered out this unexpected alarm from Con Son LORAN Station: THERE IS A CHOPPER ON THE STATION THAT SAYS THAT WE ARE SUPPOSED TO BE EVACUATED NOW REQUEST INSTRUCTIONS SHOULD WE LEAVE NOW OR WAIT FOR NAVY EVAC.

The pilot of the Air America helicopter performing the frenetic task of plucking Americans out of the country to naval ships offshore told the station he was taking off in an hour and not coming back. A hasty abandonment meant leaving important equipment behind. The station advised that if a cargo plane could be sent in to take out the gear its men would clear the runway of wrecked and broken South Vietnamese aircraft. After making rapid queries SEASEC advised Con Son that a C-130 was en route.

Con Son then mentioned a further development—that surrounding the station were a thousand South Vietnamese who had gone almost overnight from free citizens to fleeing refugees. They seemed placid for the moment, yet the possibility existed that when the C-130 landed it might be mobbed, endangering the plane, its crew, and station evacuation. At this point SEASEC ordered the equipment destroyed, suggesting ruining the generators by running them without oil, and then for them to get out on that helicopter. Shortly before one o'clock that afternoon Con Son stopped transmitting. The next day South Vietnam surrendered.

The remaining LORAN stations in Thailand functioned until they were closed in the middle of September. On 3 October, SEASEC was disestablished, bringing to a close the U.S. Coast Guard's Vietnam era.

The only sure avenue of escape from the rampaging Communists was the sea. Hordes of South Vietnamese fled for their lives in commandeered naval vessels. Six of the seven former Coast Guard HECs, teeming with refugees, made port in the Philippines. The seventh, the *Absecon,* fell into enemy possession. The North Vietnamese renamed her the *Pham Ngu Lao* and in the mid-1980s modernized her armament with surface-to-surface missiles. She was still operational well into the 1990s. Of the 26 Squadron One cutters only the *Point Clear* escaped. She too made it to the Philippines. The other WPBs were rounded up and taken north, but for lack of replacement parts, languished, dying from disuse.

On 22 and 23 May 1975, Commander Albert L. Olsen Jr., Senior Coast Guard Officer, Philippines, and three other Coast Guardsmen took the initiative to inspect the former HECs anchored in Subic Bay and sent their findings to headquarters. Understandably, conditions below decks compared to a "garbage scow," but the rats did not mind. The ships showed signs of hasty evacuation, with logs and publications undisturbed and bridge equipment intact. The *Bering Strait* held ten tons of rice (a good grade of Louisiana, U.S.A. type), the *Castle Rock*'s reefers were full, while the *Yakutat* still carried plenty of canned food and baby milk. Engineering spaces had various degrees of flooding and machinery failure. One of the *Cook Inlet*'s engine rooms had water three feet deep above the deck plates. The *Bering Strait* was rated overall in the best shape and *McCulloch* next; the *Chincoteague* was judged the cleanest. Clearly, drydocking would restore the ships for duty. Headquarters thanked the inspectors for their "illuminating report," but the cutters were not wanted back.

At least the story of the 14-year-old blind girl, whom Coast Guardsmen sent to school in the United States, had a satisfying outcome. Nguyen Thi "Maria" Chien graduated from the Perkins School for the Blind in Watertown, Massachusetts, with honors. Moving over to Brandeis University, in Waltham, she earned a bachelor of arts degree in psychology in 1976. Her education did not stop there. She attended Boston College Graduate School, where she got a masters degree in educational and counseling psychology. Afterward she moved to San Francisco, where she went to work as a caseworker for a refugee resettlement center.

A close bond developed between many Coast Guardsmen and the South Vietnamese officers and petty officers who served in liaison capacity aboard the cutters. When the crew of the *Point Ellis* learned that Chief Boatswain's Mate Tran Van Sang needed to leave Danang for Saigon to be with his critically ill father and his expectant wife, they reached into their wallets to come up with the round trip air fare. The cutter's skipper, Lieutenant (j.g.) Gene E. Bowen, praised his liaison sailor: "If they were all like him, we wouldn't have to be over here...he's fantastic." Hardworking and unselfish, Tran Van Sang on one occasion dived off the *Point Ellis* to rescue an unconscious man who had fallen off a U.S. Navy ship. Then there was Petty Officer First Class Le Chung of the *Point Hudson,* showing his feelings by naming his sixth child, a son, Le Hudson, after the cutter.

These counterparts were cruelly treated under the Communist regime. Those who were not murdered outright found themselves in such callous imprisonment that some took their own lives for relief. Through the years some managed to escape to other countries. The ordeal of Petty Officer Second Class Nguyen Van Tien, a former liaison petty officer for the *Point Orient,* is a sample of what took place after North Vietnam crushed South Vietnam.

Upon becoming draft-eligible Tien joined the South Vietnamese Navy. Following boot camp he was sent to an Army school in San Antonio, Texas, to learn English, and then on to San Diego, California, to learn electronics at a Navy school. He began liaison duty on the PCFs. Tien's commanding officer approved of his performance and reassigned him to the WPBs of Division Twelve, where the patrols were longer. In 1968, at the age of 21, he began to frequently ride the *Point Orient,* where he formed close friendships. His wife and children lived in Danang. His father, sister, and brother resided just north of Saigon.

When the North Vietnamese took Danang, Tien was in the hospital. Amid the confusion of the takeover, a week later he fell in with an assorted group of displaced military men and began walking to Saigon. Some dropped out, some lagged behind, and the strongest kept pace. They subsisted on what food villagers along the way could spare, mostly red potatoes. Tien reached Saigon almost 20 days later. By then the city, too, had fallen. Tien was arrested by the North Vietnamese and taken, at night, shoeless and hands tightly bound behind his back, into the jungle, where he was locked in a bamboo structure that he believed had been a storage area for enemy supplies during the war. Aware that those who had served in the military were treated differently from other citizens, he knew he had no future, especially when he received word that he was being sent to North Vietnam, a common procedure for American sympathizers that usually ended in death. Tien's father, who had saved his money earned from driving a big bus in the better days, knew his son's only chance to live was escape. The prison guards, without any real possessions, provided the opportunity. Tien's father used a simple ploy, one that rarely failed in these circumstances: bribery. In this instance, the lure was ounces of gold. One night, without explanation, a guard took Tien outside, pointed to a jungle path, and told him to go. Unaware that this was his father's doing, he ran, knowing that this might be his sole chance for escape.

When he reached his father's house two days later his father greeted him with angry fear, telling his son to go to Danang to his wife. If he stayed around Saigon he would be caught again. The next morning he used his brother's voting card—something issued by the new government but without photographs—for identification to buy a train ticket to Danang.

For the next 12 years Tien existed in a prison of fear. Every knock on the door brought dread. The police were relentless in their community searches to capture men who had served in the South Vietnamese armed forces. Some nights he avoided detection by sleeping on his roof. While trying to avoid recapture he struggled to feed his family, taking jobs as he found them. He gathered hardwood from the jungle, selling it for cooking fires. He worked as a porter carrying large bags of rice, he unloaded trucks—yet he still lacked money to send his children to school for basic education. Danger never left him, like one's shadow; although it cannot always be seen, it is there. He could not take a steady job because of the risk of being caught. When he labored in public he hoped that police would notice only that he was a hard worker and, for that alone, leave him be. It was a rueful existence.

His distraught wife repeatedly urged him to leave the country. An opportunity arose in 1987, when others in a similar plight asked him to join them in escaping because he had been a sailor and the sea was their path to freedom. Several plans were proposed, but it was Tien's that was accepted. They bought a boat from a fishing village with a few ounces of gold and cached it at the base of Monkey Mountain—ironically, not far from where Division Twelve cutters had once moored.

As Tien was getting ready to leave for the rendezvous his oldest daughter, now 14, told him she wanted to go with him. He gave her the timeless fatherly response, "Ask your mother." Mother said yes.

Before dawn on a Sunday in July, 13 people, including three children, ages 16, 14, and 11, in a sampan less than 25 feet long and propelled by a tiny motor, left their homeland and loved ones for a better life. The time and day had been chosen after protracted observations of naval and police patrols. Sunday morning had been picked because the authorities showed less activity and vigilance then. Using a compass and an ordinary geography map, Tien navigated them in two days to their first landfall: Hainan Island. Villagers on this Chinese possession gave the refugees food and gasoline. After the war against the Americans had ended, the new Vietnam began fighting China, its former ally. Therefore, it made sense to these people that aiding refugees was opposing Vietnam. Strong winds from the south helped their progress and five days later they unerringly entered their destination, Hong Kong Harbor. Later, when Tien was asked by a former executive officer on *Point Orient* how he came to do such a good job of navigation, Tien replied that he learned from watching the Coast Guard.

Tien and his daughter were clothed, fed, and well-treated at the Chimawan Closed Camp for Vietnamese refugees. South Vietnamese having served in the government or military received priority attention, but proof was needed. Amazingly, Tien, after all these years, still had his military identification card. However, to fulfill the dream of reaching the United States, sponsorship by an American citizen was required. Once again Tien's resourceful nature came to his rescue. All this time he had kept a small piece of paper with the address of the mother of one of the *Point Orient* skippers, should he need to get in touch. He sent a letter to the former skipper by way of his parents in Tennessee, who passed it on to their son, who gladly gave his sponsorship. While the emigration process moved at turtle speed, Tien and his daughter were moved to a refugee camp in the Philippines. There he passed time teaching English to other Vietnamese and served as an interpreter.

The journey that began in 1975 by walking from Danang to Saigon ended at one o'clock in the morning of 28 August 1988 when Tien and his daughter stepped off an airplane in Washington, DC for a joyous reunion with James B. Ellis III, former commanding officer of the *Point Orient*. This ending became happier in 1992 when Tien was joined in the United States by his wife and six other children. In the United States Tien was able to earn a living for his family and to put all his children into college. He even found time to earn a degree for himself.

Many Vietnam War veterans felt let down for their country's mishandling of the entire affair. For the nation, guilty of this misconduct, it provided a lesson, at least in the near future, to be more purposeful in any such bloody involvements. Veterans, meanwhile, take solace in knowing that their performance was testimony to their duty and honor, and therefore are proud of their Vietnam service. Disagreements on the United States' involvement and conduct will go on forever, but one proud combat veteran, Admiral Paul A. Yost Jr., USCG (Retired), summed up the conflict rather well one day in his office. Yost was Commandant of the Coast Guard from 1986 to 1990. In Vietnam, from 1969 to 1970, he commanded the Gulf of Thailand Surveillance Group, with Navy and Coast Guard units under his command. His conspicuous gallantry on 12 April 1969 was rewarded with a Silver Star Medal. After his convoy of PCFs fought clear of a river ambush, he realized that one of his boats was missing. He reentered the fire zone with another boat to find the PCF aground on the riverbank, the surviving crewmen behind the PCF in knee deep water using the hull for a shield. Yost led the attack against the ambushers, recovering the boat's survivors and dead.

Pressing the tips of his fingers together, Yost rested his chin on the point of the triangle his hands made, and reflected:

> I could tell a lot of war stories, but in closing just let me say I think we should have been in Vietnam. The thing that we did for Vietnam couldn't have been done any other way, that is we gave the Vietnamese an opportunity to save their country. We went over there, we put in the infrastructure, the supply, the ammunition, the command presence, the communications, the know-how, and the training. We put in everything that was needed to win that war. And had they been valiant, had they been willing to get rid of the graft in their own country, to get the feelings of nationalism, to fight for their country, to inspire their troops instead of ripping them off and stealing from them, to put down the black market instead of selling the U.S. supplies on the black market, to use them where they were supposed to be used, to risk their equipment and their lives for their country, they had a chance to win the war. As it turned out, when we moved out the backbone of the operation moved out, and they were not willing to risk their materials, to risk their lives. The government was shot through with graft and corruption. The officer corps often didn't lead, wasn't professional, stole from their people by not paying them, taking kickbacks, and all sorts of things. And they lost the war. Whether they could have won it had they been valiant I don't know, but they had a chance, an opportunity to win it which they didn't take. I don't feel a bit badly about us being there. We provided a nation with the opportunity to stay free. The fact that that nation did not stay free that's on their heads. That blood is on their heads, not on mine, and not on the forces of the United States, and I feel very positive about having participated in that war.
>
> That's it!

GLOSSARY

ATON — Aids to Navigation.
CINCPAC — Commander in Chief, Pacific.
COMCOGARDACTV — Commander Coast Guard Activities, Vietnam.
COMCOGARDRONE — Commander Coast Guard Squadron One.
COMNAVFORV — Commander Naval Forces, Vietnam.
COMUSMACV — Commander United States Military Assistance Command, Vietnam.
CSC — Coastal Surveillance Center.
CZ — Contiguous Zone—the waters three to twelve miles off the coast.
DER — Radar-Picket Destroyer Escort.
DMZ — Demilitarized Zone.
ELD — Explosives Loading Detachment. Coast Guard unit that supervises dangerous cargo transfer to or from a ship.
FAC — Forward Air Controller.
HEC — High Endurance Cutter.
JSARC — Joint Search and Rescue Center. Control and coordination post at Tan Son Nhut Air Base for rescuing downed aviators.
Junk Force — A paramilitary force of primarily local fishermen started in 1960 to counter Viet Cong infiltrations. This motorized and sail junk fleet was absorbed into the South Vietnamese Navy in 1965 and designated Coastal Force, but it was still popularly known as the Junk Force.
Kit Carson Scout — A former Viet Cong guerilla fighting with South Vietnam.
LORAN — Long Range Navigation. An electronic network for mariners and aviators for locating position.
MARAD — Maritime Administration.
MEDCAP — Medical Civil Action Program.
MSTS — Military Sealift Transportation Service.
M/V — Motor Vessel.
NGFS — Naval Gunfire Support.
PCF — Patrol Craft, Fast. In Vietnam the U.S. Navy's 50-foot "Swift Boat."
PSWD — Port Security and Waterways Detail. Coast Guard advisors to the U.S. Army in Vietnam.

RS — Rescue Specialist. Aircrew member specially trained to leave a rescue helicopter to assist an injured aviator on the ground or in the water. Also known as pararescueman or parajumper (PJ).

RSSZ — A 400-square-mile region bounded on the west by the Soi Rap River, on the south by the South China Sea, and on the east and north roughly by the highway running between Saigon and Vung Tau. Primarily dense mangrove swamp, with sampan the major means of transportation. A Viet Cong stronghold.

SAM — Surface-to-Air Missile.

SEASEC — Southeast Asia Section. The command post for LORAN-C units in South Vietnam and Thailand.

USAID — United States Agency for International Development.

WPB — Coast Guard patrol boat. In Vietnam, specifically the 82-foot-long class.

CHRONOLOGY

February 16, 1965	North Vietnam arms trawler found unloading in South Vietnam.
March 8, 1965	First American combat troops arrive when U.S. Marines reach Danang.
April 29, 1965	Defense and Treasury announce that U.S. Coast Guard cutters will operate with U.S. Navy in Vietnam.
May 27, 1965	Squadron One commissioned in ceremony at USCG Base, Alameda, California.
June 17, 1965	First Coast Guard WPBs arrive by merchant ship at U.S. Naval Base, Subic Bay, Republic of Philippines.
July 16, 1965	Division Twelve WPBs leave Subic Bay for Danang.
July 20, 1965	Division Twelve WPBs arrive at Danang.
July 21, 1965	Coast Guard *Market Time* patrolling begins with five WPBs deployed along the Demilitarized Zone.
July 24, 1965	Division Eleven WPBs leave Subic Bay.
July 31, 1965	Division Eleven WPBs arrive at An Thoi.
September 21, 1965	White-hulled WPBs ordered painted gray.
September 29, 1965	Nine more WPBs ordered to Vietnam.
December 1, 1965	Defense asks Coast Guard to install LORAN-C network in Southeast Asia.
December 12, 1965	Division Thirteen established, forms in Subic Bay.
January 31, 1966	Coast Guard Activities, Vietnam, formed in Saigon, absorbs Squadron One command.
February 18, 1966	Division Thirteen WPBs leave Subic Bay for Cat Lo.
April 24, 1966	USCGC *Planetree* arrives at Vung Tau. First Coast Guard buoy tender deployed to Vietnam.
May 10, 1966	Coast Guard makes *Market Time*'s first major counter-infiltration success when *Point Grey* intercepts a North Vietnamese arms trawler. Vessel destroyed.
June 4, 1966	First Coast Guard Explosives Loading Detachments arrive in Vietnam.

June 20, 1966	Second trawler battle. *Point League* makes intercept. Vessel captured with 100 tons of weapons, ammunition, and other supplies.
August 8, 1966	USCG Southeast Asia LORAN network on the air.
August 11, 1966	*Point Welcome* taken for enemy craft, attacked by U.S. Air Force. Two Coast Guardsmen killed.
October 15, 1966	USCG Port Security and Waterways Detail arrives in Vietnam.
October 28, 1966	LORAN-C network fully operational.
December 3, 1966	Coast Guard Shipping Advisor arrives in Vietnam. Forerunner of Merchant Marine Detail.
December 19, 1966	Three-man Coast Guard navigational aids team arrives to assess needs for vessel traffic safety. Forerunner of Aids to Navigation Detail.
January 1, 1967	*Point Gammon* and two PCFs battle trawler. Vessel explodes.
March 14, 1967	*Point Ellis* and U.S. Navy units fight trawler. Vessel destroyed.
April 25, 1967	Squadron Three commissioned, ceremony at U.S. Naval Base, Honolulu, Hawaii.
April 26, 1967	Five-ship Squadron Three en route for Subic Bay.
May 10, 1967	Squadron Three arrives Subic Bay, sets up headquarters.
May 15, 1967	*Gresham, Bering Strait,* and *Barataria* begin Squadron Three's *Market Time* patrolling.
July 15, 1967	*Point Orient* leads attack on North Vietnamese trawler. Her accurate, killing mortar fire on pilothouse prevents any self-destruction effort. Trawler is captured.
March 1, 1968	Four trawlers attempt to run *Market Time* blockade with desperately needed supplies. Three are destroyed in battle with Squadron One and Three cutters, and other units. The fourth trawler flees.
April 3, 1968	Coast Guard helicopter pilots arrive to fly combat search and rescue with the U.S. Air Force.
June 9, 1968	Lieutenant Jack C. Rittichier, Coast Guard pilot, is killed with his crew after his helicopter is shot down in a rescue attempt.
May 16, 1969	Vietnamization is in progress. The *Point League* and *Point Garnet* are first Squadron One cutters given to the South Vietnamese Navy.
June 5, 1969	Division Eleven disestablished.
March 16, 1970	Division Twelve disestablished.
August 15, 1970	Division Thirteen disestablished when last two WPBs, *Point Cypress* and *Point Marone,* are turned over to South Vietnam. Squadron One is decommissioned.
November 21, 1970	Squadron Three's *Rush* and *Sherman* destroy North Vietnamese trawler.

January 1, 1971	Squadron Three's *Yakutat* and *Bering Strait* turned over to South Vietnamese Navy.
April 12, 1971	Squadron Three cutters *Morgenthau, Rush,* and USS *Antelope* intercept and destroy North Vietnamese trawler.
December 21, 1971	Squadron Three's *Cook Inlet* and *Castle Rock* turned over to South Vietnam.
January 31, 1972	Squadron Three decommissioned.
February 11, 1973	ATON Detail, PSWD, and ELDs are disestablished.
May 1, 1973	Merchant Marine Detail disestablished.
March 19, 1975	North Vietnam on the offensive. Tan My LORAN Station evacuated.
April 29, 1975	Con Son LORAN Station evacuated.
April 30, 1975	South Vietnam surrenders.
October 3, 1975	USCG Southeast Asia LORAN-C network disestablished.

APPENDIX A

SQUADRON ONE CUTTERS

NAME
  COMMISSIONED
    U.S. HOMEPORT
      VIETNAM HOMEPORT
	TURNED OVER TO SVN
	NEW NAME
	HULL NO.

Point Arden (WPB 82309)
  1 February 1961
    Point Pleasant, New Jersey
      Danang
	14 February 1970
	Pham Ngoc Chau
	(HQ-710)

Point Banks (WPB 82327)
  13 December 1961
    Woods Hole, Massachusetts
      An Thoi
	26 May 1970
	Ngo Van Quyen
	(HQ-718)

Point Caution (WPB 82301)
  5 October 1960
    Galveston, Texas
      Danang
	29 April 1970
	Nguyen An
	(HQ-716)

Point Clear (WPB 82315)
  26 April 1961
    San Pedro, California
      An Thoi
	15 September 1969
	Huynh Van Cu
	(HQ-702)

Point Comfort (WPB 82317)
  24 May 1961
    Benicia, California
      An Thoi
	17 November 1969
	Dao Thuc
	(HQ-704)

Point Cypress (WPB 82326)
   22 November 1961
     Newport, Rhode Island
     Cat Lo

15 August 1970
Ho Duy
(HQ-724)

Point Dume (WPB 82325)
   1 November 1961
     Bayshore, New York
     Danang

14 February 1970
Thuong Tien
(HQ-709)

Point Ellis (WPB 82330)
   28 February 1962
     Port Townsend, Washington
     Danang

9 December 1969
Le Ngoc Thanh
(HQ-705)

Point Gammon (WPB 82328)
   31 January 1962
     San Francisco, California
     Danang

11 November 1969
Nguyen Dao
(HQ-703)

Point Garnet (WPB 82310)
   15 March 1961
     Norfolk, Virginia
     An Thoi

16 May 1969
Le Phuoc Duc
(HQ-700)

Point Glover (WPB 82307)
   7 December 1960
     Fort Hancock, New Jersey
     An Thoi

14 February 1970
Dao Van Dang
(HQ-711)

Point Grace (WPB 82323)
   27 September 1961
     Crisfield, Maryland
     Cat Lo

16 June 1970
Ho Dang La
(HQ-720)

Point Grey (WPB 82324)
   11 October 1961
     Norfolk, Virginia
     An Thoi

14 July 1970
Huynh Bo
(HQ-722)

Point Hudson (WPB 82322)
   30 August 1961
     Panama City, Florida
     Cat Lo

11 December 1969
Dang Van Hoanh
(HQ-707)

Point Jefferson (WPB 82306)
   7 December 1960
      Nantucket, Massachusetts
      Cat Lo

Point Kennedy (WPB 82320)
   19 July 1961
      San Juan, Puerto Rico
      Cat Lo

Point League (WPB 82304)
   9 November 1960
      Morgan City, Louisiana
      Cat Lo

Point Lomas (WPB 82321)
   9 August 1961
      Port Aransas, Texas
      Danang

Point Marone (WPB 82331)
   14 March 1962
      San Pedro, California
      An Thoi

Point Mast (WPB 82316)
   10 May 1961
      Long Beach, California
      An Thoi

Point Orient (WPB 82319)
   28 June 1961
      Fort Pierce, Florida
      Danang

Point Partridge (WPB 82305)
   23 November 1960
      Beals, Maine
      Cat Lo

Point Slocum (WPB 82313)
   12 April 1961
      St. Thomas, Virgin Islands
      Cat Lo

21 February 1970
Le Dgoc An
(HQ-712)

16 March 1970
Huynh Van Ngan
(HQ-713)

16 May 1969
Le Van Nga
(HQ-701)

26 May 1970
Van Dien
(HQ-719)

15 August 1970
Troung Ba
(HQ-725)

16 June 1970
Dam Thoai
(HQ-721)

14 July 1970
Nguyen Kim Hung
(HQ-723)

27 March 1970
Bui Viet Thanh
(HQ-715)

11 December 1969
Nguyen Ngoc Thach
(HQ-706)

Point Welcome (WPB 82329)
    14 February 1962
      Everett, Washington
      Danang

29 April 1970
Nguyen Han
(HQ-717)

Point White (WPB 82308)
    18 January 1961
      New London, Connecticut
      Cat Lo

12 January 1970
Le Dinh Hung
(HQ-708)

Point Young (WPB 82303)
    26 October 1960
      Grand Isle, Louisiana
      An Thoi

16 March 1970
Tran Lo
(HQ-714)

APPENDIX B

Squadron Three Cutters

NAME/HOME PORT	DEPLOYMENT
First Group:	
USCGC *Barataria* (WHEC 381) Portland, Maine	4 May 1967 – 25 December 1967
USCGC *Bering Strait* (WHEC 382) Honolulu, Hawaii	4 May 1967 – 18 February 1968
USCGC *Gresham* (WHEC 387) Alameda, California	4 May 1967 – 28 January 1968
USCGC *Half Moon* (WHEC 378) New York, New York	4 May 1967 – 29 December 1967
USCGC *Yakutat* (WHEC 380) New Bedford, Massachusetts	4 May 1967 – 1 January 1968
Second Group:	
USCGC *Androscoggin* (WHEC 68) Miami, Florida	4 December 1967 – 4 August 1968
USCGC *Campbell* (WHEC 32) Portland, Maine	14 December 1967 – 12 August 1968
USCGC *Duane* (WHEC 33) Boston, Massachusetts	4 December 1967 – 28 July 1968
USCGC *Minnetonka* (WHEC 67) Long Beach, California	5 January 1968 – 29 September 1968
USCGC *Winona* (WHEC 65) Port Angeles, Washington	25 January 1968 – 17 October 1968
Third Group:	
USCGC *Bibb* (WHEC 31) Boston, Massachusetts	4 July 1968 – 28 February 1969

USCGC *Ingham* (WHEC 35)
    Norfolk, Virginia
16 July 1968 –
3 April 1969

USCGC *Owasco* (WHEC 39)
    New London, Connecticut
23 July 1968 –
21 March 1969

USCGC *Wachusett* (WHEC 44)
    Seattle, Washington
10 September 1968 –
1 June 1969

USCGC *Winnebago* (WHEC 40)
    Honolulu, Hawaii
20 September 1968 –
19 July 1969

Fourth Group:

USCGC *Klamath* (WHEC 66)
    Seattle, Washington
7 July 1969 –
3 April 1970

USCGC *Mendota* (WHEC 69)
    Wilmington, North Carolina
28 February 1969 –
3 November 1969

USCGC *Sebago* (WHEC 42)
    Pensacola, Florida
2 March 1969 –
16 November 1969

USCGC *Spencer* (WHEC 36)
    New York, New York
11 February 1969 –
30 September 1969

USCGC *Taney* (WHEC 37)
    Alameda, California
14 May 1969 –
31 January 1970

Fifth Group:

USCGC *Chase* (WHEC 718)
    Boston, Massachusetts
6 December 1969 –
28 May 1970

USCGC *Dallas* (WHEC 716)
    New York, New York
3 November 1969 –
19 June 1970

USCGC *Hamilton* (WHEC 715)
    Boston, Massachusetts
1 November 1969 –
25 May 1970

USCGC *Mellon* (WHEC 717)
    Honolulu, Hawaii
31 March 1970 –
2 July 1970

USCGC *Pontchartrain* (WHEC 70)
    Long Beach, California
9 May 1970 –
3 September 1970

Sixth Group:

USCGC *Bering Strait* (WHEC 382)
    Honolulu, Hawaii
17 May 1970 –
31 December 1970

USCGC *Sherman* (WHEC 720)
    Boston, Massachusetts
22 April 1970 –
25 December 1970

USCGC *Yakutat* (WHEC 380)
    New Bedford, Massachusetts
17 May 1970 –
31 December 1970

Seventh Group:

USCGC *Morgenthau* (WHEC 722)
    New York, New York
6 December 1970 –
31 July 1971

USCGC *Rush* (WHEC 723)
    Alameda, California
28 October 1970 –
15 July 1971

Eighth Group:
  USCGC *Castle Rock* (WHEC 383)   9 July 1971 –
    Portland, Maine   21 December 1971
  USCGC *Cook Inlet* (WHEC 384)   6 December 1970 –
    Portland, Maine   21 December 1971

Ship, Dates Transferred to South Vietnam, New Name

USCGC *Bering Strait* (WHEC 328)
  1 January 1971 – *Tran Quang Khai* (HQ-02)
USCGC *Yakutat* (WHEC 380)
  1 January 1971 – *Tran Nhat Duat* (HQ-03)
USCGC *Castle Rock* (WHEC 383)
  21 December 1971 – *Tran Binh Trong* (HQ-05)
USCGC *Cook Inlet* (WHEC 384)
  21 December 1971 – *Tran Quoc Toan* (HQ-06)
USCGC *Chincoteague* (WHEC 375)
  21 June 1972 – *Ly Thoung Kiet* (HQ-16)
USCGC *McCulloch* (WHEC 386)
  21 June 1972 – *Ngo Kuyen* (HQ-17)
USCGC *Abescon* (WHEC 374)
  15 July 1972 – *Tham Ngu Lao* (HQ-15)

APPENDIX C

OTHER CUTTER DEPLOYMENTS TO VIETNAM

Buoy Tenders

    USCGC *Basswood* (WLB 388)
        14 October 1967 – 27 November 1967
        16 October 1967 – 10 December 1967
        15 March 1972 – 5 May 1972

    USCGC *Blackhaw* (WLB 390)
        13 March 1968 – 6 May 1968
        24 June 1968 – 18 July 1968
         9 September 1968 – 11 October 1968
        16 January 1969 – 4 March 1969
        16 April 1969 – 3 May 1969
        16 June 1969 – 3 July 1969
        24 October 1969 – 7 December 1969
        17 January 1970 – 6 March 1970
        23 April 1970 – 18 May 1970
        22 June 1970 – 7 July 1970
        25 August 1970 – 10 September 1970
        24 October 1970 – 10 November 1970
        13 January 1971 – 7 March 1971
        25 April 1971 – 17 May 1971

    USCGC *Ironwood* (WLB 297)
         9 July 1967 – 8 August 1967

    USCGC *Planetree* (WLB 307)
        24 April 1966 – 1 June 1966
        28 February 1967 – 1 March 1967
        10 March 1967 – 2 April 1967

Cargo Vessel

USCGC *Nettle* (WAK 169)
15 May 1966 – 16 May 1966
23 May 1966 – 28 May 1966
25 May 1967 – 27 May 1967
2 June 1967 – 4 June 1967

Appendix D

USCG Patrol Boat: 82-Footer

Designed by the U.S. Coast Guard for search and rescue and law enforcement, the 82-footer was built at the Coast Guard Curtis Bay Shipyard outside of Baltimore, Maryland. The A and B class craft used in Vietnam were constructed in 1960 and 1961. The boat had a steel hull, an unmanned engine room controlled from the bridge, power steering, and air conditioning. The 82-footer was named after points of land.

Characteristics of the 26 Vietnam-deployed WPBs:

Length	82' 10"
Width	17' 7"
Draft	5' 11"
Maximum Speed	16.8 knots
Range, Maximum Speed	500 nautical miles
Economical Speed	8 knots
Range, Economical Speed	1,400 nautical miles
Full Displacement	67.5 tons
Propellers	two (5-bladed, 42"×42")
Diesel Engines	two Cummins VT-12, 600-hp
Water Capacity	1,550 gallons
Fuel Capacity	1,840 gallons
Frozen Food Storage	23 cubic feet
Accommodations	13
Armament	a dual-mount 81-mm mortar and .50-caliber machine gun on bow and four .50-caliber machine guns aft
Crew	two officers, nine enlisted

All twenty-six 82-footers were turned over to the South Vietnamese Navy between May 1969 and August 1970.

APPENDIX E

STATISTICS

Gathering of wartime statistics is imprecise. Passage of time and many interpretations of statistics create discrepancies that cannot be resolved. Nonetheless, the figures presented here are representative and as accurate as possible. The numbers of Coast Guard members serving in Southeast Asia, and wounded-in-action, are based on the author's research. The Squadron One figures come from the Military Readiness Section, U.S. Coast Guard Headquarters, and those of Squadron Three from Eugene N. Tulich's monograph on the Coast Guard in Southeast Asia produced by Coast Guard Headquarters.

* * *

Coast Guardsmen in Southeast Asia between 1965 and 1975: 8,000.

Killed: 7   Wounded: 63

Squadron One (27 May 1965–15 August 1970):

Miles cruised	4,215,116
Vessels detected	839,299
Vessels inspected	283,527
Vessels boarded	236,396
Persons detained	10,286
Naval gunfire missions	4,461
Enemy killed or wounded	1,232
Structures damaged or destroyed	4,727
Vessels damaged or destroyed	1,811

Squadron Three (25 April 1967–31 January 1972)

> Miles cruised 1,292,094
> Vessels detected 69,517
> Vessels inspected 50,000
> Vessels boarded 1,094
> Persons detained 138
> Naval gunfire missions 1,368
> Enemy killed or wounded 772
> Structures damaged or destroyed 5,288

SOURCE NOTES

Introduction
1. Department of Defense, Selected Manpower Statistics, Fiscal year 1986, Table 2-22, U.S. Military Personnel in South Vietnam 1960 through 1973, p. 109.
2. The Junk Force began as a paramilitary force of civilian irregulars, largely local fishermen, in 1960, to detect inshore infiltration. In 1965 it was absorbed into the South Vietnamese Navy and designated the Coastal Force, but was still popularly called the Junk Force. Hence, Junk Force and Coastal Force are used interchangeably here. Because many Junk Force bases were located in isolated areas, South Vietnamese naval officers considered them undesirable assignments and infrequently filled these posts. Nonetheless, each base was assigned American naval advisors, both officer and enlisted.
3. Tilford, Jr., Captain Earl H., USAF. *Search and Rescue in Southeast Asia,* 1961–1975, p. 3.

Chapter 1
1. Tulich, Lieutenant Eugene N., USCG. "The United States Coast Guard in South East Asia," p. 2.
2. Spector, Barbara. "New Jersey Coast Guard Crew Is Ready For Vietnam." *Newark Evening News* 2 May 1965, 1 ff.

Chapter 2
1. Commander, Coast Guard Activities, Vietnam, Unit Diary, 20 June 1966.
2. Eifler, Major General Charles W., USA, Commander, 1st Logistical Command, letter to Commander, Coast Guard Activities, Vietnam, 11 June 1967.
3. Gillette, Homer W., Master, *SS North Platte Victory,* Master's Voyage Report, Part III, Final: Danang - Seattle, 21 May 1967, At Sea.
4. Kneip, Captain Donald G., USCG (Ret.).

Chapter 3

1. Translation of ARVN analysis based on the report of rallier Nguyen Van Xuan. Extracted from MACJ21, USMACV Log #06-003-66 of 24 June 1966.
2. Sheehan, Neil. "Sea Watch for Foe Off Vietnam Long and Tedious." *The New York Times* 12 July 1966.
3. Erdheim, Judith C. "Market Time" p. iv.

Chapter 4

1. Commander, Coast Guard Squadron Three, News Release 47-68, "Coast Guard's Circuit Riding Chaplain Belongs To Navy" by Chief Journalist Dale E. Cross, USCG, 11 June 1968.
2. Cruisebook, USCGC Dallas in Vietnam 1967–1968, p. 42.
3. U.S. Coast Guard Squadron Three Booklet, page on Operations Summary.
4. Port Information Report, Sattahip, Thailand, 7–11 June 1967, p. 8.
5. Westmoreland, General William C., USA (Ret.). *A Soldier Reports,* p. 418.
6. ———, p. 436.

Chapter 5

1. Commanding Officer, USCGC *Blackaw* (WLB 390) letter 9 March 1969, paragraph 8.
2. Momyer, General William W., USAF (Ret.). *Air Power in Three Wars,* p. 309.
3. Lavalle, Major A.J.C., USAF, Ed. *Air Power and the 1972 Spring Invasion,* pp. 45–46.

Chapter 6

1. Board of Investigation Proceeding, p. 85.
2. Westmoreland, General William C., USA (Ret.). *A Soldier Reports,* p. 256.
3. Board of Investigation Proceeding, p. 4.
4. ———, p. 64.
5. ———, Appendix: Transcript of Circuit S-3 (4085kcs), Northern Coordinating and Reporting Net.
6. Commanding Officer, USCGC *Point Caution,* to CTG 115.1, letter 5000, 12 August 1966, Subject: Summary of Events, 11 August 1966.

Chapter 7

1. Kendall, Lane C. "U.S. Merchant Shipping and Vietnam," p. 146.
2. Letter from Commandant, U.S. Coast Guard to Commander, Western Area, 13 February 1967, Subject: CG Squadron One, Policy Guidance for, paragraph 2.

Chapter 8

1. Tilford, Jr., Captain Earl H., USAF. *Search and Rescue in Southeast Asia 1961–1975,* p. 70.
2. Rittichier, Lieutenant Jack C., USCG. "Coast Guard Aviators In Vietnam," p. 4.
3. ———
4. Tilford Jr., Captain Earl H., USAF. *Search and Rescue in Southeast Asia 1961–1975,* p. 91.

5. Robinson, Anthony. *Weapons of the Vietnam War,* p. 100.
6. Tilford Jr., Captain Earl H., USAF. *Search and Rescue in Southeast Asia 1961–1975,* p. 155.

Chapter 9

1. Webber, Warrant Officer Bernard C., USCG (Ret.). *Chatham: The Lifeboatmen,* p. 46.
2. Commander, U.S. Naval Forces, Vietnam, News Release #525-67, 20 December 1967, "Three U.S. Coast Guardsmen Aid Philippine Tug in Rough Sea."
3. Commander, Coast Guard Division Twelve, to Secretary of the Navy, letter 1650, 4 April 1968, Subject: Navy Unit Commendation in the case of USCGC *Point Arden* (WPB 82309).
4. Stewart, Commander William H., USCG, war diary, 24 December 1967.

Chapter 10

1. Taylor, Captain LeRoy, USN. "Naval Operations In Confined Waters and Narrow Seas." *U.S. Naval Institute Proceedings,* June 1960.
2. Carson, Commander R.J. USCG and Lieutenant Commander W.F. Tighe Jr., USCG. "Developments and Problems in Coast Guard Cutter Design," p. 187.

Chapter 11

1. Henneberry, Commander Paul D., Commanding Officer, USCGC *Bering Strait,* Monthly Summary Report of War Operations, 1–31 October 1970, paragraph 6.
2. Commander, U.S. Coast Guard Squadron Three, Unit Diary, June 1971.
3. Commander, Coast Guard Activities, Vietnam, to Commandant (OAN), letter 11135, 14 November 1968, Subject: Turnover of Assets to the GVN; information concerning, paragraph 2.
4. ———, letter 11400, 21 June 1969, Subject: Vietnam Aids to Navigation program; status of, paragraph 4.

BIBLIOGRAPHY

Books

Bloomfield, Howard V.L. *The Compact History of the United States Coast Guard.* New York: Hawthorn, 1966.

Davidson, Lieutenant General Phillip B., USA (Ret.). *Vietnam At War: The History: 1946–1975.* Novato, CA: Presidio Press, 1988.

Drendel, Lou. *C-130 Hercules in Action.* Carrollton, TX: Squadron/Signal Publications, 1984.

Eschmann, Karl J. *Linebacker: The Untold Story of the Air Raids Over North Vietnam.* New York: Ballantine Books, 1989.

Gettleman, Marvin E., Ed. *Vietnam: History, Documents, and Opinions on a Major World Crisis.* Greenwich, CT: Fawcett, 1965.

Kaplan, H.R. and Lieutenant Commander James F. Hunt, USCG. *This Is the Coast Guard.* Cambridge MD: Cornell Maritime Press, 1972.

Karnow, Stanley. *Vietnam: A History.* New York: Viking Press, 1983.

Lavalle, Major A.J.C. USAF, Ed. *Air Power and the 1972 Spring Invasion.* Washington DC: U.S. Government Printing Office, 1976.

Mesko, Jim. *B-57 Canberra in Action.* Carrollton, TX: Squadron/Signal Publications, 1986.

Momyer, General William W., USAF (Ret.). *Air Power in Three Wars (WWII, Korea, Vietnam).* Department of the Air Force, 1978.

Nalty, Bernard C., George M. Watson, and Jacob Neufeld. *The Air War Over Vietnam: Aircraft of the Southeast Asia Conflict.* New York: Arco, 1981.

Robinson, Anthony, Antony Preston, and Ian V. Hogg, Eds. *Weapons of the Vietnam War.* New York: Gallery Books, 1983.

Scheina, Robert L. *U.S. Coast Guard Cutters & Craft 1946–1990.* Annapolis, MD: Naval Institute Press, 1990.

———. U.S. Coast Guard Cutters & Craft of World War II. Annapolis, MD: Naval Institute Press, 1982.

Tilford, Jr., Captain Earl H., USAF. *Search and Rescue in Southeast Asia, 1961–1975.* Washington, DC: Office of Air Force History, United States Air Force, 1980.

Webber, Warrant Officer Bernard C. USCG (Ret.). *Chatham: The Lifeboatmen.* Orleans, MA: Lower Cape Publishing, 1985.

Westmoreland, General William C., USA (Ret.). *A Soldier Reports.* New York: Dell, 1980.

Articles

Carson, Commander R.J., USCG and Lieutenant Commander W.F. Tighe Jr., USCG. "Developments and Problems in Coast Guard Cutter Design." *Naval Review,* 1964, 174–197.

Goodfellow, Jim. "I'm Getting Married Today." *News-Call Bulletin,* San Francisco, 30 April 1965.

Green, Lieutenant D.L., USCG. "The 82-Foot Class Patrol Boat." *The Engineer's Digest,* March–April 1962, 2–5.

Hodgman, Captain James A., USCG. "Market Time in the Gulf of Thailand." *Naval Review,* 1968, 36–67.

Kaplan, H.R. "The Coast Guard's Other War in Vietnam." *Defense Transportation Journal,* July–August 1968, 2–7.

Kendall, Lane C. "U.S. Merchant Shipping and Vietnam." *Naval Review,* 1968, 130–147.

Judd, Commander Ralph W., USCG (Ret.). "The LORAN station on Con Son Island was one of many U.S. Coast Guard Contributions to the Vietnam War." *Vietnam,* n.d., 10 ff.

Murphy, Lieutenant R.P.W., USNR and Colonel Edwin F. Black, USA. "The South Vietnamese Navy." *U.S. Naval Institute Proceedings,* January 1964, 52–61.

Oliver, Captain Edward F., USCG. "The Largest Maritime Police Beat in the World." *U.S. Naval Institute Proceedings,* April 1970, 120–122.

Rittichier, Lieutenant Jack C., USCG. "Coast Guard Aviators in Vietnam." *Coast Guard Activities, Vietnam Newsletter,* 5-68.

Schreadley, Commander R.L., USN. "The Naval War in Vietnam, 1950–1970." *Naval Review,* 1971, 180–209.

Searle, Jr., Commander W.F., USN. "The Case for Inshore Warfare." *Naval Review,* 1966, 2–23.

Thomas, William. "Going West—To War." *San Francisco Chronicle,* 1 May 1965.

Documents

Coast Guard Activities, Vietnam, News Release VN 32-68, 25 July 1968, "Coast Guardsmen Extinguish Fire Aboard Burning Craft Loaded with Ammunition."

———, News Release VN 7-68-1, 25 March 1968, "After It Was Over, I Started Thinking of My Wife and Children," by JO2 D.L. Jimenez, USCG.

———, News Release VN 65-68, 19 September 1968, "Safety Is the Name of His Game in South Vietnam," by JO2 E.M. Conlon, USCG.

———, News Release VN 19-68, 5 June 1968, "Vietnam Lamplighter Logs Thousands of Miles to Maintain Warzone Aids," by JO2 D.L. Jimenez, USCG.

———, "Maritime Aids to Navigation in Vietnam: A Staff Study," 13 April 1967.

Commander, Coast Guard Squadron One to Commander, Western Area, letter 3480, Serial No. 010-66, 14 March 1966: Summary of Point White river battle.

Commander, Coast Guard Squadron One/Commander, Coast Guard Activities, Vietnam/Senior Coast Guard Officer, Vietnam: Unit Diaries and Supplements, May 1965–February 1973.

Commander, Coast Guard Squadron Three: Monthly Summaries and Supplements, 1967–1973.

Commander, Naval Forces, Vietnam: Monthly Historical Summaries.

Commanding Officer, USCGC *Basswood* (WLB 388) to Commander, 14th Coast Guard District, letter, 5 January 1968. Subject: Vietnam Trip—OPORD 20-67.

Commanding Officer, USCGC *Blackhaw* (WLB 390) to Commander 14th Coast Guard District, letters of 26 August 1968 and 9 March 1969. Subject: ATON Vietnam.

Con Son LORAN Station General Information booklet, October 1966.

Debriefing of 10 May 1966 trawler incident by Commanding Officer (A.E. Katz) of USCGC *Point Cypress*. May 1966.

Debriefing report of LTJG B.F. Thomson III, Commanding Officer, USCGC *Point Slocum*, covering 20D2 Incident of 20 June 1966. Dated 25 June 1966.

Debriefing report of LTJG Stephen T. Ulmer, Commanding Officer, USCGC *Point League*, covering 20D2 Incident 20 June 1966. Dated 24 June 1966.

Department of Defense Intelligence Information Report #6 075 355266, 30 July 1966: "Trawler Captured on 20 June 1966 off Vinh Binh Province."

Erdheim, Judith C. "Market Time." Center for Naval Analyses, Arlington, VA, September 1975.

1st Logistical Command, U.S. Army, Regulation Number 190-36, "Security Against Underwater Swimmer Attack," 9 June 1969.

Grutzik, Major Robert K., USAF, unit historian, "History of the HQ 3d Aerospace Rescue and Recovery Group: 1 April–30 June 1968."

Lampang LORAN Station General Information booklet, August 1971.

Master, USNS *Greenville Victory* T-AK(237), letter 5213, serial 15, 3 February 1967: BM1 Albert F. Earle, USCG, 340728, Explosive Loading Detachment, Cat Lai; recommendation for commendation of.

Memorandum for the Secretary of the Navy, OP-332E/1mr, Ser. 001575P33, 8 March 1967, from Chief of Naval Operations; Subject: Additional Coast Guard Cutters for Assignment with U.S. Naval Forces in South Vietnam.

Record of Proceedings of a Formal Board of Investigation to inquire into an attack upon USCGC Point Welcome which occurred on 11 August 1966. Convened at Danang, Republic of Vietnam by order of Commander, U.S. Military Assistance Command, Vietnam.

Roland, Admiral Edwin J., USCG, (Ret.), Interview by John T. Mason, Jr., 1976, U.S. Naval Institute Oral History Program, Annapolis, MD.

Sattahip LORAN Station General Information booklets, September 1967 and September 1973.

Speaker, Jr., Commander John B., USCG. Memorandum to Commandant, 21 November 1961; Subject: Visit to South Vietnam with RAdm H.S. Persons, USN.

Stewart, Commander William H., USCG, war diary, 3 November 1967–2 September 1968.

Tan My LORAN Station General Information booklet, 1970.

37th Aerospace Rescue and Recovery Squadron, Danang Air Base, quarterly history reports 1 April 1968–30 November 1972.

Tulich, Lieutenant Eugene N., USCG. "The United States Coast Guard in South East Asia." Washington DC: U.S. Coast Guard Historical Monograph Program, 1986.

Udorn LORAN Station General Information booklet, September 1973.

Ulmer, Stephen T. "Account of Events on 20 June 1966, Republic of Vietnam." A personal recollection, 4 April 1983.

USCGC *Androscoggin* (WHEC-68), letter 3300, 6 March 1968, to Commander, Naval Forces, Vietnam; Subject: Combat Operations After Action Report.

USCGC *Rush,* Action Report Infiltration Trawler SL-3-70; Surveillance and Infiltration Attempt 17–22 November 1970.

——— (WHEC 723), Action Report Infiltration Trawler SL-8-71; Surveillance and Infiltration Attempt 11–12 April 1971.

Vietnam War Veterans Interviewed by Author

Bauman, Richard A.
Bell, Ross
Butchka, Richard V.
Clarino, Salvatore J.
Eagan, Lance A.
Franks III, Richard B.
Fremont-Smith, Richard
Gillespie, Christopher R.
Herbert, Baker W.
Hertica, Raymond C.
Judy, Marion W.
Kelleher, Martin J.
Kepler, William N.
Kneip, Donald G.
Lehr, William E.
McKenney, Mark D.
Mixon, Lonnie L.
Moody, Joseph E.
Morris, Kenneth J.
Mosher, Charles B.
Nguyen Van Tien

O'Connor, David E.
Oldford, Harry J.
Oliver, Edward "Frank"
Patterson, Richard H.
Perkins, David E.
Pierzchala, Richard P.
Quinn, James "Casey"
Ritchie, Robert T.
Riutta, Ernest R.
Russell, Billy R.
Sargent III, Thomas R.
Thomson III, B. Foster
Ulmer, Stephen T.
Venzke, Norman C.
Webber, Bernard C.
Wells, William R.
White, Joseph
Williams, Virgil G.
Wolf, Jr., William H.
Yost, Jr., Paul A.

INDEX

1st Logistical Command 23–25, 31–33
3rd Aerospace Rescue and Recovery Group (ARRGp) 129, 133, 141
17th Parallel 101–103
31st Aerospace Rescue and Recovery Group (ARRGp) 129
37th Aerospace Rescue and Recovery Squadron (ARRSq) 129–130, 133, 136, 139, 141
39th Aerospace Rescue and Recovery Group (ARRGp) 129, 133, 139
40th Aerospace Rescue and Recovery Group (ARRGp) at Nakhon Phanom 136
82-footer (USCG) 165–166, 178

A-1 141
A-1E 133
A-1 Skyraider 134
Absecon (USCGC) 192, 198
ACTOV 184
Aerospace Rescue and Recovery Squadrons (ARRSq) 129–130, 133, 136, 139, 141
Ahrens, Lieutenant Richard E. 160
Aids to Navigation (ATON) 79–80, 84, 88–89, 193, 195
Allen, Boatswain's Mate 1st Class 83
Alyee 151
Androscoggin (USCGC) 65, 68, 70–72, 74–77, 156–157
Antelope (USS) 78
An Thoi 14–16, 18, 61
Aubert, Captain N.T. 26–27

Austin, Commissaryman 2nd Class Donald L. 105, 112
Aviation Cadet Program 131

Banks, Captain William N. 83, 158, 160
Banks, Priscilla C. 162
Barataria (USCGC) 59–61, 157
Basswood (USCGC) 89, 194–195
Baton Victory 115
Bauman, Lieutenant Commander Richard A. 160
Bear 146–148
Bell, Lieutenant (j.g.) Ross 102–106, 108–109, 112
Berea Victory (SS) 29
Bering Strait (USCGC) 59–60, 63, 155, 188, 191, 198
Blackhaw (USCGC) 84–86, 89
Booth, Major Robert E. 143
Boston Whaler 38–39, 169, 177
Bowen, Lieutenant (j.g.) Gene E. 198
Brister (USS) 43–45
Brock, Commander Harold R. 93
Brostrom, Lieutenant (j.g.) David C. 104–105, 110–111
Butchka, Lieutenant Richard V. 131–132, 135, 140–143

Ca Mau Peninsula 41–42, 47, 49–50, 54, 70
Campbell (USCGC) 58, 71

231

Cam Ranh Bay 24, 36, 84
Cape San Martin 121
Carr, Master Chief Boatswain's Mate Ralph H. 36
Carroll Victory (SS) 27
Castle Rock (USCGC) 192, 198
Cat Lai 28, 30, 34, 82, 193
Cat Lo 17, 61, 80, 86, 162
Chase (USCGC) 70, 154
Chieu Hoi 171
Chincoteague (USCGC) 192, 198
Chung, Petty Officer 1st Class Le 198
Clements, Chief Engineman Robert 9
Clements, Lieutenant Richard J. 81–82
Cluff, Chief Warrant Officer Daniel W. 148
Coastal Surveillance Centers (CSC) 18
Coast Guard Activities, Vietnam (COGARDACTV) 150, 192
COINSERE 10
Commander, Coast Guard Activities, Vietnam (COMCOGARDACTV) 84
Commander, Naval Forces, Vietnam (COMNAVFORV) 69, 80, 176
Commander, U.S. Military Assistance Command, Vietnam (COMUSMACV) 8, 16, 23–24, 54, 110
Comstock (USS) 75
Con Son Island 15, 91, 96
Cook Inlet (USCGC) 192, 198
Corson, Commander Peter D. 194
Cote, Lieutenant Arthur J. 105–106, 108–109
Cotter, Lieutenant (j.g.) William S. 28
Creacy, Petty Officer Oliver W., Jr. 28
Cuu Long 83, 84, 194

Dallas (USCGC) 70, 157
Danang 14, 16, 18, 74, 79, 93, 129
Davidson, Fireman Houston J. 105, 109, 112
Davis, Chief Boatswain's Mate Bruce D. 52
Day, Captain John E. 59, 60, 62
Dead-end kids 158
Demilitarized Zone (DMZ) 18, 69, 86, 93, 101–102, 107, 110, 177, 179
Detachment One 136
Division Eleven 14–16, 20, 42, 187
Division Thirteen 17–18, 20, 25, 49, 154, 188

Division Twelve 14, 16, 29, 176, 187
Duane (USCGC) 67

Eagan, Lieutenant Lance A. 129–130, 133, 137–138, 141
Earle, Boatswain's Mate 1st Class Albert F. 26–28
Edwards, Chief Boatswain's Mate Donald 9
Eifler, Major General Charles W. 24, 28–29, 32–34, 38
Eisenhower, President Dwight D. 183–184
ELD #1 24–26, 33
ELD #2 24–25
ELD #3 29
ELD #4 29
ELD #5 29
ELDs 24, 26, 28–29
Ellis, James B., III 200
Emelio, Petty Officer Dominic 25
Endurance (USS) 78
Energy (USS) 78
Enid Victory 118–119
Explosive Loading Detachments. *See* ELD

Flak jackets 167
Floyd County (LST-726) 14
Fontaine, Lieutenant Commander Maynard J. 93
Forster 60
Fourth Coastal Zone Advisor 20
Fremon-Smith, Lieutenant Richard 14
Frischmann, Thomas F. 129
Fritz, Lieutenant Ronald E. 173

Gamon (SS) 28
Gates, Gunner's Mate 2nd Class Lester K. 6
Gillespie, Lieutenant (j.g.) Christopher R. 185–186
Glenn, Gunner's Mate 1st Class Joseph R. 28
Goff, Gunner's Mate 2nd Class Willis J. 177
Greene, General Wallace M. 6
Greenville Victory 26
Gresham (USCGC) 59–60, 72
Guadalupe (USS) 71

Gulf of Thailand 15, 70, 93, 153, 174
Gunfire support 176

Half Moon (USCGC) 58–59, 67, 70, 151, 154
Hambleton, Lieutenant Colonel Iceal E. 98–99
Hamilton, Alexander 145
Hamilton, Commander Joseph L. 122
Haverfield (USS) 52
HC-130 134, 140
HC-130P 139
Healy, Captain Michael A. 147
Helicopters 129, 131–137, 139–140
Henneberry, Commander Paul D. 190
Herbert, Chief Warrant Officer Baker W. 92, 93
Hertica, Commander Raymond C. 31–33, 35, 39–40
Hessel, Damage Controlman 3rd Class Ronald J. 151
HH-3E 131–137
HH-43B 132–133
HH-43B Huskie 129
HH-53 139
HH-53B 133–135
HH-130P 132
Hickey, Lieutenant Eugene J., Jr. 5–7
Hodgman, Commander James A. 8, 12–13, 20
Hoffman, Captain Roy 69
Hong Kong Station 63–65
Hoover, Captain Richard E. 191
Horne, Seaman Richard 9
Hudson, Damage Controlman 1st Class Arley N. 151
Hue 74
Hue, Tram Thi 159–160
Hunt, Lieutenant James F. 154

Ironwood (USCGC) 83
Istock, Lieutenant Commander Howard H. 29

Jarvis, Lieutenant David H. 146–148, 150
Jason (USS) 59
Jennings County (USS) 152–153
Johnson, Colonel Vern E. 35

Johnson, President Lyndon B. 9, 114, 183–184
Joint Search and Rescue Center (JSARC) 129, 135
Joy Taylor 150–151
Junk Force 2, 5–6, 77, 102, 109, 203

Kelleher, Gunner's Mate 1st Class Martin J. 15, 31, 44–45
Kennedy, President John F. 183
Kepler, Commissaryman 2nd Class William N. 44
Kipkowski, Boatswain's Mate 1st Class Russell 151
Knapp, Lieutenant Commander Richard J. 14
Kneip, Lieutenant Donald G. 31, 33–34
Krishna (USS) 16

Langham, Captain Charles D. 142
Laverty, Major Wayne B. 155
Lehr, Lieutenant Commander William E., Jr. 16, 18
Life-Saving Service 146
Lima Sites 136
Limited war 184
Loforte, Captain Robert J. 20–21, 24, 29, 31, 79–83, 111, 116–118, 157, 160, 162
Loma Victory 122, 123
Long Range Navigation. *See* LORAN stations
Longview Victory (SS) 29
Loomis, Lieutenant James M. 131–132, 135, 140–142
LORAN stations 90–91, 93–97, 99, 203
Lynch, Captain Herbert J. 76

Maritime Administration (MARAD) 32, 116
Mascots 172–173
Mattaponi (USS) 71
Mattila, Commander Risto A. 23–25, 34
McCullogh (USCGC) 192, 198
McKenney, Gunner's Mate 3rd Class Mark D. 102–107, 109, 112
McNamara, Secretary of Defense Robert S. 184

Medical Civil Action Program (MEDCAP) 154
Merchant marine detail 113–114, 117, 119, 124–125
MiG-21 140
Military Sea Transport Service (MSTS) 32, 113–118
Minnetonka (USCGC) 67, 77–78
Misty-11 141, 143
Mitchell, Lieutenant Robert R. 68
Mixon, Lieutenant Commander Lonnie L. 127–130, 137, 143
Modica, Lieutenant Colonel Jack 136–138
Monsoon 14, 16, 42, 79, 89, 167, 174–175
Moody, Engineman 1st Class Joseph E. 5–6
Morgenthau (USCGC) 66, 78, 150
Morse, Commander Richard M. 60
Mortar 164, 176
Mosher, Lieutenant (j.g.) Charles B. 42–45, 48
Mullins, Engineman 1st Class Raymond C. 189

Nail-53 139
Napalm 27, 35, 134
National Defense Reserve Fleet 114
Naval Gunfire Support (NGFS) 69, 164, 203
Neva West (SS) 30
New Jersey (USS) 86
Nguyen Thi "Maria" Chien 160–162, 198
Nha Be 24–25, 27, 34
Niesz, Captain Ralph W. 187
Nixon, President Richard M. 89, 184, 188
Nolan, Commander Joseph D. 108–109
North Vietnam's 125th Naval Transportation Group 47
North Vietnamese swimmer commando 36
North Vietnamese Trawlers, chart 56
Nuoc mam 156, 189

O'Connor, Seaman David E. 105–106, 109, 112
O'Donnell, Lieutenant Commander Jack A. 87
O'Keefe, Lieutenant (j.g.) Edward G. 25–26, 33

Oldford, Commander Harry J., Jr. 68
Old Westbury (SS) 34
Oliver, Commander Edward "Frank" 117–125
Olsen, Commander Albert L., Jr. 198
Operation Beau Charger 179
Operation Game Warden 16
Operation Jackstay 179
Operation Linebacker II 89
Operation Market Place 55
Operation Market Time 3, 8, 16, 18–20, 47, 57, 61–63, 69, 74, 110, 163, 175–176, 182
Operation Tight Reign 91–92

Page, Timothy J. 105, 109, 112
Patterson, Chief Boatswain's Mate Richard H. 104, 106–108, 110, 112
PBR (patrol boat, river) 38, 39
PCF (patrol craft, fast) 16, 22, 24, 61–62, 72, 75–77, 163, 203
PCF-9 164
PCF-39 164
Perkins School for the Blind 160, 198
Persons, Rear Admiral Henry S. 7–8
Phillips, Engineman 2nd Class Jerry 105–106, 109
Pierzchala, Captain Richard P. 108–109
Planetree (USCGC) 80–81
Point Arden (USCGC) 9, 152, 164, 170
Point Banks (USCGC) 9, 177
Point Caution (USCGC) 105, 109, 176
Point Clear (USCGC) 176, 198
Point Clover (USCGC) 18
Point Comfort (USCGC) 172
Point Cypress (USCGC) 45, 46, 60, 151, 187–188
Point Dume (USCGC) 61, 164, 166, 173, 175, 177–181
Point Ellis (USCGC) 165, 186, 198
Point Gammon (USCGC) 9, 48, 176
Point Garnet (USCGC) 165, 185, 187
Point Grace (USCGC) 172
Point Grey (USCGC) 41–47, 49, 75, 176
Point Hudson (USCGC) 52, 153, 172–173, 198
Point Kennedy (USCGC) 151, 179
Point League (USCGC) 17, 48, 50–53, 153, 185, 187

Point Marone (USCGC)   18, 187–188
Point Orient (USCGC)   48, 163–164, 178, 199–200
Point Partridge (USCGC)   170
Point Slocum (USCGC)   52
Point Welcome (USCGC)   75–76, 101–105, 107–110, 111, 166
Point White (USCGC)   5, 6, 186
Point Young (USCGC)   158
Political considerations   183, 185
Ponchartrain (USCGC)   67
Porster (USS)   17

Queen's Victory (SS)   28
Qui Nhon   28–29
Quinn, Lieutenant James "Casey"   129, 139

Rescue Specialist (RS)   204
Revenue Cutter Service   145–146, 147
Richards, Lieutenant (j.g.) Milton C., Jr.   162
Richards, Petty Officer Carlton C.   162
Riddle, Commander Walter H.   35
Ritchie, Lieutenant (j.g.) Robert T.   131, 135, 139–143
Rittichier, Lieutenant Jack C.   129–133
Riutta, Lieutenant Ernest R.   97–98
Roland, Admiral Edwin J.   6, 29
Rosado, Electrician's Mate 1st Class Candido   87
Royer, Boatswain's Mate 1st Class Edward   9
Rung Sat Special Zone (RSSZ)   5, 16
Rush (USCGC)   78
Russell, Boatswain's Mate 1st Class Billy R.   105–107, 112

Saigon Blind School for Girls   159
Sang, Chief Boatswain's Mate Tran Van   198
Sargent, Captain Thomas R., III   90–92, 94
Saunders, Major Alan W.   129
SCATTOR   185–188
Scotch-3   136, 138
Sebago (USCGC)   68
Semper Paratus   162

Senior Coast Guard Officer, Vietnam (SCGOV)   192–195
Silver Star   31, 177, 201
Skyraider   134. *See also* A-1
Smith, Admiral Willard J.   29
Snohomish County (USS)   14
Snyder, Lieutenant Commander Carl W., Jr.   86
Song Ong Doc   70, 155–157
Southeast Asia Section (SEASEC)   94, 192, 197, 204
South Vietnamese Navy   7, 20
Speaker, Commander John B., Jr.   7–8
Spencer (USCGC)   58
Spring Offensive   194
Squadron One   9, 12–13, 16, 20, 54, 83, 167, 176, 185, 188, 198
Squadron Three   54, 57, 59, 61–62, 65, 67, 69, 154–155, 188, 191–192
Stewart, Commander William H.   74–76
Subic Bay   57, 60, 68, 198
Swimmer commando   36

Tacoma (USS)   78
Talley, Airman 1st Class Joel   137, 139, 143
Tally Ho   102, 110
Taney (USCGC)   154
Tan My LORAN Station   96–97
Taylor, Captain LeRoy   165, 175–176, 178
Tet Offensive   34, 47, 73–74
Thieu, President Nguyen Van   73, 184
Thomson, Lieutenant B. Foster, III   52
Tien, Petty Officer 2nd Class Nguyen Van   198–200
Tom Green County   86
Tourist (USS)   30

Ulmer, Lieutenant (j.g.) Stephen T.   48–51
Underway replenishment (UNREP)   70–71
United States Agency for International Development (USAID)   33, 80, 82, 84, 159, 193

Van Boskerck, Captain Francis Saltus   162
Vaughn, Engineman 2nd Class Daniel R.   50
VECTOR   185

Vien, Lieutenant (j.g.) Do Viet   105
Villarreal, Engineman 2nd Class Larry D.   177
Vireo (USS)   43, 45
Vung Ro Bay   3, 8, 47, 54

Walters, Lieutenant Commander Everett G.   82–83
Ward, Rear Admiral Norvell G.   80
Ward, Thomas   9
Webber, Boatswain's Mate 1st Class Bernie C.   148, 150
Westmoreland, General William C.   8, 73, 80
White, Chief Hospital Corpsman Joseph   154, 190
Williams, Electronics Technician 2nd Class Virgil G.   105, 109, 112
Willis, Lieutenant Gerald T.   122–123

Winona (USCGC)   62, 70, 77
Wise, Chief Boatswain's Mate Charles D.   32–33, 35–36
Wolf, Chief Engineman William H.   104, 106–108, 112
WPB   204
Wright, Gunner's Mate 2nd Class Albert J., Jr.   50–51

Yakutat (USCGC)   59, 152–153, 188–189, 191, 198
Yered, Engineman 1st Class Robert J.   30–31
Yost, Admiral Paul A., Jr.   200–201

Zimmer, Electrician's Mate 1st Class   83
Zumwalt, Vice Admiral Elmo   69

WELCOME TO
HELLGATE PRESS

Hellgate Press is named after the historic and rugged Hellgate Canyon on southern Oregon's scenic Rogue River. The raging river that flows below the canyon's towering jagged cliffs has always attracted a special sort of individual—someone who seeks adventure. From the pioneers who bravely pursued the lush valleys beyond, to the anglers and rafters who take on its roaring challenges today, Hellgate Press publishes books that reflect this adventurous spirit. Our books are about military history, adventure travel, and outdoor recreation. On the following pages, we would like to introduce you to some of our latest titles and encourage you to join in the celebration of this unique spirit.

Look for Hellgate Press books in your favorite bookstore, or order by calling *1-800-228-2275* or online at www.psi-research.com/hellgate.htm

MIGHTY MIDGETS AT WAR
The Saga of the LCS(L) Ships from Iwo Jima to Vietnam   ISBN: 1-55571-522-2
by Robin L. Rielly   270 pages, Paperback: $18.95

Extensively researched, *Mighty Midgets at War* accurately chronicles the history of the Mighty Midgets—Landing Craft Support vessels—and the terror-filled duty into which sailors aboard them were thrust. Based exclusively on original sources such as ship's logs, action reports, and correspondence and interviews with actual wartime participants, it includes over 100 photos and illustrations, and follows the careers of these great ships from WWII to Vietnam. In several cases, it follows these ships to their eventual retirement or sale to other countries.

WIDOW-MAKERS & RHODODENDRONS
Loggers: The Unsung Heroes of WWII   ISBN 1-55571-525-7
by Doris Winter Hubbard   172 pages, Paperback: $19.95

A vivid account of life in a logging community during WWII, when men risked their lives to fill the sky-rocketing demand for wood for the contonments, packaging, dunnage for ships, explosives, and paper vital for our victory. It is a compassionate look at the families who worried whether their men would make it home from the muddy slopes.

THE PARROT'S BEAK
U.S. Operations in Cambodia   ISBN: 1-55571-543-5
by Paul B. Morgan   200 pages, Paperback: $14.95

By the author of *K-9 Soldiers: Vietnam and After,* Morgan's latest book divulges secret insertion techniques and information about Nixon's secret war that the government still refuses to acknowledge.

TO ORDER OR FOR MORE INFORMATION
1-800-228-2275 *(telephone)*
info@psi-research.com *(email)*
www.psi-research.com *(Website)*

COAST GUARD ACTION IN VIETNAM
Stories of Those Who Served ISBN: 1-55571-528-1
By Paul Scotti 250 pages, Paperback: $17.95

Written by the author of *Seaports: Ships, Piers, and People* and *Police Divers*, this well-crafted lively and engaging history will rejuvenate one's pride in the American miliary with its little-known details of the Coast Guard's involvement in Vietnam. The fact that they were in Vietnam at all is a surprise to many. What they were doing there will be an even bigger surprise!

THE UNEXPECTED STORM
The Gulf War Legacy ISBN: 1-55571-542-7
by Steven Manchester 260 pages, Hardcover: $21.95

After rigorous physical exams, soldiers were trained to fight, infused with rage, and sent to strike—only to watch biology and technology do their jobs for them. Operation Desert Storm was a war like no other. What our troops brought home with them as a result of experimental vaccines, radioactive depleted uranium, and so much pent-up rage, is just beginning to surface. This is one soldier's story.

HOW IT WAS
A Vietnam Story ISBN: 1-55571-516-8
by John Patrick O'Hara 125 pages, Paperback: $12.95

How it Was is not a blow-by-blow record, but a shoebox of memories presented as they flashed inside the mind of a Vet trying to come to terms with what he had seen and done during his tour. It is a non-traditional, thought-provoking journey into a war-torn mind.

HONOR & SACRIFICE
The Montagnards of Ba Cat, Vietnam ISBN: 1-55571-533-8
by Anthony J. Blondell 250 pages, Hardcover: $21.95

Special Forces (Green Beret) A-Team member, Anthony Blondell, tells an action-packed story of the exploitation of the Montagnards, and what happens when the South Vietnamese government not only backs out of a nearly completed, $5,000-per-day Special Forces mission, but tries to sabotage it to keep from paying.

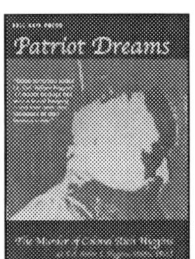

PATRIOT DREAMS
The Murder of Colonel Rich Higgins ISBN: 1-55572-527-3
by Lt. Col. Robin Higgins 200 pages, Hardcover: $21.95

In 1988, while serving the final months of his assignment as chief of the United Nations Military Observer Group in Lebanon, Lt. Col. Rich Higgins was yanked from his jeep and kidnapped by Iran-backed Hezbollah terrorists. More than a year elapsed before a gruesome videotape was released by his captors that documented his murder by hanging. His wife, then-Major Robin Higgins, who was serving as a Marine Corp public affairs officer, hid her Jewish identity as well as her frustration with the U.S. government and dedicated her life to finding him and bringing him home.

1-800-228-2275

ADDITIONAL INFORMATION ONLINE
http://www.psi-research.com/hellgate.htm

LIFE IN THE FRENCH FOREIGN LEGION
How to Join and What to Expect When You Get There ISBN: 1-55571-532-X
by Evan McGorman 250 pages, Hardcover: $22.95

Five years is a long time to commit to anything—especially when your life could be at stake. Consider, prepare, and plan before you enlist. *Life in the French Foreign Legion* is based on this insider's account of what life is really like in one the most mysterious military organizations in the world.

RIGHT FOOT IN THE PACIFIC, LEFT FOOT IN THE ATLANTIC
An Adventure Across America ISBN: 1-55571-521-4
by David Stoess 350 pages, Paperback: $17.95

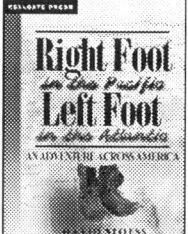

The story of a solitary 3,800-mile, five-and-a-half month walk from Los Angeles, through the south, to the Empire State Building in New York. This book tells an uplifting story of the everyday people David encountered along the way, filled with humorous and harrowing tales of flash floods, fire ants, nuts, and naked Samaritans.

PILOTS, MAN YOUR PLANES!
A History of Naval Aviation ISBN: 1-55571-466-8
by Wilbur H. Morrison **474 pages, Hardbound: $33.95**

An account of naval aviation from Kitty Hawk to the Gulf War, *Pilots, Man Your Planes!* tells the story of naval air growth from a time when planes were launched from battleships to the major strategic element of naval warfare it is today. This book is filled with rare photographs, detailed maps, and accurate accounts that can be found nowhere else. Ideal for anyone interested in aviation.

ARMY MUSEUMS
West of the Mississippi ISBN: 1-55571-395-5
by Fred L. Bell, SFC, Retired 318 pages, Paperback: $17.95

A guide book for travelers through 23 museums of the west. *Army Museums* contains detailed information about the contents of each museum and the famous soldiers stationed at the forts and military reservations where the museums are located. It is a colorful look at our heritage and the settling of the American West.

LEGACY OF LEADERSHIP
Lessons from Admiral Lord Nelson ISBN: 1-55571-510-9
by Joseph F. Callo 144 pages, Hardbound: $17.95

A penetrating view of modern history's most famous naval commander. It goes beyond the events of his life to illuminate the personal qualities that made Vice Admiral Lord Nelson such an exceptional leader—qualities that can be applied to today's military and business leaders. It is a unique analysis of what made the hero of the Battles of the Nile, Copenhagen, and Trafalgar so consistently and spectacularly successful in the ultimate test of combat.

1-800-228-2275 VISIT YOUR FAVORITE BOOKSTORE
OR ORDER DIRECT
Hellgate Press, P.O. Box 3727, Central Point, OR 97502

BYRON'S WAR
I never will be young again...
by Byron Lane

ISBN: 1-55571-402-1
298 pages, Hardcover: $21.95

Offered by The Aviators' Guild Book Club, *Byron's War* is based on letters and a personal journal that tell the story of WWII through the eyes of a young air crew officer. It is a tribute to the changes he experiences as he goes through cadet training, flies the North Atlantic as a crew member, and faces awesome responsibility during those critical times.

FROM HIROSHIMA WITH LOVE
by Raymond A. Higgins

ISBN: 1-55571-404-8
320 pages, Paperback: $18.95

Written from detailed notes and diary entries, *From Hiroshima With Love* is the remarkable story of Lieutenant Commander Wallace Higgins and his experiences in Hiroshima. As Military Governor, Higgins was responsible for helping rebuild a ravaged nation. In doing so, he developed an unforeseen respect for the Japanese, their culture, and one special woman.

WALKING AWAY FROM THE THIRD REICH
The Experiences of a Teenager in Hitler's Army
by Claus W. Sellier

ISBN: 1-55571-513-3
308 pages, Paperback: $15.95

Seventeen-year-old boys are the same everywhere. This is a gripping story of a well-to-do German boy who is eager to serve, but learns the hard way that war is not a game. From the shelter of his private boys' school, to the devastating battle fields of Germany, he learns what is truly important to him.

REBIRTH OF FREEDOM
From Nazis and Communists to a New Life in America
by Michael Sumichrast

ISBN: 1-55571-492-7
324 pages, Paperback: $16.95

"...a fascinating account of how the skill, ingenuity and work ethics of an individual, when freed from the yoke of tyranny and oppression, can make a lasting contribution to Western society. Michael Sumichrast's autobiography tells of his first loss of freedom to the Nazis, only to have his native country subjected to the tyranny of the Communists. He shares his experiences of life in a manner that makes us Americans, and others, thankful to live in a country where individual freedom is protected."

— General Alexander M. Haig, Secretary of State

IMMIGRANT SOLDIER
From the Baltics to Vietnam
by Vic Pakis

ISBN: 1-55571-512-5
240 pages, Paperback: $15.95

The story of a family whose fortunes changed dramatically due to the rise of Communism and Nazism and a flight for freedom to the United States. A son describes his family's experiences as they flee Latvia, and how he joins the U.S. Army to fight against Communism and oppression in Southeast Asia.

SURVIVAL
Diary of an American POW in World War II ISBN: 1-55571-514-1
by Samuel G. Higgins **228 pages, Paperback: $14.95**

A patriotic southerner joins the army and is captured in one of the most intense battles of WWII. During his three-month incarceration in the infamous Stalag IXB, he secretly made notes in the margins of his Bible. Fifty years later, the hundreds of entries trigger recollections of the outrage he felt, the squalid living conditions, the treatment of the Jewish prisoners, and the starvation and death that surrounded him. It is a testament to what the human spirit can endure.

WHERE DUTY CALLS
Growing Up in the Marine Corps ISBN: 1-55571-499-4
by Charlie Romine **114 pages, Paperback: $12.95**

An eighteen-year-old, out to experience the world for the first time, joins the Marine Corp in 1942 and serves during World War II and Korea. He had never been away from home, but when the Japanese bombed Pearl Harbor, he rushed to join. This is his personal coming-of-age story.

THE WAR THAT WOULD NOT END
U.S. Marines in Vietnam, 1971-1973 ISBN: 1-55571-420-X
by Major Charles D. Melson, USMC, Retired **388 pages, Paperback: $19.95**

When South Vietnamese troops proved unable to take over the war from their American counterparts, the Marines had to resume responsibility. Covering the period 1971-1973, Major Charles D. Melson describes the battle strategies of the units that broke a huge 1972 enemy offensive. The book contains a detailed look at this often ignored period of America's longest war. Featured as an alternate selection in the DoubleDay Book Club.

PROJECT OMEGA
Eye of the Beast ISBN: 1-55571-511-7
by James E. Acre **228 pages, Paperback: $13.95**

"CNN tried its level best to dishonor the reputation of the brave men of Special Operations Group. . . . Acre's beautifully written and accurate portrayal of some of the actions of that noble unit will allow the reader to see how these daring young men made accomplishing the impossible routine and to also set the record straight."
— David Hackworth, Author of *About Face* and *Hazardous Duty*

REGRET TO INFORM YOU ISBN: 1-55571-509-5
Experiences of Families Who Lost A Family Member in Vietnam
by Norman Berg 168 pages, Paperback: $16.95

How do you cope with the knowledge that a loved one is missing in action, remains not recovered? Thirty years later, real people still wait for the war in Vietnam to end—to know what happened to their loved ones. *Regret to Inform You* is a moving glimpse at the human strength and persistence it takes to survive the maze of government bureaucracy, miscommunication, and inconclusive evidence. Eight families relate their stories as only they can.

Gulf War Debriefing Book
An After Action Report
by Andrew Leyden

ISBN: 1-55571-396-3
318 pages, Paperback: $18.95

Available in the George Bush Presidential Library Museum Store. Now you can draw your own conclusion as to what happened during the seven-month period between late 1990 and early 1991. The *Gulf War Debriefing Book: An After Action Report* provides you with a meticulous review of the events. It includes documentation of all military units deployed, the primary weapons used during the war, and a look at the people, places, and politics behind the military maneuvering.

Order of Battle
Allied Ground Forces of Operation Desert Storm
by Thomas D. Dinackus

ISBN: 1-55571-493-5
407 pages, Paperback: $17.95

Contains photographs of medals, ribbons, and unit patches
Based on extensive research—containing information not previously available to the public—*Order of Battle: Allied Ground Forces of Operation Desert Storm* is a detailed study of the Allied ground combat units that served in the conflict in the Persian Gulf. In addition to showing unit assignments, it includes the type of insignia and equipment used by the various units in one of the largest military operations since the end of WWII.

Night Landing
A Short History of West Coast Smuggling
by David W. Heron

ISBN: 1-55571-449-8
136 pages, Paperback: $13.95

Night Landing reveals the true stories of smuggling off the shores of California from the early 1800s to the present. It is a provocative account of the many attempts to illegally trade items such as freon, drugs, AK-47s, sea otters, and diamonds. This unusual chronicle profiles each of these ingenious, but over-optimistic criminals and their eventual apprehension.

This Woman's Army
The Dynamics of Sex and Violence in the Military
by Marie deYoung

ISBN: 1-55571-507-9
392 pages, Paperback: $16.95

A powerful, personal account of one officer's exposure to the social problems and gender conflicts that are endemic throughout the Army. It defends women's rights to serve in any role where they can "hold their own," at the same time placing responsibility for much sexual misconduct squarely on their shoulders. It deals with the eroded standards for physical, mental, and emotional fitness at the root of the Army's problems.

Keeping Australia on the Left
A Catamaran Odyssey Around Australia
by Mark Stewart Darby

ISBN: 1-55571-508-7
232 pages, Paperback: $13.95

A wonderful tale of an Australian man, his American girlfriend, and a small open catamaran called *Tom Thumb*. It is a precarious adventure that unfolds among the desolate seaports and motley characters of the Australian coastline. Sharks, crocodiles, deadly jellyfish, storms, wild seas, and limestone cliffs are only part of this unique two-year journey.

A DYING BREED
The Courage of the Mighty Eighth Air Force ISBN: 1-55571-529-X
by Neal B. Dillon 225 pages, Paperback: $15.95

"… the true story of a WWII air combat crew's amazing courage, touching camaraderie, uplifting faith and indomitable spirit … I applaud *A Dying Breed* for preserving the lore. What had to be told has now been told."

– Lt. Gen. Stephen B. Croker, USAF, retired
Former Commander of the Eighth Air Force

"Neal Dillon is a brilliant writer who puts you into that sturdy B-17 at 28,000 feet and takes you where the flak is intense and seventy-five Luftwaffe fighter aircraft are attacking from all directions. Even before you finish reading, you will be recommending it to your friends and family."

– Major General Perry M. Smith, USAF, retired
Author, *A Hero Among Heroes* and *Rules and Tools for Leaders*

AFTER THE STORM
A Vietnam Veteran's Reflection ISBN: 1-55571-500-1
by Paul Drew 132 pages, Paperback: $14.95

Even after 25 years, the scars of the Vietnam War are still felt by those who were involved. *After the Storm: A Vietnam Veteran's Reflection* is more than a war story. It concerns itself more with the mood of the nation during the war years, and covers the author's intellectual and psychological evolution as he questions the political and military decisions that resulted in nearly 60,000 American deaths.

GREEN HELL
The Battle for Guadalcanal ISBN: 1-55571-498-6
by William J. Owens 284 pages, Paperback: $18.95

This is the story of thousands of Melanesian, Australian, New Zealanders, Japanese, and American men who fought for a poor insignificant island in a faraway corner of the South Pacific Ocean. For the men who participated, the real battle was of man against jungle. This is the account of land, sea, and air units covering the entire six-month battle. Stories of ordinary privates and seamen, admirals and generals who survived to claim the victory that was the turning point of the Pacific War.

K-9 SOLDIERS
Vietnam and After ISBN: 1-55571-495-1
by Paul B. Morgan 196 pages, Paperback: $13.95

A retired U.S. Army officer, former Green Beret, Customs K-9 and Security Specialist, Paul B. Morgan, has written *K-9 Soldiers*. In his book, Morgan relates twenty-four brave stories from his lifetime of working with man's best friend in combat and on the streets. They are the stories of dogs and their handlers who work behind the scenes when a disaster strikes, a child is lost, or some bad guy tries to outrun the cops.

1-800-228-2275   VISIT YOUR FAVORITE BOOKSTORE
OR ORDER DIRECT
Hellgate Press, P.O. Box 3727, Central Point, OR 97502

OH, WHAT A LOVELY WAR

by Stanley Swift, transcribed and edited by Evelyn Luscher

ISBN: 1-55571-502-8
96 pages, Paperback: $10.95

This book tells you what history books do not. It is war with a human face. It is the unforgettable memoir of British soldier Gunner Stanley Swift through five years of war. Intensely personal and moving, it documents the innermost thoughts and feelings of a young man as he moves from civilian to battle-hardened warrior under the duress of fire.

THROUGH MY EYES

91st Infantry Division, Italian Campaign, 1942-1945
by Leon Weckstein

ISBN: 1-55571-497-8
208 pages, Paperback: $14.95

Through My Eyes is the true account of an Average Joe's infantry days before, during, and shortly after the furiously fought battle for Italy. The author's front row seat allows him to report the shocking account of casualties and the rest-time shenanigans during the six weeks of the occupation of the city of Trieste. He also recounts in detail his personal roll in saving the historic Leaning Tower of Pisa.

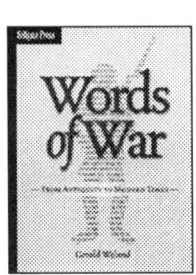

WORDS OF WAR

From Antiquity to Modern Times
by Gerald Weland

ISBN: 1-55571-491-9
176 pages, Paperback: $13.95

Words of War is a delightful romp through military history. Lively writing leads the reader to an understanding of a number of soldierly quotes. The result of years of haunting dusty libraries, searching obscure journals, and reviewing microfilm files, this unique approach promises to inspire many casual readers to delve further into the circumstances surrounding the birth of many quoted phrases.